# GERMAN CONSTITUTIONAL DOCUMENTS SINCE 1871

# GERMAN CONSTITUTIONAL DOCUMENTS SINCE 1871

*Selected Texts and Commentary*

EDITED BY

Louise W. Holborn
Gwendolen M. Carter
John H. Herz

PRAEGER PUBLISHERS
New York · Washington · London

**PRAEGER PUBLISHERS**
111 Fourth Avenue, New York, N.Y. 10003, U.S.A.
5, Cromwell Place, London S.W.7, England

Published in the United States of America in 1970
by Praeger Publishers, Inc.

© 1970 by Praeger Publishers, Inc.

Library of Congress Catalog Card Number: 69–10518

Printed in the United States of America

# Contents

## 5. Executive and Administration

## 6. Legal System and Basic Rights

## 7. Berlin and East Germany

## 8. German Foreign Policy

# *Preface*

Germany, as a modern political unit, is almost one hundred years old. In this period it has undergone more frequent and more radical changes than most of the older established nations. The Germans have witnessed, experienced, and provoked almost every one of the modern political and governmental alternatives: monarchy and republic, authoritarianism and democracy, liberalism and extreme totalitarian dictatorship. Germany has been federal in structure, centralized, and, recently, partitioned. The regimes of the units into which Germany is presently divided exemplify the two major political systems in opposition to each other in the world today.

During the first half of this period, when the Bismarckian empire (*Deutsches Reich*) was in existence, German attitudes toward society and government were formed. Will the second half of the twentieth century prove to be as critical for the present and future generations of Germans? The post-World War II system has lasted longer than that of the Weimar Republic or the twelve years of Hitler's "Thousand-Years" realm. Given peace and a minimum level of prosperity, the liberal-democratic institutions of the major portion of Germany can be expected to mold attitudes as the conservative-authoritarian structure of the Empire molded those of the previous generations. However, we must expect that, if partition continues, the Communist portion may assume its own way of life, and Germans in the two Germanys will be alienated from each other as were populations such as the Austrians, which formerly belonged to the German nation. Among the many questions raised by the variegated history of Germany is whether Germans in the eastern portion will become a separate nation.

To document present German politics and government, one must thus take into account not only the current multiplicity of units (the Federal Republic, the Democratic Republic, and West Berlin, a semi-autonomous unit) but also the events in the period since 1871, for the successive political systems have affected the present ones. Wherever possible, related characteristics of the successive systems have been presented synoptically so that similarities, divergences, and influences can be easily seen. For constitutional provisions, laws, etc., this synoptical arrangement facilitates comparison of documents of the Empire, the Weimar Republic, and the Federal Republic. The totalitarian Nazi regime and the government of the Democratic Republic do not lend themselves to such an approach, for written documents like laws and constitutions are either lacking or, where they exist, frequently fail to accurately reflect the political realities. Therefore, only selected documents from the Nazi period have been inserted into the synoptical framework. Documents of the Democratic Republic are presented in a separate chapter.

Each chapter has an explanatory introduction followed by documents.

Chapter 1 deals with the status of Germany in 1945 and the establishment of the two Germanys. The second chapter concerns the basic constitutional and governmental framework. Other chapters contain documents about political parties, elections, the legislative process, the working of the executive, the legal system, and basic rights. Chapter 7 deals with Berlin and East Germany; chapter 8 handles international relations, particularly the issues of partition and reunification.

The source of the documents designated simply "Empire," "Weimar," and "Federal Republic" is as follows. "Empire" documents are excerpts of the 1871 Constitution, which appears in the *Federal Law Gazette* (1871), pp. 63–85. "Weimar" documents are excerpts from the Weimar Constitution, which appears in the *Federal Law Gazette* (1919), pp. 1385ff. "Federal Republic" documents are excerpts from the Basic Law of the Federal Republic of Germany, which appeared in the *Federal Law Gazette* (1949). The sources of other documents are indicated in the text.

A system of cross-referencing to enable the reader to locate related topics throughout the text has been established. A sample cross reference is "see 5:1:54(1)." This means to see chapter 5, document 1, article 54, paragraph 1.

For help in obtaining documentary material, we would like to express our thanks to the following organizations: the German Information Center, New York; the Embassy of the Federal Republic of Germany, Washington, D.C.; the Bundesministerium für Gesamtdeutsche Fragen, Bonn; the Sozial-Demokratische Partei, Bonn; the Christlich-Demokratische Partei, Bonn; and the Freie Demokratische Partei, Bonn. We are grateful to Dr. Christa Tecklenberg-Johns for her generous help in translating the documents. Special appreciation for his continuous interest and unstinting aid goes to Ministerialrat Werner Blischke, Bonn, and to Balbine von Diest, of the Foreign Affairs Office, Bonn, for her help. For indefatigable typing and retyping of the manuscript, special thanks to Mrs. Geraldine Brunell-Fink, Evelyn Katrak, and Jane Martin.

L. W. H.
G. M. C.
J. H. H.

Summer, 1969

# GERMAN CONSTITUTIONAL DOCUMENTS SINCE 1871

# *1. International Status and Establishment of the Two Germanys*

## INTRODUCTION

For German government, 1945 constituted the year zero. Although prevailing theory in the West affirms the continuity of the German Reich in its various forms—monarchical empire (1871–1918), democratic republic (1918–33), and Nazi dictatorship (1933–45)—in actual fact the Germans, in both East and West, had to start from scratch.

In February, 1945, shortly before the end of the Second World War, the Big Three—the United States, Great Britain, and the Soviet Union—met at Yalta. There, they agreed that, upon the surrender of the Third Reich, the victorious Allies would assume supreme authority over all Germany and that the former Reich would be divided into four zones of military occupation (document 1). The implication of this agreement was that the indigenous German central authority would cease to exist. Upon Germany's defeat, the Allies put this agreement into effect. They assumed full authority (document 2) and established four zones of occupation as well as an Allied Control Council with headquarters in Berlin (document 3). The city of Berlin remained outside the zones of occupation and was placed under the control of an inter-Allied command (*Kommandatura*). In the Potsdam Declaration of August, 1945, the Allies laid down principles for the future government of Germany (document 4). The declaration envisaged the gradual reintroduction of indigenous German government both locally and regionally and the eventual re-establishment of a democratic central government to which the powers exercised by the Allies would be transferred. Pending this development, Germany was to be under a military government. The territories east of the Oder-Neisse line, however, were placed under Polish administration, except the northern portion of East Prussia that was to be under that of the Soviet Union. Each of the four occupation zones was to be administered under directives from the Allied Control Council in Berlin in order to preserve some "uniformity of treatment of the German population throughout Germany" (document 4).

Government was established in the four zones, but, despite the avowed intention, there was no uniformity of treatment because the Allied Control Council failed to agree on uniform directives. The Soviet Union, on the one hand, and France, Great Britain, and the United States, on the other, thereupon proceeded to establish German governments in their respective spheres: the German Democratic Republic (G.D.R.) in the east. and the Federal Republic of Germany (F.R.G.) in the west.

In the west, the establishment of the Federal Republic was preceded by the merger of the British and American zones under bizonal arrangements that, structurally and politically, anticipated a good deal of what subsequently became the Bonn government. In 1948, a London conference of six Western nations authorized the heads of the regional units (*Länder*), which had been established in the interim, to convene a constituent assembly for the purpose of drafting a constitution for West Germany (document 6; for Soviet protest, see document 5). The assembly, calling itself the Parliamentary Council, convened and drafted the document known as the Basic Law (*Grundgesetz*); this was ratified by all *Länder* except one, and it was duly promulgated on May 23, 1949 (document 7). With the establishment of the chief bodies of government as provided in the Basic Law—the election of the parliament (Bundestag), the formation of the government, and so forth—the Federal Republic of Germany began to function in the fall of 1949.

For almost six more years, however, West Germany remained under an occupation regime. Concurrent with the establishment of the Federal Republic, the three occupying powers had issued an occupation statute that reserved ultimate authority as well as many specific government powers for the Allies acting through their high commissioners. By agreement with the Bonn government, these powers were gradually scaled down. The occupation regime ended in 1955 with the coming into force of the Paris Agreements concluded in 1954 between the three occupying powers and the Federal Republic (document 10). With the exception of certain rights retained by the three powers—especially those referring to Berlin and to "Germany as a whole," that is, to the question of reunification with the eastern (Soviet) zone—full internal and external sovereignty was transferred to Bonn. Allied troops continued to be stationed on West German territory by special agreements. The reserved rights on behalf of these troops and of German security were relinquished with the coming into effect of the Emergency Legislation of 1968 (see the introduction to Chapter 2).

In the Soviet zone, a similar process led to the establishment of the German Democratic Republic. Authorized by the Soviet occupation regime, a People's Council (*Volksrat*) drafted a constitution; without further ratification, this document was declared in force in October, 1949 (document 8; for U.S. reaction, see document 9), and the government of the Democratic Republic began to function.

Consequently, since 1955, Germany has been administered by two government units—the Federal Republic in the west and the Democratic Republic in the east. In both theory and practice, east and west hold different opinions on whether these units constitute separate and independent states under international law and whether either or both continue the statehood of the pre-1945 German Reich. The Soviet Union and the German Democratic Republic consider the two units to be sovereign states (documents 11 and 13) under international law, neither of which is identical with the prewar German state. The West considers the German Democratic Republic a nonstate—a regime still under Soviet occupation (document 12)

—and the Federal Republic of Germany a state that is not only the successor to the prewar German state but also the only legitimate international representative of all of Germany.

# DOCUMENTS

## 1. YALTA CONFERENCE, FEBRUARY 4–11, 1945

### III. DISMEMBERMENT OF GERMANY

It was agreed that Article 2a of the surrender terms for Germany should be amended to read as follows: "The United Kingdom, the United States, and the Soviet Union shall possess supreme authority with respect to Germany. In the exercise of such authority, they will take such steps, including the complete disarmament, demilitarization, and dismemberment of Germany as they deem requisite for future peace and security." . . .

### IV. ZONE OF OCCUPATION FOR THE FRENCH AND CONTROL COUNCIL FOR GERMANY

It was agreed that a zone in Germany, to be occupied by the French forces, should be allocated to France. This zone would be formed out of the British and American zones, and its extent would be settled by the British and Americans in consultation with the French provisional government. It was also agreed that the French provisional government should be invited to become a member of the Allied Control Council for Germany. . . .

FROM *DSB*, XII, pp. 213–14.

## 2. ALLIED POWERS, DECLARATION ON THE DEFEAT OF GERMANY AND THE ASSUMPTION OF SUPREME AUTHORITY, BERLIN, JUNE 5, 1945

The German armed forces on land, at sea, and in the air have been completely defeated and have surrendered unconditionally. . . . There is no central government or authority in Germany capable of accepting responsibility for the maintenance of order, the administration of the country, and compliance with the requirements of the victorious powers. . . . The governments . . . of the United States, the Soviet Union, the United Kingdom, and the provisional government of the French Republic hereby assume supreme authority with respect to Germany, including all the powers

FROM *DSB*, XII, pp. 1051–55.

possessed by the German government, the High Command, and any state, municipal, or local government or authority. The assumption, for the purposes stated above, of the said authority and powers does not effect the annexation of Germany. . . . In virtue of the supreme authority and powers thus assumed by the four governments, the Allied representatives announce the following requirements arising from the complete defeat and unconditional surrender of Germany with which Germany must comply:

ART. 1  Germany, and all German military, naval, and air authorities, and all forces under German control shall immediately cease hostilies in all theaters of war against the forces of the United Nations [Allies] on land, at sea, and in the air. . . .

ART. 13  a. In the exercise of the supreme authority with respect to Germany assumed by the governments of the United States, the Soviet Union, the United Kingdom, and the provisional government of the French Republic, the four Allied governments will take such steps, including the complete disarmament and demilitarization of Germany, as they deem requisite for future peace and security.

b. The Allied representatives will impose on Germany additional political, administrative, economic, financial, military, and other requirements arising from the complete defeat of Germany. . . . All German authorities and the German people shall carry out unconditionally the requirements of the Allied representatives and shall fully comply with all such proclamations, orders, ordinances, and instructions. . . .

### 3. GOVERNMENTS OF THE UNITED STATES, THE SOVIET UNION, THE UNITED KINGDOM, AND THE PROVISIONAL GOVERNMENT OF THE FRENCH REPUBLIC, STATEMENT ON ZONES OF OCCUPATION IN GERMANY, JUNE 5, 1945

1. Germany, within her frontiers as they were on December 31, 1937, will, for the purposes of occupation, be divided into four zones, one to be allotted to each power as follows: an eastern zone to the Soviet Union, a northwestern zone to the United Kingdom, a southwestern zone to the United States, a western zone to France. The occupying forces in each zone will be under a commander-in-chief designated by the responsible power. Each of the four powers may, at its discretion, include among the forces assigned to occupation duties under the command of its commander-in-chief auxiliary contingents from the forces of any other Allied power that has actively participated in military operations against Germany.

2. The area of Greater Berlin will be occupied by forces of each of the four powers. An inter-Allied governing authority [in Russian, *Kommandatura*] consisting of four commandants, appointed by their respective commanders-in-chief, will be established to direct jointly its administration. [See 7:1:2; 7:7.]

FROM *DSB*, XII, p. 1059.

## 4. POTSDAM CONFERENCE, JULY 17–AUGUST 2, 1945

### II. THE PRINCIPLES TO GOVERN THE TREATMENT OF GERMANY IN THE INITIAL CONTROL PERIOD

#### A. Political Principles

1. In accordance with the Agreement on Control Machinery in Germany, supreme authority in Germany is exercised, on instructions from their respective governments, by the commanders-in-chief of the armed forces of the U.S.A., the U.K., the U.S.S.R., and the French Republic, each in his own zone of occupation, and also jointly, in matters affecting Germany as a whole, in their capacity as members of the Allied Control Council.

2. So far as is practicable, there shall be uniformity of treatment of the German population throughout Germany.

3. The purposes of the occupation of Germany by which the Allied Control Council shall be guided are to: (1) completely disarm and de-militarize Germany and eliminate or control all German industry that could be used for military production; . . . (2) convince the German people that they have suffered a total military defeat and that they cannot escape responsibility for what they have brought upon themselves, since their own ruthless warfare and the fanatical Nazi resistance have destroyed the German economy and made chaos and suffering inevitable; (3) destroy the NSDAP and its affiliated and supervised organizations, dissolve all Nazi institutions, ensure that they are not revived in any form, and prevent all Nazi and militarist activity or propaganda; (4) prepare for the eventual reconstruction of German political life on a democratic basis and for eventual peaceful cooperation in international life by Germany.

4. All Nazi laws that provided the basis of the Hitler regime or estab-lished discriminations on grounds of race, creed, or political opinion shall be abolished. No such discriminations, whether legal, administrative, or other-wise, shall be tolerated.

5. War criminals and those who have participated in planning or carrying out Nazi enterprises involving or resulting in atrocities or war crimes shall be arrested and brought to judgment. Nazi leaders, influential Nazi sup-porters, and high officials of Nazi organizations and institutions, and any other persons dangerous to the occupation or its objectives shall be arrested and interned.

6. All members of the Nazi Party who have been more than nominal participants in its activities and all other persons hostile to Allied purposes shall be removed from public and semipublic office and from positions of responsibility in important private undertakings. Such persons shall be re-placed by persons who, by their political and moral qualities, are deemed capable of assisting in the development of genuine democratic institutions in Germany.

FROM *DSB*, XIII, pp. 26–32.

7. German education shall be controlled so as to eliminate completely Nazi and militarist doctrines and to make possible the successful development of democratic ideas.

8. The judicial system will be reorganized in accordance with the principles of democracy, of justice under law, and of equal rights for all citizens, without distinction of race, nationality, or religion.

9. The administration in Germany should be directed toward the decentralization of the political structure and the development of local responsibility. To this end: (1) local self-government shall be restored throughout Germany on democratic principles and, in particular, through elective councils as rapidly as is consistent with military security and the purposes of military occupation; (2) all democratic political parties with rights of assembly and of public discussion shall be allowed and encouraged throughout Germany; (3) representative and elective principles shall be introduced into regional, provincial, and state administration as rapidly as may be justified by the successful application of these principles in local self-government; (4) for the time being, no central German government shall be established. Notwithstanding this, however, certain essential central German administrative departments headed by state secretaries shall be established, particularly in finance, transport, communications, foreign trade, and industry. Such departments will act under the direction of the Allied Control Council.

10. Subject to the necessity of maintaining military security, freedom of speech, press, and religion shall be permitted, and religious institutions shall be respected, Subject likewise to the maintenance of military security, the formation of free trade unions shall be permitted.

·        ·        ·

## B. Economic Principles

12. At the earliest practicable date, the German economy shall be decentralized for the purpose of eliminating the present concentration of economic power as exemplified, in particular, by cartels, syndicates, trusts, and other monopolistic arrangements.

13. In organizing the German economy, primary emphasis shall be given to the development of agriculture and peaceful domestic industries.

·        ·        ·

16. In the imposition and maintenance of economic controls established by the Allied Control Council, German administrative machinery shall be created, and the German authorities shall be required to the fullest extent practicable to proclaim and assume administration of such controls. Thus, it should be brought home to the German people that the responsibility for the administration of such controls and any breakdown in these controls will rest with themselves. Any German controls that may run counter to the objectives of occupation will be prohibited.

·        ·        ·

19. Payment of reparations should leave enough resources to enable the German people to subsist without external assistance. In working out the economic balance of Germany, the necessary means must be provided to pay for imports approved in Germany by the Allied Control Council. The proceeds of exports from current production and stocks shall be available primarily for payment of such imports.

### 5. GOVERNMENT OF THE SOVIET UNION, NOTE TO THE GOVERNMENTS OF THE UNITED STATES, THE UNITED KINGDOM, AND FRANCE ON THE LONDON CONFERENCE, FEBRUARY 13, 1948

It has become known to the Soviet government from press reports that the governments of Great Britain, the United States of America, and France intend to call in London, on February 19, a conference to discuss questions regarding Germany. According to the reports that have been published, it is intended at this conference to consider the following questions: the common policy of Great Britain, the United States, and France with regard to Germany; the future status of western Germany; control over the Ruhr; problems of security; reparation; etc.

The Soviet government deems it necessary to draw the attention of the government of Great Britain to the fact that the calling of such a conference for the consideration of questions falling under the competence of all occupying powers in Germany and involving other European countries would constitute a violation of the Potsdam Agreement and of other Four Power decisions, according to which responsibility for the administration of Germany and for defining policy with regard to Germany lies jointly in the hands of the occupying powers, and this is incompatible with separate actions. . . . The convening of the said conference in London constitutes a violation of the Agreement on Control Machinery in Germany and also a violation of the Potsdam Agreement, which provides for the treatment of Germany as a single unit.

In connection with the above, the Soviet government deems it necessary to inform the government of Great Britain that it will not consider as legitimate the decisions that will be taken at that conference.

FROM *The Soviet Union and the Berlin Question* (Moscow, 1948), pp. 5–6.

### 6. LONDON DOCUMENTS, DIRECTIVES ABOUT THE FUTURE POLITICAL ORGANIZATION OF GERMANY, FRANKFURT, JULY, 1, 1948

The military governors of the U.S.A., U.K., and French zones of occupation in Germany, in accordance with the decisions of their respective governments, authorize the ministers president of the states of their respective

FROM U.S. Department of State, *Germany, 1947–49: The Story of Documents*, Office of Public Affairs, pub. 3556 (Washington, D.C.: U.S. Gov't. Printing Office, March, 1950), pp. 275–77.

zones to convene a constituent assembly to be held not later than September 1, 1948. The delegates to this assembly will be chosen in each of the existing *Länder* under such procedure and regulations as shall be adopted by the legislative body of each of these *Länder*. The total number of delegates to the constituent assembly will be determined by dividing the total populations at the last census by 750,000 or some similar figure as may be recommended by the ministers president and approved by the military governors. The number of delegates from each *Land* will be in the same proportion to the total membership of the constituent assembly that its population is to the total population of the participating *Länder*. The constituent assembly will draft a democratic constitution, which will establish for the participating *Länder* a government structure of federal type, which is best adapted to the eventual re-establishment of German unity at present disrupted and which will protect the rights of the participating *Länder*, provide adequate authority, and contain guarantees of individual rights and freedoms. If the constitution, as prepared by the constituent assembly, does not conflict with these general principles, the military governors will authorize the submission for ratification. . . .

### 7. THE BASIC LAW OF THE FEDERAL REPUBLIC OF GERMANY, MAY 23, 1949

ART. 144   1. This Basic Law requires ratification by the representative assemblies in two-thirds of the German *Länder* in which it is for the time being to apply. [See 2:4:23.]

ART. 145   1. The Parliamentary Council shall note in public session, with the participation of the representatives of Greater Berlin, the ratification of this Basic Law and shall sign and promulgate it.

2. This Basic Law shall come into force at the end of the day of promulgation.

3. It shall be published in the *Federal Law Gazette*.

ART. 146   This Basic Law shall cease to be in force on the day on which a constitution adopted by a free election of the German people comes into force.

FROM *FLG* (May 23, 1949), official translation, Bonn. The Basic Law was adopted by the Parliamentary Council on May 8, 1949, and ratified May 16–22, 1949, by the representative assemblies of more than two-thirds of the participating *Länder*. It has been amended several times.

### 8. LAW ON THE CONSTITUTION OF THE G.D.R., OCTOBER 7, 1949

ART. 1   The Constitution of the G.D.R., created with the participation of the entire German people, passed on March 19, 1949, by the German People's Council and confirmed on May 30, 1949, by the Third German People's Congress, is hereby put into effect.

ART. 2   This law comes into effect upon its adoption. . . . [See 7:20.]

FROM *GB*, No. 1, pp. 4–16.

### 9. Dean Acheson, U.S. Secretary of State, Statement on the Illegality of the East German Government, October 12, 1949

The U.S. government considers that the so-called G.D.R., established on October 7 in Berlin, is without any legal validity or foundation in the popular will. This new government was created by Soviet and Communist fiat. It was created by a self-styled People's Council, which itself had no basis in free popular elections. . . . The eastern government rests on no constitution written by democratic representatives of the states of the Soviet zone. The new government is not the outcome of a free popular mandate . . . it will be a subservient and controlled government since its actions will be dictated behind the scenes, not by the people of the Soviet zone but by the Communist Party directed from Moscow. Such a government cannot claim by any democratic standard to speak for the German people of the Soviet zone; much less can it claim to speak in the name of Germany as a whole. . . . The U.S. government and the governments associated with it will . . . continue to give full support to the government of the F.R.G. at Bonn in its efforts to restore a truly free and democratic Germany.

From *DSB*, XXI, pp. 634–35.

### 10. Convention on Relations Between the Three Powers and the F.R.G., May 26, 1952

ART. 1    1. On the entry into force of the present convention, the United States, the United Kingdom, and the French Republic (hereinafter and in the related conventions sometimes referred to as the Three Powers) will terminate the occupation regime in the F.R.G., revoke the Occupation Statute, and abolish the Allied High Commission and the offices of the *Land* commissioners in the F.R.G.

2. The F.R.G. shall have accordingly the full authority of a sovereign state over its internal and external affairs.

ART. 2    In view of the international situation, which has so far prevented the reunification of Germany and the conclusion of a peace settlement, the Three Powers retain the rights and the responsibilities, heretofore exercised or held by them, relating to Berlin and to Germany as a whole, including the reunification of Germany and a peace settlement. The rights and responsibilities retained by the Three Powers relating to the stationing of armed forces in Germany and the protection of their security are dealt with in articles 4 and 5 of the present convention.

ART. 3    1. The F.R.G. agrees to conduct its policy in accordance with the principles set forth in the Charter of the United Nations and with the aims defined in the Statute of the Council of Europe.

From *U.S. Treaties and Other International Agreements*, No. 3425, Vol. 6, Part IV (1955), pp. 4117–5687. This convention was amended by the Paris Protocols of October 23, 1954.

2. The F.R.G. affirms its intention to associate itself fully with the community of free nations through membership in international organizations contributing to the common aims of the free world. The Three Powers will support applications for such membership by the F.R.G. at appropriate times.

3. In their negotiations with states with which the F.R.G. maintains no relations, the Three Powers will consult with the F.R.G. in respect of matters directly involving its political interests.

4. At the request of the federal government, the Three Powers will arrange to represent the interests of the F.R.G. in relations with other states and in certain international organizations or conferences, whenever the F.R.G. is not in a position to do so itself.

ART. 4   1. Pending the entry into force of the arrangements for the German defense contribution, the Three Powers retain the rights, heretofore exercised or held by them, relating to the stationing of armed forces in the F.R.G....

2. The rights of the Three Powers, heretofore exercised or held by them, which relate to the stationing of armed forces in Germany and which are retained, are not affected by the provisions of this article insofar as they are required for the exercise of the rights referred to in the first sentence of article 2 of the present convention. The F.R.G. agrees that, from the entry into force of the arrangements for the German defense contribution, forces of the same nationality and effective strength as at that time may be stationed in the F.R.G....

ART. 5   ... 2. The rights of the Three Powers, heretofore held or exercised by them, which relate to the protection of the security of armed forces stationed in the F.R.G. and which are temporarily retained, shall lapse when the appropriate German authorities have obtained similar powers under German legislation enabling them to take effective action to protect the security of those forces, including the ability to deal with a serious disturbance of public security and order. To the extent that such rights continue to be exercisable they shall be exercised only after consultation, insofar as the military situation does not preclude such consultation, with the federal government and with its agreement that the circumstances require such exercise. In all other respects, the protection of the security of those forces shall be governed by the forces convention or by the provisions of the agreement that replaces it and, except as otherwise provided in any applicable agreement, by German law.[1]

ART. 6   1. The Three Powers will consult with the F.R.G. in regard to the exercise of their rights relating to Berlin.

2. The F.R.G. will cooperate with the Three Powers in order to facilitate the discharge of their responsibilities with regard to Berlin.

ART. 7   The signatory states agree that an essential aim of their common policy is a peace settlement for the whole of Germany, freely negotiated between Germany and former enemies, which should lay the founda-

[1] This paragraph was relinquished by the Three Powers. See exchange of letters, June 18, 1968, in *FLG*, I (1968), pp. 714–16.

tion for a lasting peace. They further agree that the final determination of the boundaries of Germany must await such a settlement.

2. Pending the peace settlement, the signatory states will cooperate to achieve by peaceful means their common aim of a reunified Germany enjoying a liberal-democratic constitution like that of the F.R.G. and integrated within the European community.

3. The Three Powers will consult with the F.R.G. on all matters involving the exercise of their rights relating to Germany as a whole.

## 11. GOVERNMENT OF THE SOVIET UNION, STATEMENT ON RELATIONS WITH THE G.D.R., MARCH 25, 1954

1. The Soviet Union establishes the same relations with the G.D.R. as with other sovereign states. The G.D.R. shall be free to decide on internal and external affairs, including the question of relations with West Germany, at its discretion.

2. The Soviet Union will retain in the G.D.R. the functions connected with guaranteeing security that resulted from the obligations incumbent on the Soviet Union as a result of the Four Power Agreement.

The Soviet government has taken note of the statement of the government of the G.D.R. that it will carry out its obligations arising from the Potsdam Agreement on the development of Germany as a democratic and peace-loving state as well as the obligations connected with the temporary stationing of Soviet troops on the territory of the G.D.R.

3. Supervision of the activities of the G.D.R. hitherto carried out by the High Commissioner of the Soviet Union in Germany will be abolished.

FROM *The Times* (London), March 26, 1954.

## 12. ALLIED HIGH COMMISSION, JOINT DECLARATION ON THE STATUS OF EAST GERMANY, APRIL 8, 1954

The Allied High Commission desires to clarify the attitude of the governments it represents toward the statement issued on March 25, by the Soviet government, purporting to describe a change in its relations with the government of the so-called G.D.R. This statement appears to have been intended to create the impression that sovereignty has been granted to the G.D.R. It does not alter the actual situation in the Soviet zone. The Soviet government still retains effective control there.

The three governments represented in the Allied High Commission will continue to regard the Soviet Union as the responsible power for the Soviet zone of Germany. These governments do not recognize the sovereignty of the East German regime, which is not based on free elections, and do not intend to deal with it as a government. They believe that this attitude will be shared by other states, who, like themselves, will continue to recognize

FROM *DSB*, XXX, p. 588.

the F.R.G. as the only freely elected and legally constituted government in Germany. The Allied High Commission also takes this occasion to express the resolve of its governments that the Soviet action shall not deter them from their determination to work for the reunification of Germany as a free and sovereign nation.

### 13. TREATY BETWEEN THE SOVIET UNION AND THE G.D.R., SEPTEMBER 20, 1955

The President of the G.D.R. and the Presidium of the Supreme Soviet of the Soviet Union . . . in view of the new situation which has arisen owing to the coming into force of the Paris Agreements of 1954; convinced that the concerted efforts of the G.D.R. and the Soviet Union to cooperate in the preservation and consolidation of peace and of security in Europe, to restore the unity of Germany as a peace-loving and democratic state, and to bring about a peace settlement with Germany in the form of a treaty are in accordance with the interest of the German people and the Soviet people and alike with the interests of the other European peoples; taking into consideration the obligations of the G.D.R. and the Soviet Union under the international agreements that concern Germany as a whole, have decided to conclude this treaty. . . .

The contracting parties solemnly confirm that the relations between them are based on complete equality of rights, mutual respect of sovereignty, and noninterference in domestic affairs.

In accordance with this, the G.D.R. is free to decide on questions of its internal and foreign politics, including those pertaining to its relations with the F.R.G., as well as those pertaining to the development of relations with other states. . . .

The Soviet troops at present stationed on the territory of the G.D.R., in accordance with the existing international agreements, remain temporarily in the G.D.R. with the approval of the government of the G.D.R. on conditions to be settled by an additional agreement between the government of the G.D.R. and of the Soviet Union.

The Soviet troops temporarily stationed on the territory of the G.D.R. will not interfere with the internal affairs of the G.D.R. and with the social and political life of the country.

There is accord between the contracting parties that it is their main aim to bring about a peaceful settlement for the whole of Germany by means of appropriate negotiations. In accordance with this, they will make the necessary efforts toward a settlement by a peace treaty and toward the restoration of the unity of Germany on a peaceful and democratic basis.

FROM U.S. House of Representatives, *Documents on Germany, 1944–59*, 86th Cong., 1st sess. (1959), pp. 156–57.

# 2. *Basic Constitutional-Governmental Framework*

## INTRODUCTION

Modern Germany has experienced several systems of government: the monarchical federal system of imperial Germany, the parliamentary system of the Weimar Republic, the totalitarian Nazi regime, the parliamentary federal system of West Germany, and the regime patterned along Soviet lines in East Germany.

The monarchical federal system was established by the Constitution of 1871. It was the result of an agreement concluded between the King of Prussia, acting on behalf of the North-German Confederation (formed in 1867 by agreement between Prussia and the German states north of the river Main), and the rulers of four southern German states. Established by previously independent states, the framework was basically federal in structure, although for many years after its formation, arguments about where sovereignty lay—with the member states or with the federation—continued unabated. The union was characterized by Prussian predominance; in the main, this was exercised through the *Bundesrat* (Federal Council), the body in which the member states were represented. Although a popularly elected parliament—*Reichstag* (Federal Diet)—existed, the executive, in the person of the emperor (Kaiser), had power to thwart any real form of popular sovereignty. He could freely appoint and dismiss the federal chancellor (*Reichskanzler*), who was not responsible to the Reichstag. The emperor also had the power to dissolve the Reichstag, and, while legislative power was not shared with the emperor, the Reichstag had to share it with the Bundesrat. Just prior to the demise of the Empire, in the last stages of World War I, the Empire Constitution was amended to introduce the parliamentary principle; under the terms of this amendment, the government was to depend on the confidence of a majority in the Federal Diet. This foreshadowed the structure of the subsequent system, the Weimar Republic.

The Weimar Constitution of 1919 (*Verfassung des Deutschen Reiches*), adopted after Germany's defeat in World War I and after the abdication of the monarchs, was drafted by a constituent assembly (*Nationalversammlung*) that convened at Weimar. The preamble and the first article define the basic nature of the Weimar Republic as that of popular sovereignty. Popular sovereignty was exercised through direct votes (plebiscites), popular election of a federal president (*Reichspräsident*), and, above all, the election of a Reichstag with strong powers. While the president had the power to dissolve parliament and to appoint the government (the chancellor and his ministers), the Reichstag had strong lawmaking powers and also controlled the government, which had to resign upon a vote of nonconfidence. The Weimar structure was federal. A Reichsrat (Federal Council) represented the *Länder* (states), but its powers were considerably more restricted than those of its predecessor under the Empire Constitution. More important than the Reichsrat as a limitation on the power of the Reichstag were the emergency powers given to the president. In addition, the powers of all government bodies were restricted by an elaborate listing of rights, which were embodied in the second part of the Weimar Constitution and called fundamental rights (*Grundrechte*).

The Weimar Constitution had ceased to function before Hitler assumed power in 1933. From 1930 to 1933, government, for the most part, was carried on by presidential emergency power; however, the Constitution was never formally abrogated and continued to exist under the Nazi regime, where it simply was not observed. In fact, the Nazi regime never acted on the basis of a written constitution; in its early stages, the Nazi regime was based on a presidential emergency decree that conferred upon the executive unlimited powers in regard to the rights of individuals and groups and on the Enabling Act of March, 1933, that gave the executive almost unlimited legislative powers. Subsequently, the powers of the executive were merged in the person of the *Führer*, Adolf Hitler, and the theory and practice of the Third Reich became based on a leadership principle in which all power was concentrated in him.

The events leading to the creation of the Bonn Constitution have been mentioned and documented in chapter 1. Characteristics of the constitution are described in subsequent chapters (see especially chapters 4, 5, and 6).

In order to place the Bonn Constitution in perspective, this chapter presents synoptically and comparatively articles of the 1871, 1919, and 1949 constitutions (and, in the case of the Nazi system, its basic decrees) that illustrate the fundamental features of each of the four government systems. Thus, the reader can, for instance, compare how the power of dissolution of the parliament, the appointment of the head of government, the election of the popularly elected part of the legislature, and emergency powers were regulated under each system.

A few words should be said here about the emergency legislation amending the original version of the Bonn constitution. Under the Occupation Statute and its modification under the Convention of 1955 (see chapter 1, document 10), the Allied powers had retained certain residual powers designed to safeguard the position of Allied armed forces serving on West German soil and to cope with internal and external subversion. They had refused to relinquish these powers until they were satisfied that the federal government had what they considered adequate comparable powers. Upon the passage of the Emergency Law of 1968, the Three Powers declared that their residual rights had lapsed.

The federal government, then under the control of the Christian Democratic Union (CDU), had favored inserting emergency provisions into the constitution and, to this end, drafted several alternative bills. The Social Democratic Party (SPD) long opposed such legislation and gave its support to the government only when, as a member of the Grand Coalition (see chapter 3), it was able to make substantial modifications. The emergency law was finally approved by the Bundestag (Federal Diet) and promulgated on June 24, 1968, despite violent opposition by extraparliamentary forces comprised of trade union elements, students, and leading intellectuals, as well as vigorous protests made by the Free Democratic Party (FDP) and segments of the SPD within the Bundesrat (Federal Council) itself.

The emergency legislation was not presented as a single block of amendments but was inserted section by section into several parts of the constitution. These constitutional modifications fall into a number of categories.[1] One of the most controversial provisions—the one amending article 10— provides the federal government with the right, formerly exercised by the Allied powers, to intercept mail and to tap telephones in the interests of national security. No notification to individuals subject to such surveillance is required and these individuals cannot bring the matter to court if they learn of this action. This provision constitutes presently applicable law in contrast to other powers that may only be used after a state of emergency or a state of defense has been proclaimed.

The bulk of the emergency legislation deals with three special situations: the "state of defense" (*Verteidigungsfall*), "the state of tension" (*Spannungsfall*), and the "internal state of emergency" (*innerer Notstand*). The state of defense (see chapter 5) can be proclaimed not only in case of war or outbreak of hostilities but also if there is an "immediate threat" of hostile action. It must be proclaimed by a two-thirds majority of both houses of parliament. If, however, parliament is not able to function, its powers will be taken over by a Joint Committee (*Gemeinsamer Ausschuss*) made up of twenty-two members of the Bundestag (appointed in proportion to the strength of the parliamentary parties) and eleven members of the Bundesrat.

The state of tension, likewise to be proclaimed by a two-thirds majority of parliament, is a situation preceding the state of defense but not otherwise defined in the legislation. In both cases, the executive can interfere with a number of basic rights and use the armed forces "for the protection of civilian objects" and for "combating organized and militarily armed insurgents."

The internal state of emergency is defined as a situation in which there is a threat to the existence of the federation or of a *Land* or a threat to the liberal-democratic basic order in either. No formal finding by parliament or any other specific body is required. Consequently, the government of a *Land* or the federal government is empowered to use all state police forces and portions of the armed forces for the removal of the threat.

[1] The categories and the location of the amendments in this book are as follows: the Joint Committee (2:8:53a), state of emergency (2:20[91]1;35[2–3], legislation (4:23: 73–80a), armed forces and state of defense (5:6:65; 20:87a–b,115a–1), basic rights (6:12:9[3],10[2],11[2],17,19[2]).

# DOCUMENTS

## *CONSTITUTIONAL FORMS*

### 1. FEDERAL REPUBLIC

PREAMBLE   The German people in the *Länder* of Baden, Bavaria, Bremen, Hamburg, Hesse, Lower Saxony, North Rhine–Westphalia, Rhineland-Palatinate, Schleswig-Holstein, Württemberg-Baden, and Württemberg-Hohenzollern, conscious of its responsibility before God and men, animated by the resolve to preserve its national and political unity and to serve the peace of the world as an equal partner in a united Europe, desiring to give a new order to political life for a transitional period, has enacted, by virtue of its constituent power, this Basic Law of the Federal Republic of Germany. It has also acted on behalf of those Germans to whom participation was denied.

The entire German people is called on to achieve by free self-determination the unity and freedom of Germany.

.    .    .

ART. 20   1. The F.R.G. is a democratic and social federal state.

2. All state authority emanates from the people. It is exercised by the people by means of elections and voting and by separate legislative, executive, and judicial organs. [See 5:1:54(1); 2:14:63(1).]

3. Legislation shall be subject to the constitutional order; the executive and the judiciary shall be bound by the law.

4. All Germans shall have the right to resist any persons seeking to remove that constitutional order, should no other remedy be possible.[1]

### 2. WEIMAR

PREAMBLE   The German people, united in their branches and animated by the will to renew and strengthen their federation in liberty and justice, to preserve peace at home and abroad, and to promote social progress have given themselves this Constitution.[2]

ART. 1   The German federation is a republic. Sovereignty emanates from the people.

[1] Article 20 was amended by the Federal Emergency Law of June 24, 1968. Paragraph 4 was added. The articles of the Federal Emergency Law have been inserted into the official text of the Basic Law.

[2] Adopted by the National Constituent Assembly on July 31, 1919, and signed by the federal government on August 11, 1919.

## 3. EMPIRE

PREAMBLE   His Majesty the King of Prussia on behalf of the North-German Federation; His Majesty the King of Bavaria; His Majesty the King of Württemberg; His Royal Highness the Grand-Duke of Baden; and His Royal Highness the Grand-Duke of Hesse and of the Rhine—the latter for the section of the Grand-Duchy situated south of the river Main—conclude a perpetual federation to protect the federal territory and the law of the land as well as to promote the welfare of the German people. This federation shall be known by the name of German Empire [*Deutsches Reich*] and shall have the following Constitution.

## *FEDERAL STRUCTURE*

## 4. FEDERAL REPUBLIC

ART. 23   For the time being, this Basic Law applies in the territory of the *Länder* of Baden, Bavaria, Bremen, Greater Berlin, Hamburg, Hesse, Lower Saxony, North Rhine–Westphalia, Rhineland-Palatinate, Schleswig-Holstein, Württemberg-Baden, and Württemberg-Hohenzollern. In other parts of Germany, it shall be put into force on their accession.[1] [See 1:7:144(1).]

.   .   .

ART. 28   1. The constitutional order in the *Länder* must conform to the principles of republican, democratic, and social government based on the rule of law, within the meaning of this Basic Law. In each of the *Länder*, counties, and municipalities, the people must be represented by a body chosen in universal, direct, free, equal, and secret elections. In the municipalities, the assembly of the municipality may take the place of an elected body.

2. The municipalities must be guaranteed the right to regulate on their own responsibilty all the affairs of the local community within the limits set by law. The associations of municipalities also have the right of self-government in accordance with the law within the limits of the functions given them by law.

3. The federation guarantees that the constitutional order of the *Länder* conforms to the basic rights and to the provisions of paragraphs 1 and 2.

ART. 29   1. The federal territory shall be reorganized by a federal law with due regard to regional ties, historical and cultural connections,

---

[1] As amended by the federal law of March 19, 1956. See *FLG*, I (1956), p. 111. By the federal law of May 4, 1951 (*FLG*, I [1951], p. 284), the *Land* Baden-Württemberg was created from the former *Länder* of Baden, Württemberg-Baden, and Württemberg-Hohenzollern. The Basic Law was made effective in the Saarland by section 1, paragraph 1, of the federal law of December 23, 1956 (see *FLG*, I [1956], p. 1011).

economic expediency, and social structure. Such reorganization should create *Länder* that, by their size and capacity, are able effectively to fulfill the functions incumbent upon them. [See 2:17:79; 5:20:115e(2).]

2. In areas that, upon the reorganization of the *Länder* after May 8, 1945, became, without plebiscite, part of another *Land*, a specific change in the decision then taken regarding the *Land* boundaries may be demanded by popular initiative within a year from the coming into force of the Basic Law. The popular initiative requires the assent of one-tenth of the population entitled to vote in *Landtag* [*Land* Diet] elections. If the popular initiative receives such assent, the federal government must include in the draft of the reorganization law a provision determining to which *Land* the area shall belong.

·     ·     ·

5. In a referendum, the majority of the votes cast decides.

6. The procedure shall be established by a federal law. The reorganization should be concluded before the expiration of three years after promulgation of the Basic Law and, should it become necessary as a result of the accession of another part of Germany, within two years after such accession.

7. The procedure regarding any other change in the territory of the *Länder* shall be established by a federal law that requires the consent of the Bundesrat and of the majority of the members of the Bundestag. [See 2:17:79(3).]

ART. 30   The exercise of government powers and the discharge of government functions is incumbent on the *Länder* insofar as this Basic Law does not otherwise prescribe or permit. [See 2:11:50; 2:17:79(3); 5:13:36(1); 8:1:32(2–3).]

ART. 31   Federal law overrides *Land* law.

·     ·     ·

ART. 37   1. If a *Land* fails to comply with its obligations of a federal character, imposed by the Basic Law or another federal law, the federal government may, with the consent of the Bundesrat, take the necessary measures to enforce such compliance by the *Land* by way of federal compulsion. [See 2:11:50.]

2. To carry out such federal compulsion, the federal government or its commissioner has the right to give instructions to all *Länder* and their authorities.

·     ·     ·

ART. 70   1. The *Länder* have the power to legislate insofar as this Basic Law does not confer legislative powers on the federation.

2. The division of competence between the federation and the *Länder* is determined by the provisions of this Basic Law concerning exclusive and concurrent legislative powers. [See 4:23:71–75; 5:20:115i.]

·     ·     ·

ART. 83   The *Länder* execute federal laws as matters of their own concern insofar as this Basic Law does not otherwise provide or permit. [See 5:10:84–86.]

## 5. Third Reich, Law for the Reorganization of the Reich, January 30, 1934

ART. 1   The popular assemblies of the *Länder* are hereby abolished.

ART. 2   1. The sovereign rights of the *Länder* are hereby transferred to the Reich.

2. The governments of the *Länder* are subordinate to the Reich government.

ART. 3   The federal governors of the *Länder* are subject to the supervision of the Reich Minister of the Interior.

ART. 4   The Reich government may lay down new constitutional laws.

ART. 5   The Reich Minister of the Interior is to issue the necessary legal decrees and administrative measures for the carrying out of this law.

ART. 6   This law becomes effective on the day it is promulgated.

From *FLG*, I (1934), p. 75.

## 6. Weimar

ART. 2   The territory of the federation consists of the territory of the German *Länder*. Other territories can be received into the federation by means of a federal law, if their inhabitants request this by virtue of the right of self-determination.

．　　．　　．

ART. 5   Sovereignty is exercised in federal affairs through organs of the federation on the basis of the federal constitution, in *Land* affairs through the organs of the *Land* on the basis of the *Land* constitution. [See 4:24:6, 7,9,77.]

．　　．　　．

ART. 12   So long and so far as the federation does not make use of its legislative power, the *Länder* retain the right of legislation. This does not hold for the exclusive legislative power of the federation. The federal government possesses a right of veto in respect to *Land* laws which refer to the subject of article 7, paragraph 13 insofar as the general welfare in the federation is affected thereby. [See 4:24:7(13).]

ART. 13   Federal law overrules *Land* law. If doubts or differences of opinion exist as to whether a provision of *Land* law is compatible with the federal law, the appropriate federal or *Land* central authorities may request the decision of the Federal Supreme Court, according to the more detailed provisions of a federal law.

ART. 14   The federal laws are executed by the *Land* authorities, insofar as the federal laws do not provide otherwise. [See 5:11:15.]

.    .    .

ART. 17   Every *Land* must have a republican constitution. The popular representatives must be elected by the universal, equal, direct, and secret suffrage of all men and women who are citizens of the federation, according to the fundamental principles of proportional representation. The *Land* government must have the confidence of the representatives of the people. The fundamental principles for election to the popular house are also valid for the local elections. However, through *Land* law the right of suffrage may be made dependent upon a period of residence in the community up to one year.

ART. 18   The division of the federation into *Länder* shall serve the highest economic and cultural development of the people, with the utmost possible consideration of the will of the population affected. Alteration of the domain of the *Länder* and the reconstruction of the *Länder* within the federation are accomplished by a law amending the constitution.

If the directly affected *Länder* consent, only an ordinary federal law is needed. An ordinary federal law is sufficient also if one of the affected *Länder* does not consent, but the territorial change or reconstruction is demanded by the will of the population and required by a preponderant national interest.

The will of the population is ascertained in an election. The federal government orders the election, if this is requested by one-third of the electors of the Bundestag who reside in the territory to be separated.

To decide upon territorial change or reconstruction, three-fifths of the votes cast, but at least a majority of all qualified electors, are required. . . . [See 2:18:76.]

ART. 48   If a *Land* does not fulfill the duties incumbent upon it according to the federal constitution or the federal laws, the federal president may compel it to do so with the aid of the armed forces. [See 2:22:48(2).]

.    .    .

ART. 127   Communities and municipal associations have the right of self-administration within the limits of the laws.


### 7. EMPIRE

ART. 1   The territory of the Empire consists of the *Staaten* of Prussia with Lauenburg, Bavaria, Saxony, Württemberg, Baden, Hesse, Mecklenburg-Schwerin, Saxe-Weimar, Mecklenburg-Strelitz, Oldenburg, Brunswick, Saxe-Meiningen, Saxe-Altenburg, Saxe-Coburg-Gotha, Anhalt, Schwarzburg-Rudolstadt, Schwarzburg-Sondershausen, Waldeck, Reuss of the Elder Line, Reuss of the Younger Line, Schaumburg-Lippe, Lippe, Lübeck, Bremen, and Hamburg.

ART. 2  Within the federal territory, the federation shall exercise the right of legislation in accordance with the provisions of this constitution. . . . The laws of the Empire shall receive their binding force by imperial promulgation, through the medium of a federal gazette. . . .

ART. 19  If the *Staaten* of the Empire fail to fulfill their constitutional duties, they may be compelled to do so by federal execution. This execution shall be decided upon by the Bundesrat and carried out by the emperor.

## *FEDERAL DIET*

### 8. FEDERAL REPUBLIC

ART. 38  1. The deputies to the German Bundestag are elected in general, direct, free, equal, and secret elections. They are representatives of the whole people, not bound by orders and instructions, and subject only to their conscience.

2. Anyone who has attained the age of twenty-one is eligible to vote; anyone who has attained the age of twenty-five is eligible for election.[1]

3. Details will be regulated by a federal law. [See 4:2:41; 4:5:39; 4:8:40, 42–48; 5:20:45b.]

. . .

ART. 53a  1. Two-thirds of the members of the Joint Committee[2] shall be deputies of the Bundestag and one-third shall be members of the Bundesrat. The Bundestag shall delegate its deputies in proportion to the sizes of its parliamentary groups; such deputies must not be members of the federal government. Each *Land* shall be represented by a Bundesrat member of its choosing; these members shall not be bound by instructions. The setting up of the Joint Committee and its procedures shall be regulated by rules of procedure to be adopted by the Bundestag and requiring the consent of the Bundesrat.

2. The federal government must inform the Joint Committee about its plans in respect of a state of defense. The rights of the Bundestag and its committees under article 43, paragraph 1, shall not be affected by the provision of this paragraph. [See 5:20:115e–1.]

### 9. WEIMAR

ART. 20  The Reichstag is composed of the deputies of the German people.

ART. 21  The delegates are representatives of the entire people. They are subject only to their conscience and are not bound by instructions.

[1] As amended by the Federal Emergency Law of 1968.

[2] This "little parliament" composed of a small number of Bundestag and Bundesrat members, has been provided for by the Emergency Law of 1968.

ART. 22    The deputies are elected by universal, equal, direct, and secret suffrage of men and women over the age of twenty, according to the principles of proportional representation. . . . The federal election law prescribes the details. [See 2:15:25; 4:3:31; 4:6:23–24; 4:9:26–30, 32–40.]

## 10. EMPIRE

ART. 20    1. The members of the Reichstag shall be chosen in a general, direct election and by secret ballot. [See 4:4:27; 4:7; 4:10.]

## FEDERAL COUNCIL

### 11. FEDERAL REPUBLIC

ART. 50    The *Länder* participate through the Bundesrat in the legislation and administration of the federation. [See 2:4:30, 37(1); 4:14:51–53.]

### 12. WEIMAR

ART. 60    A Reichsrat is formed to give the German *Länder* representation in the lawmaking and administration of the federation. [See 4:15:61,63–67.]

### 13. EMPIRE

ART. 6    The Bundesrat shall consist of representatives of the members of the Confederation, among which the votes shall be divided in such manner that Prussia . . . shall have 17 votes; Bavaria, 6; Saxony, 4; Württemberg, 4; Baden, 3; Hesse, 3; Mecklenburg-Schwerin, 2; Saxe-Weimar, 1; . . . all others, 1; total, 58 votes . . . the votes of each state shall be cast only as a unit. [See 4:16:7–10,12–15; 5:4:11(2–3).]

## FEDERAL GOVERNMENT

### 14. FEDERAL REPUBLIC

ART. 62    The federal government consists of the federal chancellor and the federal ministers.

ART. 63    1. The federal chancellor is elected, without debate, by the Bundestag on the proposal of the federal president. [See 4:8:45(2); 5:20:115h (2).]

2. The person obtaining the votes of the majority of the members of the Bundestag is elected. The person elected must be appointed by the federal president.

3. If the person proposed is not elected, the Bundestag may, within fourteen days of the ballot, elect a federal chancellor by vote of more than one-half of its members.

4. If no candidate has been elected within this period, a new ballot shall take place without delay, in which the person obtaining the largest number of votes is elected. If the person elected obtained the votes of the majority of the members of the Bundestag, the federal president must appoint him within seven days of the election. If the person elected did not receive this majority, the federal president must, within seven days, either appoint him or dissolve the Bundestag.

ART. 64   1. The federal ministers are appointed and dismissed by the federal president upon the proposal of the federal chancellor. [See 5:6:64(2), 65–66.]

.     .     .          .

ART. 67   1. The Bundestag can express its lack of confidence in the federal chancellor only by electing a successor by the majority of its members and by requesting the federal president to dismiss the federal chancellor. The federal president must comply with the request and appoint the person elected.

2. Forty-eight hours must elapse between the motion and the election.

ART. 68   1. If a motion of the federal chancellor for a vote of confidence is not assented to by the majority of the members of the Bundestag, the federal president may, upon the proposal of the federal chancellor, dissolve the Bundestag within twenty-one days. The right to dissolve lapses as soon as the Bundestag, by the majority of its members, elects another federal chancellor.

2. Forty-eight hours must elapse between the motion and the vote thereon. [See 2:20:81(1); 5:6:69.]

## 15. WEIMAR

ART. 25   The federal president may dissolve the Reichstag but only once for one and the same reason. New elections shall take place at the latest on the sixtieth day after dissolution.

.     .     .

ART. 52   The federal government consists of the federal chancellor and the federal ministers.

ART. 53   The federal chancellor and, on his recommendation, the federal ministers are appointed and dismissed by the federal president.

ART. 54   The federal chancellor and the federal ministers require for the exercise of their office the confidence of the Reichstag. Any one of them must resign if the Reichstag by formal resolution withdraws its confidence. [See 5:7.]

## 16. EMPIRE

ART. 15   The federal chancellor, to be appointed by the emperor, shall preside in the Bundesrat and supervise the conduct of its business. . . . [See 4:21:16.]

ART. 24   . . . 2. The Reichstag may be dissolved during that time [i.e. the five-year legislative period] by a resolution of the Bundesrat with the consent of the emperor. [See 4:7:24.]

ART. 25   In case of a dissolution of the Reichstag, new elections shall take place within a period of sixty days, and the Reichstag shall be called together within a period of ninety days after its dissolution. [See 4:7:26.]

## *AMENDMENTS*

### 17. FEDERAL REPUBLIC

ART. 79   1. The Basic Law can be amended only by laws that expressly amend or supplement the text thereof. . . .[1]

2. Any such law requires the affirmative vote of two-thirds of the members of the Bundestag and two-thirds of the votes of the Bundesrat.

3. Amendments of this Basic Law affecting the division of the federation into *Länder*, the participation in principle of the *Länder* in legislation, or the basic principles laid down in articles 1 and 20 is inadmissible. [See 2:1:20; 2:4:29(1,7); 2:11:50; 6:12:1; 8:1:32(3).]

### 18. WEIMAR

ART. 76   The constitution may be amended by law, but acts . . . amending the constitution can only take effect if two-thirds of the legal number of members present and at least two-thirds of those present consent. [See 2:6:18.]

### 19. EMPIRE

ART. 78   Amendments to the constitution shall be made by legislative enactment. They shall be considered as rejected when fourteen votes are cast against them in the Bundesrat.

[1] As amended by federal law, March 24, 1954. See *FLG*, I (1954), p. 45.

## EMERGENCY POWERS

### 20. FEDERAL REPUBLIC

ART. 81   1. Should in the circumstances of article 68 [see 2:14:68] the Bundestag not be dissolved, the federal president may, at the request of the federal government and with the consent of the Bundesrat, declare a state of legislative emergency with respect to a bill, if the Bundestag rejects the bill although the federal government has declared it to be urgent. The same applies if a bill has been rejected although the federal chancellor had combined with it the motion under article 68.

2. If, after a state of legislative emergency has been declared, the Bundestag again rejects the bill or adopts it in a version declared to be unacceptable to the federal government, the bill is deemed to have been passed insofar as the Bundesrat consents to it. The same applies if the bill is not adopted by the Bundestag within four weeks of its reintroduction.

3. During the term of office of a federal chancellor, any other bill rejected by the Bundestag may become law in accordance with paragraphs 1 and 2 of this article within a period of six months after the first declaration of a state of legislative emergency. After expiration of this period, a further declaration of a state of legislative emergency is inadmissible during the term of office of the same federal chancellor.

4. The Basic Law may not be amended or be repealed or suspended in whole or in part by a law passed pursuant to paragraph 2.

.   .   .

ART. 91[1]   1. In order to ward off imminent danger to the existence or to the free democratic basic order of the federation or of a *Land*, a *Land* may request the services of the police forces [civil defense corps, emergency civil engineering corps, fire department, etc.] and facilities of other administrative authorities and of the federal border police. [See 5:20:87a(4).]

2. If the *Land* where such danger is imminent is not willing or able to combat the danger, the federal government may place the police in that *Land* and the police forces of other *Länder* under its own instructions and commit units of the federal border police. The order for this shall be canceled after the removal of the danger or else at any time upon the request of the Bundesrat. If the danger extends to a region larger than a *Land*, the federal government may, insofar as is necessary for effectively combating such danger, issue instructions to the *Land* governments; the first and second sentences of this paragraph shall not be affected by this provision.

ART. 35[2]   ... 2. In order to deal with a natural catastrophe or an especially grave accident, a *Land* may request the assistance of the police forces of

[1] As amended by the Federal Emergency Law of 1968.
[2] As amended by the Federal Emergency Law of 1968.

other *Länder* or of forces and facilities of other administrative authorities or of the federal border police or the armed forces.

3. If the natural catastrophe or the accident endangers a region larger than a *Land*, the federal government may, insofar as this is necessary effectively to deal with such danger, instruct the *Land* governments to place their police forces at the disposal of other *Länder* and may commit units of the federal border police or the armed forces to support the police forces. Measures taken by the federal government pursuant to the first sentence of this paragraph must be revoked at any time upon the request of the Bundesrat and, in any case, without delay upon removal of the danger.

### 21. THIRD REICH, PRESIDENT VON HINDENBURG, DECREE FOR THE PROTECTION OF THE PEOPLE AND STATE, FEBRUARY 28, 1933

By virtue of article 48, paragraph 2 [see 2:22] of the German Constitution, the following is decreed as a defensive measure against Communist acts of violence, endangering the state:

1. Articles 114, 115, 117, 118, 123, 124, and 153 of the constitution of the German federation are suspended until further notice. Thus, restrictions on personal liberty, on the right of free expression of opinion, including freedom of the press, on the right of assembly, and on the right of association, and infractions of the privacy of postal, telegraphic, and telephone communications, and warrants for house-searches, orders for confiscations, as well as restrictions on property are also permissible beyond the legal limits otherwise prescribed.

·   ·   ·

6. This decree enters into force on the day of its promulgation.[1]

FROM *FLG*, I (1933), p. 83.

### 22. WEIMAR

ART. 48   . . . 2. If the public safety and order in the federation are seriously disturbed or endangered, the federal president may take the measures necessary for the restoration of public safety and order and may intervene if necessary with the assistance of the armed forces. For this purpose he may temporarily set aside, in whole or in part, the fundamental rights established in articles 114, 115, 117, 123, 124, and 153. [See 6:4; 6:13:115, 118,123,124.] The federal president must immediately inform the Reichstag of all measures taken in conformity with paragraph 1 or 2 of this article. The measures are to be revoked upon the demand of the Reichstag. In case of imminent danger, a *Land* government may take for its territory temporary measures of the nature described in paragraph 2. The measures are

[1] This emergency decree remained in force throughout the Nazi regime.

to be revoked upon the demand of the federal president or of the Reichstag. A federal law shall prescribe the details. [See 2:6:48.]

### 23. EMPIRE

ART. 68   The emperor shall have the power, if public security within the federal territory is threatened, to declare martial law in any part of the Empire. . . .

# 3. Political Parties

## INTRODUCTION 1: LEGAL BASIS OF PARTIES IN THE FEDERAL REPUBLIC

Organized parties existed in Germany even before unification in 1871. They ran candidates for and were represented in the parliaments of the German states. From the outset, they were strongly organized. In the parliaments, representatives of the various parties acted much as they do today—as disciplined units (*Fraktionen*). Neither the Constitution of 1871 nor the Weimar Constitution officially recognized parties as organizations participating in the formation of the popular will. Under the Nazi regime, all parties but one were suppressed by law, and any attempt to organize such a group was made a punishable offense; however, the one official party was given important prerogatives (document 3).

The Nazi Party (NSDAP) was outlawed by the Allied occupation authorities, who licensed the formation of four "democratic" parties in Germany: the Social Democratic Party (SPD), the Christian Democratic Union (CDU), the Liberal Democratic Party (LDP)—subsequently renamed the Free Democratic Party (FDP)—and the Communist Party (KPD). In the Soviet zone, the SPD underwent a forced merger with the KPD and the two became the Socialist Unity Party (SED), now the state party in the German Democratic Republic. Although the two "bourgeois" parties (CDU and LDP) were not dissolved and two additional parties were permitted to form later, all parties in the German Democratic Republic are joined in a National Front, and every party must accept the National Front's basic principles and policies: These are identical with those of the SED.

In West Germany, with the termination of Allied licensing, additional political parties were formed. Some—such as the rightist Socialist Reich Party (SRP) and its successor, the National Democratic Party (NPD), and the leftist *Friedensunion* (FU)—were radical. Some, such as the Bavarian Party (BP), were regional in character. Others represented special interests. Apart from the NPD, which is represented in some *Land* parliaments and, in the 1969 election, just barely failed to get into the Bundestag, these parties have by now either disappeared or are insignificant. The trend has been toward a two-party system composed of the CDU (in Bavaria the CDU is organized as the Christian Social Union or CSU) and the SPD; the FPD is now the only remaining third party represented in the Bundestag.

The Basic Law officially recognizes political parties and prescribes requirements for their activities (document 1). In accordance with these requirements, parties hostile to "the free democratic basic order" of Bonn can be declared unconstitutional by a decision of the Federal Constitutional Court. Two parties have thus far been outlawed: the SRP and the KPD (documents 4 and 5). Attempts to reorganize outlawed parties, form substitutes for them, or pursue activities reflecting their policies are punishable by law.

The Basic Law also envisaged legislation that would regulate in some detail the structure and activities of political parties. After protracted disagreement, especially over the problem of how to regulate party financing, parliament finally enacted a Law on Parties in 1967 (document 2). In addition to prescribing rules concerning internal party government—for example, on acquisition and possible loss of membership and on composition and powers of party organs—the law strikes a compromise between those opposing any regulation of party finances and those advocating virtually complete party subsidization by the state. It allows for reimbursement of election expenses but not of general party expenses from public funds. The distinction was rendered necessary by a 1966 Constitutional Court decision (document 6), which permitted a loophole in regard to specific campaign expenditures but prohibited the practice of general state financing of parties, a practice that had arisen in the 1960's. Prior to that, another decision had declared tax deductions of campaign contributions—which, in view of the large amounts contributed by corporations and businessmen, tended to favor the CDU and the FDP—unconstitutional on the ground that they violate equal opportunities for all parties. The Law on Parties permits contributions but prescribes disclosure for larger ones. Financially, German parties now rely most heavily on reimbursement of direct election expenses by the government and membership fees as well as on contributions from private sources.

# DOCUMENTS

## 1. FEDERAL REPUBLIC

ART. 21  1. The political parties participate in the formation of the political will of the people. They may be freely formed. Their internal organization must conform to democratic principles. They must publicly account for the sources of their funds.

2. Parties that by reason of their aims or by the behavior of their adherents seek to impair or destroy the free democratic basic order or to endanger the existence of the F.R.G. are unconstitutional. The Federal Constitutional Court decides on the question of unconstitutionality.

3. Details will be regulated by federal legislation. [See 3:2.]

## 2. Federal Republic, Law Concerning Political Parties, July 24, 1967

PART I: GENERAL REGULATIONS

### Article 1: Constitutional Position and Tasks of the Parties

1. The parties are a constitutionally necessary element of the free and democratic basic order. Through their free and continuous participation in the process of the formation of the political will of the people, the parties fulfill a public duty. They are obliged to do so by the Basic Law, and their right to do so is guaranteed to them by the Basic Law.

2. The parties participate in the formation of the political will of the people in all aspects of public life by influencing in particular the formation of public opinion, by stimulating and deepening political education, by furthering the active participation of citizens in political life, by training capable citizens to assume public responsibility, by participating in the federal elections and in the elections of the *Länder* and the municipalities, by nominating candidates, by influencing the political process in parliament and in government, by introducing their political goals into the process of forming a national political will, and by continuously maintaining a close relationship between the people and the state organs.

3. The parties define their political goals in party programs.

### Article 2: Concept of a Party

1. Parties are associations of citizens who want to influence permanently or for a long period of time the formation of the political will in the federation or in a single *Land* and who want to participate in the representation of the people in the German Bundestag or in a *Landtag*. With respect to the over-all conditions and, in particular, with regard to the size and strength of their organization, to the size of their membership, and to their public appearance they must, however, give sufficient guarantee of the seriousness of their goals. Only individuals can be members of a party.

2. An association loses its legal position as a party if, after six years, it has participated neither in an election of the Bundestag nor of a *Landtag* by nominating candidates from its own ranks. . . .

### Article 3: Active and Passive Legal Identity of a Party

1. A party can sue or can be sued under its name. The same holds for its district units at the highest level, unless the party statute states otherwise.

### Article 4: Name of a Party

The name of a party must be clearly distinguished from the names of already existing parties; the same holds for abbreviations. During the election campaign and during the electoral process, the name of a party or its abbreviation can only be used as defined in its statute. Additional names must not be mentioned.

## Article 5: Equal Treatment

If a holder of public power places certain institutions at the disposal of one party or grants it public funds, all other parties should be treated in the same way. The size of the grant can be graduated according to the importance of the party and can be reduced to the minimum amount necessary for reaching its political goals. The importance of a party is determined in particular by the results of the preceding elections for representative bodies of the people. . . .

PART II: INTERNAL ORDER

## Article 6: Statute and Program

1. The party must have a written statute and a written program.

2. The statute must contain regulations concerning (1) the name of the party and, if used, its abbreviation, as well as its headquarters and the range of its activity; (2) admission and resignation of members; (3) rights and duties of the members; (4) allowable penalties against members and regulations concerning their expulsion (article 10, paragraphs 3–5); (5) allowable penalties against district units; (6) general structure of the party; (7) structure and rights of the party leadership and of the rest of the party organs; (8) matters that, according to article 9, are reserved to the decision of the meeting of the party members and deputies; (9) prerequisites, form, and time interval for the convocation of the meeting of the party members and deputies as well as for the documentation of the decisions; (10) district units and organs that have the right to submit the nomination of candidates for election to the representative organs of the people if no legal regulations exist; (11) a poll of the entire membership as part of the procedure to be followed should the party conference decide to dissolve the party or the district unit or to fuse it with other parties according to article 9, paragraph 3. According to the result of the poll of the entire membership, this decision must be considered as confirmed, modified, or annulled.

3. The party executive must inform the federal election supervisor about (1) the statute and the program of the party; (2) the names of the federal party leaders and of the leaders of the party units in the *Länder*, as well as their functions; (3) the dissolution of the party or of a party unit in a *Land*. Changes must be reported by December 31 of every year. . . .

4. The party regulations in this law are valid for the *Land* whose party organizations are restricted to a *Land* [*Landesparteien*].

## Article 7: Structure

The parties are composed of district units. The size of the district units is determined by the party statute. The district structure must be such that the individual party member can exert a proper influence on the process of forming the will of the party. . . .

### Article 8: Organs

Conventions of members and of party leaders are necessary organs of the party and of its district units. It can be stated in the statute that, in units comprising more than one district, the meeting of the members is replaced by the meeting of the deputies, who are elected for a maximum of two years by the meeting of the members or of the deputies of lower units. . . .

### Article 9: Conventions of Members and Delegates

1. A meeting of the members or delegates is the highest organ of any district unit. . . .

2. The party leaders, the members of other organs of the district unit, as well as the members of the categories listed in article 11, paragraph 2, can join a deputy meeting according to the statute, but they may only have up to one-fifth of the vote of all members represented at the meeting, as determined by the statute.

3. Within the framework of the rights of the district units of the party, the party congress decides the party programs, statute, regulations concerning membership fees, regulations concerning arbitration, dissolution of the party, and fusion with other parties.

4. The party congress elects the party leader of the district unit, his deputy, other party leaders, members of other party organs (if they exist), and deputies in the organs of higher district units, if these are not determined otherwise by this law.

5. At least every two years, the party congress receives a report of the activities of the party leaders and votes upon it. The financial part of this report is to be examined by auditors elected by the party congress before the report is submitted.

### Article 10: Rights of Members

1. The responsible organs of the party decide independently and on the basis of detailed instructions contained in the statute about the admission of members. No reason need be given for the rejection of a membership application. A general or temporary ban on admission is not allowed. Persons whose civic or voting rights have been legally abrogated by a penal sentence cannot become members of a party.

2. The party members and the deputies in the party organs have equal voting rights. According to detailed regulations of the statute, the exercise of the right to vote can be made dependent on whether the member has paid his membership fee. The member has the right to withdraw from the party immediately and at any time.

3. The statute must contain regulations concerning (1) the penalties allowed against members; (2) the reasons justifying these penalties; (3) the party organs allowed to administer these penalties. A reason must be given for the decision to remove a party member from his party office or to disqualify him from holding office.

4. A party member can only be expelled from the party if he intentionally

contravenes the statute or to a considerable extent violates the principles or rules of the party, thus harming the party seriously.

5. According to the regulations for arbitration, the responsible court of arbitration decides on the expulsion of a party member.

### Article 11: Party Leadership

1. The party leadership is elected at least every two years. It must consist of at least three members.

2. According to the statute, representatives and other prominent persons in the party may belong to the party leadership if they obtained their offices or mandates by an election. . . .

3. The leadership controls the district unit and conducts its affairs according to the law and statute as well as according to the decisions of the superior party organs. . . .

4. To carry out the decisions of the leadership and to conduct the current affairs and the most urgent affairs of the leadership, an executive body can be formed from the ranks of the leadership. Its members can also be elected by the leadership or can be determined by the statute.

.     .     .

### Article 13: Structure of Meetings of the Deputies

The structure of a meeting of the deputies or of any other organ consisting completely or partly of deputies from district units must be defined by the statute. The number of deputies of a district unit must be determined according to the number of members represented by them. The statute determines that the remaining number of deputies, which may amount at most to half of the total number, may be assigned to the district units in accordance with the proportion of votes obtained in the district area during preceding elections for representative bodies of the people. . . .

### Article 14: Courts of Arbitration of the Party

1. For the arbitration of and decision on conflicts between the party or of a district unit and individual members as well as of disputes over the interpretation and application of the statute, arbitration courts have to be formed at the higher level of the party and of the district units.

2. The members of the arbitration courts are elected for a maximum period of four years. They may not be members of the party leadership or of the leadership of a district unit; they may not be employed by the party or by a district unit; and they may not get their general income through the party or its units. They are independent and not bound by instructions. . . .

### Article 15: Formation of the Political Will in the Organs

1. The organs make their decisions by a simple majority vote, unless the law or the statute prescribes the use of more than a majority vote.

2. Balloting for members of the leadership and for deputies to deputy meetings and to higher district units is secret. Votes in other elections can be cast openly if, upon consultation, there is no objection to this procedure.

3. The right to submit motions must be defined so that a democratic formation of the political will remains guaranteed and minorities, in particular, can get sufficient discussion of their proposals. . . .

### Article 16: Disciplinary Measures Concerning District Units

1. The dissolution and the expulsion of lower district units as well as the dismissal from office of whole district unit organs is committed only if the principles or the rules of the party have been seriously violated. It must be determined under the statute (1) the reasons that permit such measures; (2) which superior district unit or organ of this unit is allowed to carry out such measures. . . .

PART III: NOMINATION OF CANDIDATES

### Article 17: Nomination of Candidates

The nomination of candidates for election to the representative bodies of the people must be by secret ballot. Electoral laws and party statutes regulate the nomination.

PART IV: REFUNDING OF ELECTION CAMPAIGN COSTS

### Article 18: Principles and Extent of Refunding

1. The necessary cost for a proper election campaign must be refunded to parties that, by nominating candidates, have participated in the election to the Bundestag. Necessary costs are calculated on the basis of a flat fee of 2.50 DM for every person eligible for election to the Bundestag.

2. The flat fee for the election campaign costs is distributed to those parties that have obtained at least: (1) 2.5 per cent of the valid second votes[1] in an electoral district or (2) 10 per cent of the valid first votes in an electoral district only if the *Land* list of a particular *Land* has not been accepted.

3. The percentage of the flat fee, that is, the amount of refund covering the election campaign costs, is (1) for parties, according to paragraph 2(1), proportional to the second votes obtained in the electoral district; (2) for a single party, according to paragraph 2(2), 2.50 DM for every first vote in electoral districts where the minimum number of votes, that is, 10 per cent, was obtained.

4. Before the exact amount of the refund is determined in accordance with paragraph 3(1), the refund obtained under paragraph 3(2) must be deducted from the flat fee received for election campaign costs.

### Article 19: Refunding Procedures

1. Determination and payment of the refund must be applied for in writing to the president of the Bundestag not later than two months after

[1] West Germans vote not only for the representative of a party (first vote) but also for the party itself (second vote). See chapter 4.

the first meeting of the Bundestag. The application can also be submitted for part of the total amount due.

2. The refund is determined and paid by the president of the German Bundestag.

### Article 20: Payment by Installments

1. All parties that fulfilled the requirements of article 18, paragraph 2, by receiving results during the preceding Bundestag elections must be granted refund installments upon applying for them. The installments may not exceed 10 per cent of the refund during the second year of the electoral term of the Bundestag, and they may not exceed 15 per cent during the third year and 35 per cent during the fourth election year.

2. The application for a payment by installments must be made in writing to the president of the Bundestag.

.  .  .

### Article 22: Refund for Election Campaign Costs in the "Länder"

In the *Länder*, the election campaign costs of the parties represented in the *Landtag* can be refunded under articles 18–20, since the requirements of article 18, paragraph 2, need not be fulfilled by national minority parties.

PART V: ACCOUNTING

### Article 23: Obligation of Public Disclosure

The party leadership must make the sources of the party's finances public during each fiscal year. . . .

### Article 24: Statement of Accounts

1. The statement of accounts itemizes the party's revenues.

2. In the revenue account, the following must be listed: membership fee; fees of the members of the parliamentary parties and other regular fees; revenues from property, party functions, the sale of pamphlets and publications, and other party activities as well as revenues from contributions; loans; refunds according to Part IV; and income from any other source.

### Article 25: Identification of Donors

Contributions to a party, or to one or several of its district units, of more than 20,000 DM per individual or 200,000 DM per legal body during one fiscal year must be recorded in the statement of accounts. The name and address of the donor as well as the total amount of the donation must be indicated.

.  .  .

### Article 28: Obligation of Bookkeeping

The parties must keep books itemizing their revenues. This must be done according to the law and the principles of orderly bookkeeping. Records of accounts must be kept for five years beginning at the end of each fiscal year.

. . .

### Article 32: Enforcement

If a party or party organization is declared unconstitutional according to article 21, paragraph 2 of the Basic Law, the authorities appointed by the governments of the *Länder* will take all legal measures necessary to enforce the sentence and any possible additional measures demanded by the Federal Constitutional Court. The highest authorities of the *Länder* have, for this purpose, the unrestricted right to give instructions to those authorities and offices of the *Land* that are responsible for the maintenance of public safety and order.

### Article 33: Prohibition of Substitute Organizations

It is prohibited to form organizations in order to continue the unconstitutional activities (substitute party organizations) of a party that has been outlawed according to article 21, paragraph 2 of the Basic Law and article 46 of the Federal Constitutional Court law. It is also illegal to use existing organizations as substitute organizations for such a party.

. . .

PART VII: FINAL DETERMINATIONS

### Article 40: Validity in the "Land" of Berlin

According to the definition given in article 13, paragraph 1, of the third transition law of January 4, 1952, this law also applies to Berlin. As long as the application of article 21, paragraph 2, sentence 2 of the Basic Law is obstructed in the *Land* of Berlin, Part IV and article 38 of this law will not be applied in the *Land* of Berlin.

3. THIRD REICH, LAW PROHIBITING THE FORMATION OF
POLITICAL PARTIES, JULY 14, 1933

1. The NSDAP is the only political party in Germany.

2. Whoever undertakes to maintain the organization of another political party or to form a new political party is punishable with imprisonment in a penitentiary for up to three years or with confinement to jail for six months to three years, unless the act is punishable with a higher penalty under other provisions.

FROM *FLG*, I (1933) p. 479.

## 4. Federal Republic, Federal Constitutional Court, Decision on Political Parties in General and the SRP in Particular, 1952

In a liberal democratic state each citizen has the right to freedom of political speech and association. But, in a democracy, it is also assured that popular sovereignty is exercised through elections and voting. In the actuality of the large modern democratic state, this popular will can emerge only through political parties operating as political units. Both concepts suggest the fundamental conclusion that no barriers may be erected against the formation and operation of political parties.

Thus the framers of the German constitution were concerned with whether this conclusion could be put into practice unadulteratedly or whether, in the light of the most recent experiences, certain limits had to be imposed.

In article 21, the Basic Law dealt with these problems. It established the principle that political parties should be formed freely, but it also provided for measures to prevent anticonstitutional activities of political parties. To prevent abuse of the first principle, article 21 authorized the Federal Constitutional Court to determine questions of unconstitutionality and, further, attempted to specify the factual requirements for such a determination.

The basic concepts underlying this regulation also furnish important guidelines for the interpretation of article 21. This applies particularly to the interpretation of the concept of a "free democratic basic order." The special position of parties in a democratic state justifies their exclusion from participation in the political process not if they attack, by legal means, individual provisions or even comprehensive institutions of the constitution but only if they seek to invalidate the basic values of a free democratic, constitutional state. . . .

A free democratic basic order can be defined as an order that excludes rule by force and arbitrariness. Instead, it constitutes a government system that respects the rule of law, popular sovereignty, the will of the majority, liberty, and equality. As a minimum, the following fundamental principles must be observed: respect for human rights embodied in the Basic Law, especially for each individual's right to life and free development; respect for popular sovereignty, separation of powers, government responsibility, administrative legality, independence of the judiciary, and a multiparty system; and respect for equal opportunities for all political parties including a constitutional guarantee of the right to exist and of the right to exercise opposition. . . . A political party can only be excluded from participation in the political process if it rejects the fundamental principles of liberal democracy.

Examination of the evidence [described in some detail in the opinion of the Court] suggests the following conclusions:

1. As its political tenets and the behavior of its members indicate, the SRP

rejects fundamental human rights—particularly the dignity of man, the right of each individual to develop freely, and the principle of equality before the law. This is particularly evident in the party's attempt to revive anti-Semitism.

2. The SRP attacks the democratic political parties of the F.R.G. not only to draw attention, by legitimate means, to its own program but also to exclude other parties from participation in the political process. In other words, the SRP does not attack individual parties but the principle of a multiparty system, which is one of the essential principles of a liberal democracy.

3. The internal organization of the SRP is characterized by the following features: it is structured hierarchically on the basis of the *Führerprinzip.* . . . Admission to the party may be denied arbitrarily. According to the party's standing orders, members can be expelled by the dissolution of entire area associations. Furthermore, proceedings against individual members are taken arbitrarily, and these proceedings are conducted without due process.

4. The SRP resembles the former NSDAP in program, ideology, and style. . . . The SRP considers itself as the successor of the NSDAP. This is shown by the composition of its leadership, which consists mainly of former National Socialists; by the attempts of the party to recruit former National Socialists as party members not despite but because of their past affiliation as National Socialists; and by the undisguised glorification of Hitler.

The SRP is therefore unconstitutional.

### 5. Federal Republic, Federal Constitutional Court, Decision on the Communist Party, August 17, 1956

. . . Examined within their proper context, these [Communist] utterances suggest only one interpretation: they represent a systematic agitation that aims at degrading and bringing into contempt the constitution of the F.R.G. Their objective is to derogate the Republic's reputation and to shake the confidence of the people in the value system established by it. The decisive factor is that these are not isolated and individual lapses, as happen sometimes in political campaigns; the origin of these utterances and their manner of being circulated clearly reveal the systematic and premeditated nature of the procedure. . . . The force behind the political will—the official Party command—is waging a systematic campaign against the constitutional organs of the F.R.G. With the help of the rigidly organized Party machinery, this action was to be given effectiveness and power that no individual Party organ could hope to achieve by independent propaganda. That is why the KPD [Communist Party] must rely on such agitation. . . .

The proper perspective for interpreting the activities of the KPD emerges against the background of the Party's attitude toward the constitutional systems of other Communist countries, which is characterized by unlimited

FROM *FCC*, III (1956), p. 133.

loyalty and unreserved agreement with existing conditions and government measures of those countries. Their devoted respect for the Communist system of government leads to blindness, even on the question of whether Communist politics and administration conform to the doctrines of Marx and Engels.

A party aiming at radical reform must have the right to criticize the existing order; this right includes the opportunity to spread mass propaganda. In this process, its political ideas become vulgarized and adapted to the emotional needs of the masses; in other words, trivial phrases and campaign slogans are used to appeal to the public sentiment. All this is harmless and, from a constitutional point of view, unobjectionable, as long as the party's behavior shows that it is conscious of its status as a political party in a free democracy.

From this is derived the fundamental objective of every political party in a free democratic state: to recognize publicly, by the form and manner of its political activities, the paramount and binding values of the constitution; to cooperate in consolidating the party's reputation among the people; and, at the very least, to refrain from degrading, insulting, or bringing into contempt the democratic order. Any party that consciously, continually, and systematically undertakes a campaign of slander and mockery against these values and against the order representing them aims at impairment and destruction. It is unthinkable that such a party could be called upon constitutionally to cooperate in the formation of the political will of a free democratic state.

### 6. Federal Republic, Federal Constitutional Court, Decision on Party Subsidies, July 19, 1966

Using the negotiations on the motion of the government of the *Land* Hesse as a basis, the Federal Constitutional Court was convinced that it was not in accord with article 20, paragraph 2, and article 21 of the Basic Law to subsidize parties with funds budgeted for activities directed at the formation of the political will and opinion of the people. . . . It is, however, in accord with the Basic Law to use funds to finance the proper election campaign of all political parties that participate in the formation of the political will of the people as a result of their participation in parliamentary elections. . . . The legislators of the Basic Law voted to support the free and open formation of the political will and opinion of the people by creating a free and democratic basic order. . . . In a democracy, the political will must be formed by the people and passed on to the state organs. It must not be formed by the state organs and passed on to the people. . . . The relations between constitutional organs and political parties are subject to the constitutional demand for an open formation of the political opinion and will, originating with the people and proceeding to the state organs without the interference of the state.

From *FCC*, XX (1966), pp. 56–118.

As regards the financial relations between the highest constitutional organs and the political parties, the state has no obligation to satisfy the financial needs of the political parties. . . . The political parties cooperate in the formation of the political will of the people by participating in elections that could not be carried out without parties. . . . Beyond this, they represent a link between the individual and the state. . . . They are the instruments by which the will of the citizens can be carried out even in periods between elections; they are the mouthpiece of the people. . . . Insofar as the parties support the government, they bring about and maintain a link between the people and their political leader. If they are minority parties, they represent the opposition and make it visible. Even as mediators, they influence the formation of public opinion. . . .

According to general opinion, the Basic Law does not permit the state to cover the financial needs of the parties completely or even largely with public funds. If the state were to help finance all political activities of the parties by annual or monthly payments, the parties would not necessarily be fitted into the state machinery. Nonetheless, they would be tied to the state machinery and would become dependent upon the state. If the parties were financed in such a way, the state organs could influence the formation of political opinion.

Article 21 of the Basic Law does not serve as a justification for party financing by the state. State financing of the political activities of the parties cannot be justified by arguing that parties could otherwise not fulfill their duties. Such an argument implies doubt about the ability and readiness of the citizens to create and maintain organizations that serve to articulate their opinion and to make political decisions. Thus, the foundations of the democratic order, upon which the constitution is based and which are still valid today, could be questioned. Granted the antipathy of indifference of some citizens toward political parties, this results either from historical experiences or from the present social, economic, and political situations.

According to article 20, paragraph 2, and article 21 of the Basic Law, the state cannot subsidize all of the political activities of the parties. It can, however, refund the costs of a proper election campaign to the political parties if the principles of freedom and equal opportunity for all parties are observed. The parliamentary elections represent the most important act in the formation of the political will in a democratic state. In a representative democracy . . . parliamentary elections must be repeated periodically in order to give the people from whom all state power emanates an opportunity to express its will. . . . Without political parties, elections cannot be held in a modern mass democracy. . . .

The continuous process of forming political opinion culminates first in the election campaign and then in the election itself. The election campaign can be separated from the party's normal activities. The election campaign is based on the assumption that the election is imminent and that it is limited in terms of time. Consequently, the cost of an election can be determined by the nature of the election. The expenses of the parties for the election campaign can be separated from other expenses. . . . Thus, the particular importance of the parties for the elections justifies refunds by the state for the costs of a proper election campaign.

If the legislature provides a refund for election campaign costs, it must respect the freedom granted to the parties by article 21 of the Basic Law. It must also take into account that the proportional distribution of funds does not disagree with the principle of equal opportunity for all parties. . . . Once the decision is made to refund the proper campaign costs of the political parties, those parties that may claim a share of the federal funds must be determined; only parties that have participated in the election campaign are eligible. However, the principle of equal opportunity for all parties requires that all parties that have participated in the election campaign must at least be considered for refunds. The principle of equal opportunity for all parties is violated if the funds are provided a priori for only those parties that were already represented in parliament or that obtained representation in parliament as a result of the election.

# INTRODUCTION 2: PARTIES AND PROGRAMS

In earlier German party life, there had been more than two major parties. The SPD was opposed by a number of nonsocialist parties. The Center Party represented Catholics who, prior to 1945, were a minority in the Reich. A conservative party represented the politically and socially ruling groups prior to 1918 (Prussian land-owning aristocracy, officialdom, many among the upper middle classes); it continued to play a role under Weimar. And various "liberal" parties represented chiefly business and lower middle classes. In the post-World War II period, this picture changed drastically. The SPD is now opposed by one big nonsocialist party, the CDU, in addition to which only the FDP has retained significance.

The CDU was organized—first locally and regionally, then nationally— by Catholics and Protestants who had formerly been members of the various middle-class parties. Its purpose was to oppose socialism by the force of Christian principles. In its early programs and policies, the party was divided on important questions of social and economic policy; its left wing opposed the free market policy and favored some degree of state regulation and the nationalization of certain industries. Adenauer became the uncontested leader of the party in 1949 and, as his *Memoirs* shows, from the outset, he favored his party's right wing, whose leader in economic policies was Ludwig Erhard. Successive party programs from the early 1950's onward solidified the victory of the right wing. As long as Adenauer was at the helm—that is, until 1963—he managed to control all deviating factions of his party. Since then, dissent has arisen over a great variety of issues. This difficulty is reflected in successive changes in the party statute: under Adenauer, detailed provisions were not important because, as party chairman, Adenauer always had his way. After his resignation as chancellor in 1963, he continued as party chairman until 1966 and matters continued much the same. In 1966, Chancellor Erhard restored the identity of party leadership with government leadership. In December, 1966, a Grand Coalition government was formed by the CDU and the SPD. Kurt-Georg Kiesinger (CDU) became the new chancellor; he also became the new chairman of the CDU. More recent amendments to the party statute indicate that Kiesinger is surrounded by prominent party members with whom he has to share control over the party. Strong influence is also exercised by regional party organizations and their leaders, in particular, by the formally autonomous Bavarian CSU (document 8).

In contrast to the CDU, the SPD, which had formerly been beset by factional strife (leftist wings on occasion going so far as to split away), has been more or less united in its policies and programs since its postwar reorganization. This is all the more remarkable because the party has undergone considerable changes in its basic outlook. Its Marxist heritage was still noticeable late in the 1940's and early in the 1950's, under party chairman Kurt Schumacher, who died in 1952 (document 10). The party's Godesberg Program of 1959 signaled the acceptance of a reformist development that shifted the party's interest from socialism to social reform (document 11). In foreign affairs, too, the party changed from neutralism and opposition to rearmament to favoring a Western-alliance orientation. In structure, the party has always been organized in such a way that the central party organs and, in particular, the party executive—a group of top party leaders who have usually known how to control the biannual party convention—have perpetuated their control for considerable periods of time. Recently, the presidium, a small group within the executive, has concentrated control in its hands (documents 12 and 13). While the SPD has controlled the government in several *Länder* (almost continuously in Hesse, Hamburg, Bremen, and Berlin) and increasingly controls the government of the major West German cities, until the formation of the CDU-SPD Grand Coalition it had failed to take over or even gain access to the central government. After the 1969 Bundestag election, the party joined forces with the FDP to form a new government in which, for the first time in postwar history, it took over the role of major group in the government coalition under its chairman's (Willy Brandt) chancellorship.

The FDP, successor to various liberal parties, has been characterized by divergent policy views and backing and by a structure that has placed more power in the regional party organizations than has been the case in the CDU and SPD. The FDP stands for free enterprise and economic competition, for secular schools, and for strong central government power (document 14). In foreign policy, its leaders have from time to time voiced unorthodox opinions, such as a strong emphasis on a détente with East Germany, even favoring close ties with the G.D.R. The party's future depends on whether it can hold the support of over 5 per cent of the electorate. In 1969, with a strong emphasis on a "leftist" orientation, the party lost most of its conservative support but managed to pass the critical 5 per cent barrier and, as the third party represented in the Bundestag, to re-enter government in coalition with the SPD. With its own support diminishing, however, its future is very much in doubt.

The National Democratic Party (NPD) is the result of a merger between remnants of smaller conservative, nationalist groups, such as the German Party (DP), and outright neo-Nazi groups. By the end of 1966, the neo-Nazi elements, among which numerous former Nazi functionaries can be found, had taken over control of the key positions in the party organization. In its program, the party denies having Nazi-type objectives and puts its emphasis on nationalism. However, this is nationalism of the xenophobic variety: jobs for Germans and an end to the entry of foreign workers; priority of domestic projects over foreign aid; an end to the "humiliating" trials of Nazi war criminals and to alleged discrimination against former Nazis; a foreign policy independent of foreign powers, particularly the United States; a refusal to renounce German territory in the east; and so forth. Anti-Semitism has been veiled ("no tributes in the form of restitution payment") but has frequently come into the open in election campaigns (document 15). Although the party failed to attain the necessary 5 per cent of the vote for entering the Bundestag both in 1965 and 1969, its support has risen steadily since its formation and it is likely to continue to be the rallying point of the rightist-nationalist elements in West German society.

Space prevents comprehensive documentation of the often changing and highly varied policy statements made by parties and party leaders. However, the documents that follow are of illustrative value. The CDU has never agreed on a basic program, and its statements usually resemble American campaign platforms. The basic principles of the CDU are in the Hamburg Program of 1953, which is still in line with the party's present policies (document 7) and the statute adopted by the party in 1967 (document 8). To illustrate the varying position of the SPD the party's Erfurt program of 1891 (document 9) and two more recent pronouncements—one by Kurt Schumacher (document 10) illustrating the transition from socialism to social reform and the Godesberg Program of 1959 (document 11), codifying the present party line—are presented. Also included is the party statute of 1966 (document 12) and its parliamentary standing order of 1962 (document 13). The Hannover "Theses" of the FDP of 1967 (document 14) not only contain the party's basic program but also reflect its former position as the only opposition group in the Bundestag. The programmatic manifesto of the NPD (document 15), the content of which is similar to the 1920 program of the NSDAP (document 16) but the form of which is as vague and unrevealing as that of most German ultra-rightist groups in the past, is likewise included.

# DOCUMENTS

### 7. FEDERAL REPUBLIC, CDU, HAMBURG PROGRAM, 1953

Under the chancellorship of Konrad Adenauer, the CDU has led the German people in the F.R.G. away from hunger, misery, and deadly isolation during the past four years. In view of the coming federal elections, we give an account of what we have achieved and announce our program for the next federal parliament.

#### BASIC DEMANDS OF NATIONAL POLICY

It is the duty of the state to serve its citizens. As a free citizen, the individual should carry the responsibility for the state. State authority has no right to become totalitarian. For this reason, we fight for the right of the family and the freedom of the individual to make morally responsible decisions. The same applies to the activities of free organizations and of social life. The primary responsibility for the fulfillment of public duties lies with the local government. The central government's responsibility begins only if local government is unable to function.

The churches have an important role to play in public life, and they must be able to fulfill their responsibilities freely independent of state control. . . .

In public administration, we want to promote the successfully tested system of a professional civil service . . . and to ensure its efficiency and viability through a reform of civil service compensation that takes into account the responsibility of the individuals and ensures the well-being of their families.

We support the German soldiers who, by their best tradition, are bound to the people by moral obligations. The injustice done after the collapse of 1945 to the German soldiers who were fulfilling their duty has not affected their honor. The just treatment of war criminals is a task particularly close to our hearts. . . .

#### ASSIMILATION OF EXPELLEES AND REFUGEES

A firm policy to deal with refugee problems serves the well-being of the entire nation. To support the unrenounceable right to their homeland is also a responsibility of the entire German nation. Federal legislation has prompted the speedy assimilation of expellees and refugees. It must be ensured that the benefits of this legislation are given without delay to all who are entitled to them.

FROM CDU, Bonn.

## ECONOMIC AND SOCIAL POLICY

At a time when production and supply reached a perilous ebb, the CDU assumed the primary responsibility for Germany's economic policy. Through a social market economy [*Soziale Marktwirtschaft*] we have freed the productive capacity of the nation from the paralysis of a state-controlled economy and have developed it through free competition. Today, the economy is viable again, and we now have to solve the following problems, using the well-tried principles of a social market economy: a further increase in production and a reduction of prices; an improved standard of living for all; the promotion of agricultural production, of free farmers, and of a middle-class economy; the development of social security legislation, especially for older employees, old-age pensioners, and war victims; and the creation of private property for a wide sector of the population. We reject an economic policy controlled by the state, because it paralyzes rather than encourages productive capacity and because it is incompatible with a free system of justice. We approve of planned influence on the economy by methods applicable to the market, of free competition based on legislation, and of the fulfillment of social obligations for which we are responsible. . . .

## AGRICULTURAL POLICY

An efficient agriculture is the basis of national nutrition and an essential part of our economy. Its most important factor—a farming population closely associated with its soil—is also a cornerstone of the social and moral life of the people. For this reason, farms—and especially family holdings— must be maintained, strengthened, and encouraged. Unified legislation for agriculture and real estate that acknowledges the principle of private property must be quickly introduced. . . .

## POLICY FOR THE MIDDLE CLASSES

The middle classes are an essential reconstructive and binding element in a soundly balanced society. Efficient and responsible persons should be able to develop their activities in their own businesses. The middle-class professions have the right to enjoy a social system that is based on self-administration, promotes community feeling, and ensures an improvement in professional efficiency. By appropriate community programs, the training of the younger generation particularly should be intensified. . . .

## FINANCE AND TAXATION POLICY

The defense of the currency is the most important task of the government and of the central bank. To achieve this, a policy of successfully balancing the national budget must be maintained. . . .

ENSURING SOCIAL SATISFACTION

Our social policy is not an appendix to a social market economy, but its objective. The immense social misery caused by the collapse after World War II could not be remedied by a single measure. Through our legislation during the past four years, we have been successful in mitigating and overcoming poverty. We have achieved material and social improvement for the unemployed, the sick, invalids, the disabled, widows, and orphans. Pensions have been greatly increased. Progressive laws to ensure just regulation of the relationship between employer and employee have been passed. In social insurance, self-administration by the participants has been re-established.

COMPANY LAW AND CODETERMINATION IN INDUSTRY

The CDU has led the way in introducing the workers' right of codetermination in industry. We have thus made a decisive contribution to securing peaceful conditions in industry and in the economy as a whole. We have introduced a similar law for public service employees. We support the principle of economic self-administration and economic partnership.

ENSURING THE RIGHT OF THE FAMILY

The well-being of the family must be promoted in every possible way. The family has the right to an adequate income as determined by legislation. Taxation, revenues, grants, assistance and old-age pensions must be determined not only for the single person but, where applicable, also for the whole family.

SOCIAL SECURITY

Our social system is based on social security. We will maintain the successfully tested form of a graduated social system. In order to present a clear picture of the effects and results of the various insurance, pension, and welfare programs, an investigation of the social security programs is urgently needed. In social health insurance, responsible cooperation between insured persons, health insurance funds, doctors, and hospitals must be ensured. . . .

PROPERTY FOR ALL CLASSES OF THE POPULATION

Human dignity and existence is severely endangered by modern tendencies toward collectivization. For this reason, we demand that all classes of our population should have the right to own property. Private property promotes the responsible attitude of individuals and families toward life. The greater the number of private property owners, the more balanced the social system and the securer social peace will become.

The division of economic power can be achieved best by combining the principles of codetermination and joint ownership. Nationalization and socialist common ownership are not the solution to social questions.

## 8. FEDERAL REPUBLIC, CDU, STATUTE ADOPTED AT THE FIFTEENTH FEDERAL PARTY CONGRESS, BRAUNSCHWEIG, MAY 23, 1967

### AIMS, NAME, AND SEAT

ART. 1  The CDU aims at democratically shaping public life in the service of the German people and the German fatherland in accordance with Christian responsibility and the Christian moral law based on individual liberty.

.  .  .

### MEMBERSHIP

ART. 4  Any person may become a member of the CDU who is willing to promote the party's aims, has reached the age of eighteen, and is in possession of his civil rights. Membership in another party precludes membership in the CDU.

.  .  .

ART. 10  Disciplinary measures may be taken against members by either the local or the federal party executive committee. Disciplinary measures may include warning, reprimand, deprivation of party offices, deprivation of eligibility to hold party office during a specified period of time, expulsion from the party. . . . In the event of expulsion from the party or of temporary or permanent deprivation of eligibility for party office, reasons must be given for the decision.

ART. 11  Proof that the member has damaged the party by his conduct or by the continued neglect of his duties as laid down by the party statute is a prerequisite for expulsion.

ART. 12  A member is deemed to have damaged the party if he is also a member of another political party; if he takes a position opposed to the declared policy of the CDU in the public meetings of political opponents, in radio and television programs, or in the press; if he publishes or reveals to a political opponent confidential party matters; or if he embezzles funds that belong to, or are at the disposal of, the party.

.  .  .

FROM CDU, Bonn.

ORGANIZATION

ART. 15   The four organizational levels of the CDU are the federal party, the *Land* associations [*Landesverbände*], the county associations [*Keisverbände*], and the local associations [*Ortsverbände*].

.     .     .

ORGANS

ART. 27   The organs of the federal party include the federal party congress, the federal committee [*Bundesausschuss*], and the federal executive committee [*Bundesvorstand*].

ART. 28   The federal party congress is composed of delegates from *Land* associations elected by *Land* and county party congresses. In addition, special delegates participate in the federal party congress (article 16). The *Land* associations designate one delegate for every seventy-five thousand votes cast for the CDU during the previous Bundestag election and an additional delegate for each thousand members or fraction thereof. The CDU of the Soviet zone of occupation (CDU in exile) shall be represented by seventy-five delegates. The representation of territories behind the Oder-Neisse line (*Land* association Oder-Neisse) shall have twenty delegates. The federal party congress shall meet at least every two years and shall be convened by the federal executive committee. It must be convened by a motion by the federal committee or by at least one-third of the *Land* associations.

ART. 29   The tasks of the federal party congress include deciding on the basic guidelines of the party's policy and program, electing in separate ballots the members of the federal executive committee, including its chairman, secretary-general (nominated by the chairman), five deputy chairmen, and federal treasurer. The members of the executive committee are elected every second calendar year; the secretary-general is elected every four years but may be relieved of his duties before then (at the suggestion of the party chairman).

Members of the federal executive committee as well as the federal chancellor and the federal president (if CDU members) and the chairman of the CDU/CSU parliamentary party of the Bundestag form the presidium [*Präsidium*]. The federal executive officer of the party attends meetings of the presidium in an advisory capacity.

The congress elects the chairman and four assessors [*Beisitzer*], as well as five deputy members of the federal party courts, according to the provisions of the party court order. The congress receives and acts upon the reports of the federal executive committee and of the federal parliamentary party; it makes decisions in matters relating to the party statutes, to party fees and finance regulations, and to party court orders.

ART. 30   The federal committee consists of ninety members elected by county and *Land* associations, eight delegates of the CDU in exile, five delegates of the *Land* association Oder-Neisse, plus the members of the federal executive committee, and the federal chairmen of the associations. The chairmen of the federal experts committees [*Bundesfachausschüsse*] participate on an advisory basis.

ART. 31    The tasks of the federal committee are as follows: the federal committee shall have jurisdiction over all political and organizational matters of the federal party insofar as they are not reserved for the federal party congress.

.   .   .

ART. 33    The federal executive committee consists of thirty members, including the chairman; the secretary-general; the five deputy chairmen; the federal treasurer; the federal chancellor and the president of the Bundestag (if members of the CDU); the chairman of the federal parliamentary party; and the federal executive officer.

ART. 34    The secretary-general supports the chairman in the fulfillment of his duties and administers party affairs in accord with [*im Einvernehmen mit*] the chairman.

.   .   .

ASSOCIATIONS [VEREINIGUNGEN]

ART. 38    The following associations are affiliated with the party: the Youth Union, the Women's Association, social committees, local political associations, and middle-class associations.

.   .   .

ART. 49    The CDU has a working partnership with the CSU of Bavaria.

### 9. EMPIRE, SPD, PROGRAM ADOPTED AT THE PARTY CONGRESS, ERFURT, OCTOBER 21, 1891

The SPD does not fight for new class privileges and rights, but for the abolition of class domination, of classes as such, and for equal rights and equal obligations, regardless of sex and origin. On the basis of these opinions, it fights not only against the exploitation and oppression of the workers but against any kind of exploitation and oppression in modern society, no matter whether it is directed against a class, a party, a sex, or a race.

Starting from these principles, the SPD makes the following demands:

1. universal, equal right to vote in all elections and plebiscites be given to all citizens of the Empire who are over twenty years of age, regardless of their sex and that such votes are to be direct and secret; that an electoral

FROM Berliner Volksblatt, *Vorwärts* (1891).

system based on proportional representation be introduced and, until this is introduced, that a new legal determination of the voters' roll be made every census; that elections occur every two years and that the day of election be declared a legal holiday; that financial compensation be given to elected representatives; and that all restrictions on political rights be abolished, except in the case of interdiction.

2. direct lawmaking by the people based on their right to make and reject proposals; self-determination and self-administration of the people in the Empire, in the *Länder*, and in the communities; election of the authorities by the people; responsibility and liability of the former; and the annual determination of tax rates by the people.

3. general military training and a people's army instead of a standing army; declaration of war and peace by the representative bodies of the people; and settlement of all international controversies by means of arbitration.

4. abolition of all laws that restrict or suppress the free expression of opinion and the right of association.

5. abolition of all laws that discriminate against women in public and private spheres.

6. declaration that religion is a private matter; abolition of all payments from public funds for ecclesiastical and religious purposes; private status of all ecclesiastical and religious societies, which are to be independent in the handling of their own affairs.

7. secular schools; obligatory attendance at public elementary schools; free classes; free educational aids; and free board in public elementary schools as well as in higher educational institutions for all students who, because of their mental abilities, are considered capable of further education.

8. free access to the courts and free legal advice; jurisdiction by judges elected by the people; appeal in criminal cases; compensation for innocent people who have been accused, arrested, and sentenced; abolition of the death penalty.

9. free medical treatment, including obstetrical care and medicines; free burial.

10. graduated income and property taxes to cover all public expenses that must be covered by taxes; obligation to self-assessment of taxes; death duties increasing gradually according to the size of the inherited property and to the nature of the relationship to the deceased; abolition of all indirect taxes, duties, and other economic measures that sacrifice the interest of all to the interests of a privileged minority.

For the protection of the working class, the SPD makes the following demands:

1. effective national and international legislation for the protection of workers based on the following principles: introduction of a normal eight-hour workday; prohibition of child labor—work by those under fourteen years of age; prohibition of night work, except for such sections of the industry that require night work for technical or public welfare reasons; an

uninterrupted thirty-six-hour rest period every week for every worker; the prohibition of payment in goods.

2. inspection of all factories; examination and regulation of working conditions in the cities and in the country by labor exchange offices of the Empire and of the districts, as well as by the Ministry of Labor.

3. equal legal status of agricultural and industrial workers; abolition of the regulations governing the rights and duties of servants.

4. guarantee of the right to organize.

5. nationalization by the Empire of insurance programs for workers with a decisive participation of the workers in their administration.

### 10. FEDERAL REPUBLIC, SPD, INTRODUCTION TO THE ACTION PROGRAM OF THE PARTY, BONN, JULY 28, 1952

The Social Democrats regard democracy as a political, human, and national opportunity for Germany and as a way to maintain peace in the world. As early as 1945, the Social Democrats declared that they did not recognize the Oder-Neisse as the borderline. The Social Democrats fought alone and without help from others against the efforts of the Soviet occupying power to enforce the union of the SPD with the Communist Party. The Social Democrats were always sure that their efforts to fight against the totalitarian regime in the east and to win the Germans to the principles of democracy would only be possible and show lasting success if this struggle was carried out on the basis of democratic, national self-confidence. German democracy must not be a function of the policy of the Western occupying powers.

The Social Democrats consider it their highest task to create not a state that restores former conditions but a new Germany, which has a new political and social content and in which the people actually can participate in the determination of their own fate in all spheres.

The policy of the present federal government [CDU] is to eliminate the participation of the people as much as possible. Instead, the Social Democrats want to mobilize the people to shape their own fate. The federal government tries to eliminate the practice of parliamentary democracy and to establish an authoritarian administrative state. . . . It is irresponsible propaganda to assert today that the Social Democrats would exercise the same policy as the present federal government does if they were to assume power. The Social Democrats start from completely different principles and try in different ways to reach different aims. For us, German unity is not a distant goal but an immediate aim. The whole program of the SPD is based on the conviction that the future of the German people lies in its energy and efficiency. Twice in the lifetime of one generation, the German worker has had to clear away mountains of debris and ruins left behind by a mad policy of power. By exemplary performance and success, the workers, technicians, and scholars have had to re-establish the good reputation of

FROM SPD, Bad Godesberg.

the German people again and again after it had been lost by national megalomania.

German youth must not get the impression that democracy is related to national decline. Out of national necessity, we are therefore the enemies of a class struggle that starts at the top and destroys all beginnings of a true community in Germany today. The omnipotent power of large property ownership and its followers must be broken in order to clear the road for the development of free German citizens as well as of a free German nation. . . .

The German working class refuses to recognize the economic structure in the Soviet occupation zone as socialization. But it is equally determined not to follow a policy that seeks to return to capitalism and to the restoration of former conditions.

The SPD believes it is its duty to be the party of German patriots and international socialists. Internationalism means the cooperation of truly equal people enjoying equal rights. Today, as in the past, Social Democrats support this internationalism. They reject national self-abnegation, which now even the Germans demand from each other. The SPD also rejects the idea that working people should atone for the guilt that the large property owners brought upon themselves before and after 1933.

It is more important to give the German people a feeling of national self-consciousness that is as far from the criminal arrogance of the past as it is from today's widespread tendency to recognize in every wish of the Allied forces the revelation of European spirit. Only a people that can shape its own destiny can be a valuable member of a community of nations.

## 11. FEDERAL REPUBLIC, SPD, BASIC PROGRAM, ADOPTED AT THE EXTRAORDINARY PARTY CONGRESS, BAD GODESBERG, NOVEMBER, 13–14, 1959

### FUNDAMENTAL VALUES OF SOCIALISM

Socialists aim at establishing a society in which every individual can develop his personality and, as a responsible member of the community, take part in the political, economic, and cultural life of mankind. . . .

Democratic socialism, which in Europe is rooted in Christian ethics, humanism, and classical philosophy, does not proclaim ultimate truths— not out of any lack of understanding for, or indifference to, philosophical or religious truths, but out of respect for the individual's choice in these matters of conscience in which neither the state nor any political party should be allowed to interfere.

The SPD is the party that represents freedom of thought. It is a community of men holding different beliefs and ideas. Their agreement is based on shared moral principles and political aims. The SPD strives for a way

FROM SPD, Bad Godesberg.

of life that is in accord with these principles. Socialism is a constant task: to fight for freedom and justice, to preserve them, and to live up to them.

### BASIC DEMANDS FOR A SOCIETY WORTHY OF MAN

From the acceptance of democratic socialism follow certain basic demands that must be fulfilled in a society worthy of man. All nations must submit to the rule of international law, which must be backed by adequate executive power. War must be ruled out as a means of policy. All nations must have equal opportunities to share in the world's wealth. Developing countries have a claim to the help of other peoples.

We are fighting for democracy. Democracy must become the universal form of state organization as well as the universal way of life, because it is founded on the respect for the dignity of man and on the principle of his individual responsibility. We resist every dictatorship, every form of totalitarian or authoritarian rule, because they violate human dignity and destroy man's freedom and the rule of law. Socialism can be realized only through democracy, and democracy can be fulfilled only through socialism.

Communists have no right to invoke socialist traditions. In fact, they have falsified socialist ideas. Socialists are struggling for the realization of freedom and justice, while Communists are exploiting the conflicts in society in order to establish the dictatorship of their party.

In a democratic state, every form of power must be subject to public control. The interest of the individual must be subordinated to the interest of the community. Democracy, social security, and individual freedom are endangered by an economic and social system in which striving for profit and power are the distinguishing features. Democratic socialism therefore strives for a new economic and social order.

All privileged access to educational institutions must be abolished. Talent and achievement should be the sole criteria of advancement. . . .

### THE ORDER OF THE STATE

The SPD of Germany exists for, and works in, the whole of Germany. It stands by the Basic Law of the F.R.G. In accordance with the Basic Law it strives for German unity in freedom. . . .

Man's life, his dignity, and his conscience take precedence over the state. Every citizen must respect the convictions of his fellow men. It is the duty of the state to protect freedom of faith and conscience. . . .

The SPD affirms its adherence to democracy. In a democracy, the power of the state is derived from the people, and the government is always responsible to parliament, whose confidence it must possess. In a democracy, the rights of the minority as well as the rights of the majority must be respected; government and opposition have different but equally important tasks; both share responsibility for the state. . . .

The legislature, the executive, and the judiciary should function separately, and it is the duty of each to serve the public interest. The existence of three levels of authority—federal, state, and local—ensures the distribution of power, strengthens freedom, and, through codetermination and coresponsibility, gives the citizen manifold access to democratic institutions. Free local communities are vital to a living democracy. The SPD therefore supports the principles of local self-government, which must be extended and given adequate financial support. . . .

Press, radio, television, and cinema fulfill public tasks. They must be independent and free to gather information wherever they wish, to comment on it, to distribute it, and to form and express their own opinions. Radio and television should remain under the control of public corporations and should be directed by free and democratic boards. They must be safeguarded against pressure from interest groups.

Judges must have structural and psychological independence if they are to serve justice in the name of the people. Lay judges should play an equally important part in jurisdiction. Only independent judges can pass judgment on criminal offenses. Neither wealth nor poverty should have an influence on the individual's access to courts or on jurisdiction. Legislation must keep pace with the development of society if justice is to be done and if the people's sense of justice is not to be violated.

### NATIONAL DEFENSE

The SPD affirms the need to defend the free, democratic society. It is in favor of national defense. National defense must be adapted to the political and geographical position of Germany; it must therefore remain within the limits imposed by the necessity of creating conditions that ease international tensions, effectively control disarmament, and reunify Germany. Protection of the civilian population is an essential part of a country's defense.

The SPD demands that the means of mass destruction be banned in the whole world by international law.

The F.R.G. must neither produce nor use atomic weapons or other means of mass destruction. . . .

The armed forces must be under the political direction of the government and under the control of parliament. A relationship of trust should exist between soldiers and the democratic institutions of the country. The soldier must retain his civic rights and duties. The armed forces must be used only for the defense of the nation. The SPD pledges itself to protect every citizen who, for reasons of conscience, refuses to do military service or to operate means of mass destruction. . . .

### CONSTANT ECONOMIC EXPANSION

The goal of social-democratic economic policy is the constant growth of prosperity, a just share of the national produce for all, and a life in freedom, undisturbed by undignified dependence and exploitation.

The second industrial revolution allows a standard of living that is higher than ever before as well as the elimination of the poverty and misery still suffered by large numbers of people. The nation's economic policy must secure full employment; it must also maintain a stable currency, increase productivity, and raise general prosperity.

To enable all people to take part in the country's growing prosperity and to adjust the economy to constant structural changes in order to achieve balanced economic development, there must be planning.

Free choice of consumer goods and services, free choice of place of work, freedom for employers to exercise their initiative, and free competition are essential conditions of social-democratic economic policy. The autonomy of trade unions and employers' associations in collective bargaining is an important feature of a free society. Totalitarian control of the economy destroys freedom. The SPD therefore favors a free market wherever free competition really exists. If a market is dominated by individuals or groups, however, every possible step must be taken to protect economic freedom. As much competition as possible—as much planning as necessary.

### OWNERSHIP AND POWER

Those who control large industrial concerns, huge financial resources, and tens of thousands of employees do not merely perform an economic function but wield decisive power over men, keeping wage and salary earners in a position of dependence not only in purely economic and material matters. . . .

Increased power through cartels and associations grants leaders of big business an influence on politics and the state that is irreconcilable with democratic principles. They usurp the authority of the state. Economic power becomes political power. . . . The key task of an economic policy concerned with freedom is, therefore, to contain the power of big business. State and society must not be allowed to become the prey of powerful sectional groups.

Private ownership of the means of production can claim protection by society as long as it does not hinder the establishment of social justice. Efficient small and medium-sized enterprises must be strengthened so that they can prevail in their competition with large-scale enterprises.

Competition by public enterprise is an important means of preventing private enterprise from dominating the market. Public enterprise should safeguard the interests of the community as a whole. Public enterprise becomes a necessity if, for natural or technical reasons, economic functions vital to the community cannot be carried out rationally unless competition is excluded. . . .

Effective public control must prevent the abuse of economic power. The most important means to this end are investment control and control over the forces dominating the market. Public ownership is a legitimate form of public control, which no modern state can do without. It serves to protect freedom against domination by large economic concerns. In these concerns, power is held today by managers who are servants of anonymous forces. Private ownership of the means of production is therefore no longer identical with the control of power. Economic power and not ownership is the central problem today. If sound economic power relations cannot be guaranteed by other means, public ownership is appropriate and necessary.

Every concentration of economic power, even in the hands of the state, harbors dangers. This is why the principles of self-government and decentralization must be applied to the public sector. The interests of wage and salary earners as well as public consumer interests must be represented on the management boards of public enterprises. Not centralized bureaucracy but responsible cooperation between all concerned serves the interests of the community best.

### DISTRIBUTION OF INCOME AND WEALTH

A competitive economy does not guarantee the just distribution of income and wealth. This can only be achieved by economic-policy measures. . . . Appropriate measures must ensure that an adequate part of the steadily growing capital of big business is widely distributed or used for public purposes. It is a deplorable symptom of our time that privileged groups of our society enjoy luxury, while important public tasks, especially in science, research, and education, are neglected in a way unworthy of a civilized nation.

### TRADE UNIONS AND THE ECONOMY

All wage and salary earners and civil servants have the right to free association in trade unions. They would be helplessly exposed to the managers and executives of private enterprises and concerns if they were unable to confront the latter with the united force of their free and democratically organized trade unions or if they could not agree freely upon working conditions. . . .

Wage and salary earners whose contribution to production is decisive have so far been deprived of effective participation in economic life. Democracy, however, demands that workers should be given a voice and that codetermination be extended to all branches of the economy. From being a servant, the worker must become a citizen of the economy.

Codetermination in the iron and steel industry as well as in coal mining marks the beginning of a new economic structure. The next step should be the establishment of a democratic organizational structure in all large enterprises. Codetermination by employees in the independent administrative bodies of the economy must be secured.

### SOCIAL RESPONSIBILITY

Every citizen has the right to receive a state pension in case of old age, of inability to earn a living, or if the family's provider dies. This pension is supplemented by other personal pension claims. In this way, the individual's standard of living will be sustained. Social allowances of all kinds, including pensions for the war-disabled and their dependents, must be regularly adjusted to rising incomes.

The SPD demands comprehensive health protection. Health policy must be perfected, and the conditions and ways of life must be shaped to make life in sound health possible. Public health protection, especially protection at work and effective methods of preventing damage to the individual's health, must be developed. . . .

Housing shortage must be eliminated speedily through effective building programs. Public housing must be encouraged, and social considerations must be taken into account when rents are determined. Speculation in real estate should be prohibited, and excessive gains from the sale of real estate should be confiscated as taxes.

### WOMAN, FAMILY, YOUTH

Women should enjoy equal rights in the legal, economic, and social spheres. Women must be given equal opportunities in educational and occupational training, in the choice and practice of professions, and in earnings. . . . Effective help should be given to the family by generous tax allowances for parents, by maternity benefits, and by family allowances.

### RELIGION AND CHURCH

Only mutual tolerance that respects the dignity of all men, regardless of different beliefs and convictions, offers a sound basis for political and human cooperation in society. Socialism is no substitute for religion. The SPD respects churches and religious societies. It affirms their public and legal status, their special mission, and their autonomy. . . .

Freedom of thought, religion, and conscience and freedom to preach the gospel must be protected. Any abuse of this freedom for partisan or anti-democratic ends cannot be tolerated.

### EDUCATION

Education must give an opportunity to all to develop their abilities and capacities freely. It must strengthen the will to resist the conformist tendencies of our time. Knowledge, the acquisition of traditional cultural values, and a thorough understanding of the formative forces of society are essential to the development of independent thinking and free judgment. . . .

Parents should have a voice in the education of their children at school, and student self-government should be developed everywhere. School systems and curricula must give the student every opportunity to develop his talents and abilities at all stages. Every gifted student should have access to advanced education and training. Attendance at all state-supported schools and universities should be free. Books and other study materials should be available to students free of charge.

The period of compulsory school attendance should be increased to ten years. Trade and technical schools should provide not only occupational training but also general education.

New paths to university education must be opened. Since not all talented young people can reach the university level by the usual elementary and high school training, other opportunities to do so must be made available through vocational work, occupational schools, and special educational institutions. . . .

Generous grants should secure for all students the full benefits of academic education. All students should be taught the basic elements of political and social science. . . .

THE INTERNATIONAL COMMUNITY

The greatest and most urgent task is to preserve peace and protect freedom. . . . Democratic states must express their solidarity, especially with the developing countries. Half of the world's population still lives in extreme poverty and ignorance. So long as the wealth of the world is not redistributed and the productivity of developing countries raised considerably, democratic development is in jeopardy, and peace continues to be threatened. All people are obliged to fight starvation, misery, and disease in a common effort. Their economic, social, and cultural development must be inspired by the ideas of democratic socialism, if they are not to become the victims of new forms of oppression.

OUR WAY

The socialist movement has a historic task. It began as a spontaneous moral protest of wage earners against the capitalist system. The tremendous development of the productive forces through science and technology brought wealth and power to a small group of people but destitution and misery to the workers. To abolish the privileges of the ruling classes and to secure freedom, justice, and prosperity for all was and remains the essence of socialism. . . .

In several countries of Europe, the foundations of a new society have been laid by social-democratic governments. Social security and the democratization of the economy are being realized more and more.

These successes represent milestones in the forward march of the labor movement, which has demanded so many sacrifices. The emancipation of the workers helped to enlarge the freedom of all men. Initially a party of the working class, the SPD has now become a party of the people. It is determined to put the forces unleashed by the industrial revolution and by the advance of technology in all spheres of life to the service of freedom and justice for all. The social forces that built the capitalist world cannot tackle this task. Their historical record is one of impressive technical and economic advance but also of destructive wars, mass unemployment, inflation that robbed people of their savings, and economic insecurity. The old forces are unable to oppose the brutal Communist challenge with a better program for a new society, in which individual and political freedom is enhanced and economic security and social justice guaranteed. . . .

Only the prospect of a society based on the fundamental values of democratic socialism can offer the world new hope—a society that is built on respect for human dignity, on freedom from want and fear, from war and oppression, and on cooperation with all men of good will. . . .

In Germany, socialists are united in the SPD, which welcomes to its ranks all who accept the fundamental values and demands of democratic socialism.

## 12. Federal Republic, SPD, Organization Statute, Adopted May 23, 1950, and Amended by Party Congress, Dortmund, 1966

### PARTY MEMBERSHIP

ART. 1 Every person who subscribes to the principles of the party and has acquired membership shall be a member of the SPD.

ART. 2 The executive committee of the local association [*Ortsverein*] shall decide on the admission to membership. If no objection is lodged within one year after the application, the admission shall be final. Any member shall have the right to lodge an objection through his appropriate executive committee. The district executive committee and the party executive committee shall, in that order, decide on objections. . . .

### STRUCTURE

ART. 3 The basis of organization shall be the district, which is made up of local associations and demarcated by the party executive committee in accordance with political and economic expediency.

### PARTY CANDIDATES FOR LOCAL OR NATIONAL OFFICE

ART. 5 Candidates for municipal representative bodies [*Gemeindevertretungen*] shall be nominated by the local associations. Candidates for county
From SPD, Bad Godesberg.

assemblies [*Kreistage*] shall be nominated by delegates from the local associations at county conferences called by the subdistrict executive committee; candidates shall be nominated in agreement with the subdistrict or' district executive committee respectively. Nominations for elections to the Bundestag or *Land* legislatures shall be compiled and decided on by the district executive committee with the agreement of the party executive committee, the expanded district executive committee, or the district convention. Nominations for *Land* elections shall be made by the *Land* districts with the agreement of the party executive committee. . . .

ART. 7  The amount of the initiation fee [*Eintrittsgeld*] shall be determined by the district executive committee. . . .

### THE PARTY CONVENTION

ART. 10  The party convention shall be the highest organ of the party. It shall be composed of thirteen hundred delegates elected in the districts, with seats distributed to the number of members for whom obligatory dues were remitted to the party executive committee during the preceding business year; and members of the party executive committee and of the control commission. Participation in the party convention as advisers shall be granted to the members of the party council, one-tenth of the federal parliamentary party [*Bundestagfraktion*], party convention delegates [*Referenten*] designated by the party executive committee and representatives of party institutions. . . .

ART. 12  A party convention shall take place every two years and shall be convened by the party executive committee. . . .

ART. 13  The date and the preliminary agenda of a party convention shall be announced at least three months in advance. . . . Resolutions by party organizations for the party convention shall be submitted to the party executive committee five weeks in advance, and the party executive committee shall publish these resolutions in the party's weekly, *Vorwärts*, at least three weeks before the party convention.

ART. 14  The tasks of the party convention shall include seeing that reports on the activities of the party executive committee, the control commission, and the federal parliamentary party are submitted; determining the location of the party executive committee's headquarters; electing the party executive committee and the control commission; voting on resolutions concerning the party organization and all matters related to the party activities and voting on the resolutions submitted to it.

### THE PARTY EXECUTIVE COMMITTEE

ART. 17  The direction of the party shall be the responsibility of the party executive committee. The executive committee shall consist of a chairman, two deputy chairmen, a treasurer, and additional members to be determined by the party convention. It must include at least four women.

To execute the decisions of the party executive committee and to conduct the party's current political and organizational business the party executive committee shall elect from among its members a managing executive committee (party presidium). The number of the presidium's members shall be determined by the party convention. . . .

The incumbent party executive committee shall present nominations for the election of the next party executive committee not later than two days before the election. The party convention may present additional nominations until one day before the election. The nominations must be supported by at least thirty delegates from at least four districts. . . .

### THE PARTY COUNCIL

ART. 22 The party council shall be composed of (1) the chairmen of the districts and other representatives elected by the district executive committees (districts with up to twenty thousand members shall elect one additional representative; those with up to fifty thousand members, two additional representatives; and those with more than fifty thousand members, three additional representatives; districts with less than twenty thousand members should elect one woman, and districts with more than twenty thousand members must elect one woman to the party council); (2) the chairman of the *Land* committees or *Land* executive committees, respectively, if several districts exist in a *Land*; (3) the chairman of the *Land* parliamentary parties [*Landtagfraktionen*]; (4) the ministers president [*Ministerpräsidenten*] or the deputy ministers president of the *Länder*; (5) the members of the federal government. . . .

ART. 23 The party council shall be convened by the party executive committee. An agenda is to be submitted. As a rule, the party council meets four times a year. . . .

ART. 24 The party council shall be consulted before the party executive committee passes resolutions on basic decisions relating to domestic or foreign policy, to fundamental organizational questions, to the establishment of central party institutions that substantially and permanently encumber the party financially, and to the preparation of Bundestag elections. The party council shall also be responsible for the coordination of the party's policies toward the federation and the *Länder*.

### THE CONTROL COMMISSION

ART. 25 The party convention shall elect a control commission consisting of nine members to supervise the party executive committee and to serve as an appeals institution for complaints against the party executive committee. . . . Supervision shall take place at least four times a year. All communications to the control commission shall be addressed to its chairman; he shall publish them in an appropriate manner. . . .

PARTY DISCIPLINARY PROCEEDINGS

ART. 27  1. Proceedings shall be conducted against any party member who, through persistent disobedience to decisions of the party convention or of a party organization, harms the interests of the party or who commits a dishonorable act or a gross violation against the principles of the party.

2. A disciplinary meeting of the party may decide to issue a reprimand, to deprive the party member temporarily of his right to hold honorary party posts, to expel him from the party. . . .

5. Any branch of the organization can ask for disciplinary proceedings against a party member regardless of whether the accused is a member of that branch. . . .

ART. 28  1. For the purpose of conducting party disciplinary proceedings, arbitration tribunals [*Schiedsgerichte*] shall be established in party subdistricts, districts, and in the party executive committee. . . .

4. The arbitration tribunal of the party executive committee shall consist of three members and three deputy members. The chairman and his deputy must, and the other members and their deputies should, belong to the party executive committee. The members and deputy members of the tribunal shall be elected by the party executive committee for a period that coincides with the term of the party executive committee. . . .

11. Appeals to the arbitration tribunal of the district against the decisions of a subdistrict arbitration tribunal shall be permitted. Appeals to the arbitration tribunal of the party executive committee against the district tribunal decision shall also be permitted, if it has been decided to expel the member or to deprive him temporarily of his right to hold honorary party posts. . . .

ART. 29  1. In cases where serious damage to the party must be averted by quick intervention and when the expulsion of the accused by the arbitration tribunal is expected, the district executive committee concerned as well as the party executive committee may—without having received a petition—expel the accused immediately. . . .

3. According to paragraph 1, the expelled member shall have the right to appeal against a decision . . . to the arbitration tribunal of the party executive committee. . . .

READMISSION TO THE PARTY

ART. 33  The application for readmission by a person expelled from the party shall be addressed to the executive committee of the district organization at the place of residence of the expellee. The organization that requested the expulsion shall be heard before a decision is made. The applicant as well as the organization that requested the expulsion shall have the right to appeal against this decision to the party executive committee. . . .

## 13. FEDERAL REPUBLIC, SPD, PARLIAMENTARY PARTY STANDING ORDERS, 1962

ART. 1   A quorum of the federal parliamentary party shall exist if over one-half of its members are present.

ART. 2   The federal parliamentary party shall designate speakers who shall present its views in the Bundestag.

ART. 3   Should a member of the federal parliamentary party wish to intervene in a debate in the Bundestag, he shall do so after notifying the appropriate committee chairman [*Obmann*] and the executive secretary of the federal parliamentary party.

ART. 4   The federal parliamentary party shall determine the composition of committees, delegations, and the like after nominations have been received from the federal parliamentary party. The procedure applicable to the election of the federal parliamentary party . . . must be employed, if five members present a motion to this effect.

ART. 5   Questions for the question period shall be submitted through the executive secretary of the federal parliamentary party. . . .

### THE EXECUTIVE COMMITTEE

ART. 10   The executive committee shall consist of a chairman, his deputies, other members elected from the federal parliamentary party, and the executive secretaries of the federal parliamentary party. If the chairmen of the working groups are not members of the federal parliamentary party, they or their deputies shall participate in the meetings of the federal parliamentary party as nonvoting members.

ART. 11   The federal parliamentary party shall elect its members by secret balloting. The chairman and the executive secretaries shall be elected by separate ballots. The first election shall be for a term of twelve months. Re-election is possible after an interval of eighteen months. The term of the executive secretaries of the federal parliamentary party shall coincide with the legislative term. . . .

### FUNCTIONS OF THE EXECUTIVE COMMITTEE OF THE FEDERAL PARLIAMENTARY PARTY

ART. 14   The federal parliamentary party shall conduct its business and plan its activities in accordance with party policies [*Richtlinien*].

ART. 15   The executive committee shall prepare meetings and shall report to the federal parliamentary party on its deliberations. The report shall also include views deviating from the majority opinion of the federal parliamentary party. The executive committee shall inform the federal parliamentary party of significant political events and conferences.

FROM SPD, Bad Godesberg.

ART. 16   The executive committee shall convene the meetings of the federal parliamentary party and shall schedule them so that careful attention can be given to all agenda items.

ART. 17   The executive committee shall present proposals to the federal parliamentary party for the composition of committees, delegations, and so forth.

### COMMITTEE ACTIVITY

ART. 20   Members of the federal parliamentary party must actively participate in the work of the Bundestag committees.

ART. 21   The federal parliamentary party shall elect a chairman for each committee.

ART. 22   The chairman shall be responsible to the federal parliamentary party for the work of the committee.

ART. 23   The chairman shall, if necessary, convene a meeting of members and deputies prior to the committee meeting in order to discuss the agenda.

ART. 24   The chairmen shall ensure the cooperation of the different committees, particularly if several committees are considering a measure.

ART. 25   The chairman shall ensure the cooperation of the experts [*Sachbearbeiter*] of the party.

### WORKING GROUPS

ART. 26   For a more thorough discussion of its work, the federal parliamentary party shall establish working groups in various areas. Each working group shall elect its chairman and deputy chairman.

### PRESS OFFICE

ART. 33   The federal parliamentary party shall establish a press office and staff it with experienced journalists.

ART. 34   It shall be the specific task of the press representative to publicize, for the formation of public opinion, the political and parliamentary activities of the Bundestag.

### SECRETARIAT

ART. 36   The federal parliamentary party shall maintain a secretariat to conduct the business of the federal parliamentary party. Members of the federal parliamentary party shall be able to use the secretariat for confidential work.

14. FEDERAL REPUBLIC, FDP, PROGRAM ADOPTED AT THE EIGHTEENTH
PARTY CONGRESS, HANNOVER, APRIL 3–5, 1967[1]

STATE AND LAW

POLITICAL TASKS OF LIBERALISM    Liberalism has created the modern constitutional state [*Rechtsstaat*] based on the security and guarantee of the
inalienable basic rights of its citizens and unable to exist in the future
without the incorporation of the principles of political liberalism. The
constitutional status of the F.R.G. must be free and progressive and thus
liberal. . . .

THE STATE OF EMERGENCY AND THE RIGHT TO VOTE    Parliament must be
a place of freedom and it must, at the same time, guarantee freedom. It
must represent the basic political convictions of our people. Because the
Free Democrats represent opposition, they regard it as their special
responsibility to protect the order of the liberal constitution of the F.R.G.
in all spheres of political life. Therefore, the FDP fights against the unjustified restriction of basic rights as contained in the proposed Emergency
Powers Bill and against the exclusion of parliament, which would transform an emergency situation into an emergency dictatorship; . . .

Furthermore, the FDP demands the retention of the present right to elect
persons on the basis of the proportional representation system and the
abstention from any manipulation of this system. . . .

ECONOMY AND FINANCES

ECONOMIC AND FINANCIAL POLICIES    The FDP supports a free market
economy. Only a free market economy preserves and creates the conditions
of a just and free order of society and of maximal economic progress. In
order to strengthen and to improve confidence in the efficiency of the free
market economy, the FDP demands the achievement of a fair balance in
the conflict between economic growth and equality and the achievement
of growth only by stability, since only a policy based on stable wages and
salaries guarantees workers and employees work and an improved living
standard as well as the opportunity for the pursuit of happiness. Only a
balanced economic policy gives stability to the achievements of social
improvement. . . .

The budget deficits of recent years and those that can be expected in
the future require that all public expenses be checked in order to determine
whether they are objectively justified and well balanced and whether they
can be defended in the light of the total capacity of the national budget.
The results of this investigation must be summarized in a concise statement
on expenditure policy. This holds not only for defense policy but also for

[1] This program is known also as the "107 Theses" or "The Aims of Progress."
FROM FDP, Bonn.

social, agricultural, and public policy as well as for police protection and rural and urban renewal. . . .

Housing policy must aim at the distribution of housing via the free market economy. Controlled housing must be abolished and rent controls must be relaxed in order to establish a balanced market and to provide adequate housing for the population. . . .

### SOCIAL PROBLEMS AND HEALTH

SOCIAL POLICY  Social policy as part of the general policy of a free society requires more freedom in the choice of life and old-age insurance as well as the guarantee that all claims will be paid by the state; affirmation of the obligation to take out sufficient insurance against risk and to provide sufficiently for one's old age; elimination of disadvantages for certain groups in regard to the form and availability of insurance; . . . the establishment of a durable and solid system of benefits and payments so that claimants and contributors will have lasting confidence in the efficiency of the social security system. . . .

### GERMANY AND EAST EUROPE: DEFENSE

FOREIGN AND GERMAN POLICY  The highest aim of German foreign policy was and is the peaceful unification of the German people in a free democratic order. To achieve this aim, the principle of national self-determination, of human rights and the principle of the right to a homeland must be taken into consideration. The federal government's renunciation of the use of force, which is internationally effective, applies to all frontiers and demarcation lines. . . .

Germany's policy to decrease tension must be aimed at everybody: at all European states as well as at the other part of Germany. The goal of such a policy is to create a peaceful European order based on balanced security. A technical step on the road to mutual understanding is the establishment of diplomatic relations with all states of the world. Germany's policy of mutual understanding must not exclude the G.D.R. Our policy will be successful only if we reach an agreement with East Berlin within the framework of our mutual interest.

A regime that does not correspond to the will of the people cannot be recognized on German soil. Nevertheless, power is exercised on German soil and over Germans in a region where the Basic Law is not valid.

The federal government, because it is responsible for the care of all Germans, has the right and the obligation to talk with all national and foreign authorities in order to bring the German people relief from the consequences of the division of their country.

In order to effect a relaxation of tensions existing between Bonn and East Berlin, negotiations must be undertaken, in agreement with our allies, about a regulated but temporary coexistence of both parts of Germany. . . . Concessions from the F.R.G. are meaningful only if they are met by equal concessions from the other side. One-sided commitments . . . are politically harmful and against the interests of all Germans.

As a result of regulated coexistence East Berlin should give up its theory of the existence of three German states, guarantee that Berlin belongs to the F.R.G. . . ., and keep all access routes to Berlin open, without check-points and detriment to the rights of the Allied forces.

To maintain their dignity and support world peace, the Germans must promote mutual understanding, and, to this end, they must discuss all problems concerning Germany and strive for their solution through an all-German commission. Among other things, this commission shall have the following tasks: to establish joint trade commissions; to create possibilities for economic cooperation and a unified economy; to facilitate financial transactions and, especially, to establish parity; to establish trade regulations within Germany; to investigate the possibilities for the F.R.G.'s participation in COMECON and the G.D.R.'s participation in the EEC, as a preliminary step toward the establishment of an all-European economic system; to establish and work out the guidelines for a cultural exchange (printed matter), a sports exchange, and the exchange of scientific and technical knowledge; to conclude technical agreements concerning communication and transportation by road, rail, air-freight, mail, and telephone; to gradually ease movement in Germany, especially in the city of Berlin, with the aim of complete freedom of movement; to conclude treaties that respect the different codes of law in each part of Germany, including aiding and abetting clauses, as long as basic rights are observed; to conclude treaties that respect the economic and social property situation; to prepare an amnesty for criminal acts that resulted from the division of Germany; to work out a development plan in which the construction projects in West and East Berlin as well as at the demarcation line are adjusted to each other; to negotiate the admission of political parties and their activities; to negotiate a mutual nonaggression agreement so that Germans might not be forced to shoot at other Germans. . . .

DEFENSE POLICY    The use of atomic weapons, even for defense purposes, in Central Europe can neither be planned nor justified because of its disastrous consequences. The atomic armament of the federal armed forces is therefore useless from a military point of view; it is politically harmful and represents an expensive, false investment.

Within the framework of the NATO agreements, the F.R.G. should leave nuclear bomb rattling to the Americans. The duty of the F.R.G. is, above all, an effective defense of the borders of the F.R.G. in case of a limited war of aggression. Modern conventional armaments suffice for this purpose. The nuclear-bomb carriers of the federal armed forces should be under U.S. control to be used within the framework of NATO. . . .

## 15. Federal Republic, NPD Manifesto, 1965

### PRINCIPLES OF OUR POLICY

1. Germany needs an order of state and society that creates a common spirit between the natural authority of a genuine democracy and each citizen's freedom to make personal decisions. . . . The waste of public means for megalomania, vain representation, and ostentatious buildings must be fought. We are opposed to the corruption spreading more and more in circles that have taken over public office. . . .

2. Farmers, the middle class, skilled workers, and independent enterprise are the most important pillars of a healthy national economy. They must be preserved, encouraged, and protected against foreign interests and unjustified demands for power by big business. . . . We oppose the infiltration of foreign capital and the sale of our basic industries to international companies. . . . We demand public price control to protect our savings and to safeguard our currency and wages. We demand a basic tax and finance reform and a uniform federal tax and finance system.

3. Not unrestrained materialism but recognition and reward according to performance, the protection of property, and the guarantee of employment must be the fundamental principles of a healthy economic and social order. German workers have a priority claim over foreign laborers to the security of their work. Only through increased work can our national productivity be increased. He who wants to work more should be encouraged. We demand, therefore, that overtime work as well as the work of pensioners be exempt from income and social security taxes. Trade unions and employers' organizations are necessary only to balance varying interests and to create peaceful working conditions. These are their obligations, and they should not claim political prerogatives. The economy and its organizations serve the state and the people, not vice versa.

4. To preserve its political independence Germany needs a healthy agriculture. Agriculture guarantees adequate food supplies. To achieve this, agricultural labor must be adjusted to industrial wages and benefits. In our industrial society, a guaranteed income for agricultural labor is necessary for the secure existence of agriculture. . . .

5. By foreign order, we pay foreign countries billions of DM, which serve neither German nor European interests. The urgent tasks of our own development are, however, neglected. Development aid to foreign countries should consist mostly of educational and technical assistance and should further German and European political aims. We oppose the continued payments of disguised contributions and demand a public statement of accounts relating to development aid, reparation costs, and military aid. . . .

7. Germany needs youth educated to recognize duty and to promote understanding in the world and able to resist the threatening enslavement by Communism and by the spiritless equalization of masses. Amid the

From NPD, Hannover.

fierce clash of different systems, we demand a uniform educational system for our German youth that encourages every gifted child, regardless of his financial means and background, and grants him an appropriate place in this order. . . .

8. Outside of the family, our youth is exposed to sex profiteers and to the demoralizing influences of a pernicious environment that is tolerated by all responsible organizations. But our youth wants and needs decent and clean examples. Thus, we demand elimination of public immorality and, in particular, the offenses against the dignity of our women. . . .

9. We need a free and responsible press, which corresponds to the cultural claims and the dignity of an old civilization. Therefore, we demand the liquidation of the destructive opinion monopolies in television, broadcasting, and cinema. We cannot continue to tolerate an unscrupulous clique that undermines and renders contemptible our national moral and ethical values. The frightening increase of criminality is a consequence of these unrestrained activities. Our women and children must no longer be fair game for violent criminals. . . . Twenty years after the war, we demand an end to one-sided reparation lawsuits [*Wiedergutmachung*], while in other countries millions of war crimes against German men, women, and children remain unpunished. The internal pacification of Germany and Europe demands that all people enjoy equal rights and that the book of Germany's past be closed by a general amnesty.

10. Germany needs a true conception of history for its political future. We oppose the glorification of high treason and the assertion that Germany alone is guilty for all the misery and woe now afflicting the world. These attitudes would lead to a moral self-destruction of our nation. We therefore demand an end to the lie that only Germany is guilty, a lie that has allowed billions of DM to be continuously extorted from our people. The bravery of the German soldiers at all times must be the leading principle of the federal army. Military service is a service of honor. The soldier must know the values for which he risks his life. Nobody should expect him to serve as a mercenary for foreign interests. As long as the fathers can be branded as criminals, in public and with impunity, their sons cannot be good soldiers.

11. Germany has the right to claim the territories in which the German people matured for centuries. We do not dispute any people's right to their original settlement areas, but, with equal determination, we insist on the right to our land. Readiness to waive our claim destroys our international legal position in representing the vital rights of the German people.

12. For two decades, the negative spirit of submission and the acceptance of collective guilt have paralyzed German politics. Only a people that is conscious of its own value and of its national dignity can gain the respect of the world and the friendship of other nations. No people will obtain help and support from others if its leaders neglect the country's vital interests in order to be friends with everybody. The free will of the European peoples must be regained and the domination by foreign powers must be ended. Therefore, we demand that all powers be exercised to awaken the will for self-determination of the German nation.

German politics must be governed by the principle that peace in Europe and in the world depends ultimately on the restoration of the center of Europe through a united and free Germany. As long as tension between foreign power blocs cuts through Germany, splitting Europe, the world will continue to face the abyss of war. In its profoundest meaning, German national policy is therefore the policy of peace.

## 16. ADOLF HITLER, NSDAP PARTY PROGRAM, MUNICH, FEBRUARY 24, 1920

1. By the right of self-determination of peoples, we demand that all Germans unite in one great Germany.

2. We also demand that the German nation be considered equal with all other nations and that the treaties of Versailles and St. Germain be abrogated.

3. We demand enough land and colonial territory to feed our people and to settle our surplus population.

4. Only German nationals can be German citizens. Irrespective of religion, only those with German blood can be members of the German nation. Consequently, no Jew can be a member of the German nation.

5. Every person who is not a German citizen shall be allowed to stay in Germany only as a guest; he must live according to the laws governing the stay of foreigners.

6. Only citizens shall have the right to decide on their leaders and on the laws of the state. Every public office of the Reich as well as of the states and of the municipalities can therefore be held only by German citizens. We reject the corrupting parliamentary practice of filling offices with people loyal to their party, without regard to character and abilities.

7. The state is obliged to give the citizen the opportunity to work and live. Since we cannot provide for all people living in our state, the citizens of foreign states must be expelled from the Reich.

8. The immigration of non-Germans must be prevented from now on. All non-Germans who immigrated to Germany after August 2, 1914, must leave the Reich immediately.

9. All citizens must possess the same rights and duties.

10. The first duty of every citizen is to work productively with mind or body. The activities of individuals must not transgress the interests of the community; they must serve the common good.

11. All income that has been acquired without labor or effort must be eliminated.

12. Out of regard to the frightful sacrifice in goods and blood that every war demands from the nation, personal enrichment through war must be designated as a crime against the nation. We demand, therefore, summary confiscation of all war profits.

13. All trusts must be nationalized.

14. Profits must be shared in large concerns.

15. The old-age pension system must be radically enlarged.

16. A sound middle class must be formed and maintained, large department stores must be made the property of the community and must be rented at low cost to small merchants, and the dealings of all small merchants with the national government, the states, and the municipalities must be strictly controlled.

17. Land reform must be adapted to our national needs, a law for the uncompensated expropriation of land must be enacted, land interests must be eliminated, and land speculation must be prevented.

18. Anyone who injures public interests by his actions must be punished. Those who commit crimes against the people, usurers, profiteers, and others must be punished by death irrespective of religion or race.

19. The Roman Law, which serves a materialistic world order, must be replaced by a legal system for all Germany.

20. In order to make higher education attainable for every capable and industrious German and to provide access to a leading position, the state is responsible for a fundamental extension of our entire educational system. The curricula of all educational institutions must be adapted to the demands of practical life. Our children must gain an understanding of national consciousness at the earliest possible age. Education must be paid by the state for especially talented children of poor parents, without regard to their profession or position.

21. The state must improve the health of the people by protecting mother and child, by prohibiting child labor, by developing the physical capabilities of the people through legislative provision of a gymnastics and sports duty and through the greatest support of all associations concerned with the physical education of youth.

22. Mercenary armies must be abolished and people's armies formed.

23. Legislation must be passed against conscious political lies and their propagation in the press. In order to create a German press, all German editors and newspaper contributors must be German citizens; non-German newspapers can only be published by special permission of the state— they cannot be published in the German language; financial participation in German newspapers by non-Germans must be prohibited, and the plants where such newspapers are produced must be closed; the non-Germans involved must be immediately expelled from the Reich. Newspapers working against the public interest must be prohibited. Legislation must be passed against artistic and literary expression that influences our national life negatively, and the institutions that stand in conflict with these demands must be closed.

24. All religions must exist freely in the state as long as they do not endanger the welfare of the state or offend the morals and the decency of the German race. The party recognizes positive Christianity without representing one particular belief. It rejects the materialistic spirit of the Jews and is convinced that a permanent convalescence of our nation can only succeed if the priority of public interest over private interest is recognized.

25. Consequently, a strong central power must be created in the Reich,

and the absolute authority of the central power over the Reich and its organizations must be recognized. Professional and trade chambers must be organized to carry out the general laws of the Reich in the federal states. The leaders of the party promise to see that the above demands are ruthlessly carried out; they are even prepared to risk their lives for this program.

# 4. *Elections and the Legislative Process*

## INTRODUCTION

### *ELECTIONS*

Universal manhood suffrage has existed in Germany since the foundation of the Reich in 1871, but in the *Länder* and, notably, in Prussia, suffrage remained unequal until 1918 and was based on criteria such as taxable wealth. The Weimar Constitution not only introduced women's suffrage but also required that national and *Länder* elections be based on proportional representation. The Basic Law of the Federal Republic of Germany prescribes universal, direct, free, equal, and secret elections to the Bundestag but leaves the determination of further requirements to federal law.

The first constitution of the German Democratic Republic also stipulated election by proportional representation (see chapter 7). In practice, however, there always has been only one over-all list of candidates. This list consists of nominees of the different groups (parties and mass organizations) that make up the National Front and is so arranged that the SED and the groups under its control are sure of a majority. The electorate can vote only for the listed candidates.

The electoral law of the Federal Republic (document 1) provides for a mixed system of voting both from single-member and multimember districts (*Länder-Listen.*) Each voter has two votes. Half of the members of parliament are elected in single-member constituencies (*Kreise*) by a simple majority (plurality) vote. The other half is elected from lists submitted by the parties in each *Land* in such a way that the total of second votes cast for each party is represented proportionally in the Bundestag. Candidates on the lists are elected in the order in which they are placed on the lists by their parties.

Candidates are nominated by party members or by conventions of member delegates. There are no primary elections. To counter the tendency inherent in proportional representation—the excess of splinter groups —the federal election law provides that, to be represented in the Bundestag, a party must either carry at least three districts or gain an over-all vote of at least 5 per cent of the total second vote cast. This provision has resulted in the elimination from the federal parliament of all parties but the CDU, SPD, and FDP. Some smaller parties once tried to have the 5 per cent clause declared unconstitutional, but the Federal Constitutional Court affirmed its constitutionality.

The minimum voting age is twenty-one; for holding office, the minimum age is twenty-five. There are few other requirements. Election campaigns are subject to few regulations. The law provides for free and equal time on radio and television for the parties and their candidates. Candidates are not required to post deposits. The *Länder* are free to regulate their own suffrage and election laws, and they have, for the most part, followed federal practices.

Under the Weimar Constitution, legislation could be subject to plebiscites and referenda; the president was elected popularly. By contrast, the Basic Law does not provide for a plebiscite (except if *Land* boundaries are to be changed) and entrusts the election of the federal president to a special assembly (see chapter 5.)

## PARLIAMENT

Because of its federal structure, Germany has always had a bicameral system. The Bundestag, the lower chamber (Reichstag under the Empire and Weimar), is elected by popular vote; however, the upper chamber, the Bundesrat (Reichsrat under Weimar) is selected neither by direct nor indirect elections. It has always consisted of representatives of the *Länder*, who have been selected for that body by their respective *Land* governments. Under the Bonn Constitution, the Bundesrat consists of members of the *Länder* governments (usually ministers) who vote according to the instructions of their governments. This means that the Bundesrat not only represents the *Länder* but also reflects the party constellations in the different *Länder*. Thus, *Länder* elections indirectly influence the composition of the Bundesrat. Each *Land* has from three to five votes, depending on its population, and each *Land* votes as a bloc.

Both chambers are organized not only by the terms of the Basic Law but also by a series of standing orders that specify voting procedures, the establishment and procedures of committees, legislative procedure, and so forth (documents 11 and 17).

Committees are established according to subject matter, and their number varies from session to session. The Basic Law prescribes the formation of certain committees (e.g. defense and foreign affairs); other committees are optional. Committee membership is allocated roughly in proportion to the party's strength in parliament.

The Bundestag is elected every four years. In contrast to the provisions under both the Empire and Weimar, it cannot be dissolved except under the exceptional circumstances of articles 63 and 68. Thus far, no Bundestag has been dissolved. The members of the Bundestag enjoy the customary privileges of deputies in democracies (such as immunity from arrest and criminal prosecution, unless the Bundestag decides otherwise); they also receive adequate compensation. Holding a seat in the Bundestag is not incompatible with holding public office; public officials elected to parliament are excused from their office during their tenure as deputies. In the Bundestag, the members of each party are organized in parliamentary parties (*Fraktionen*).

## LEGISLATIVE POWERS

Lawmaking is by joint action of the Bundestag and Bundesrat. The legislative powers of the two chambers have varied under the different constitutions. The influence of the Bundesrat of the Federal Republic lies between that of the powerful Bundesrat of the Empire and the weaker Reichsrat of Weimar. It has an absolute veto in certain cases, but only a suspensive veto (which can be overridden by either ordinary or two-thirds majority of the Bundestag) in others. In case of deadlock, a conference committee, established jointly by both chambers, takes over (document 22).

German constitutions have always carefully distinguished between the legislative powers of the federal parliament and those of the *Länder*. In this respect they differentiate among "exclusive" law-making powers of federation or member units, their "concurrent" legislative authority, and the power of the federation to legislate "principles" (leaving implementation to the *Länder*). As a result, the German constitutions have always reflected the relative strength of the *Länder* vis-à-vis the federation.

In contrast to previous constitutions, the Bonn Constitution does not give the executive a share in lawmaking. Indirectly, however, the influence of the executive is considerable. While bills may be initiated in the Bundestag or even in the Bundesrat, most bills are introduced by the federal government. They are drafted in the respective ministries and approved, as bills, by the cabinet. They are then submitted (not yet for final vote but merely for stating its position) to the Bundesrat. After discussion, voting, and adoption by the Bundestag, the legislation is placed before the Bundesrat for consent. A law enacted by parliament is then signed by the federal president and promulgated in the *Federal Law Gazette*.

Laws frequently authorize the issuance by the executive of ordinances having the force of law. In many instances, such ordinances can be issued only with the consent of the Bundesrat. (On other powers of parliament, in particular on emergency powers, see chapters 2 and 5.)

The constitutional provisions in this chapter are arranged as follows. The first section presents the rules on the composition and operation of the Bundestag, the rights and duties of its members, its organization, and so forth, and it includes excerpts from such relevant laws as the federal election law, the standing orders of the Bundestag, and its rules on the question period (document 12). The second section deals with the corresponding rules of the Bundesrat. The third section contains the provisions for the legislative process per se and, in particular, the constitutional provisions for the delineation of federal and state legislative powers and the standing orders of the conference committee. The last section concentrates on fiscal jurisdiction (documents 26–28).

# DOCUMENTS

## *VOTING AND ELECTIONS*

### 1. FEDERAL REPUBLIC, FEDERAL ELECTORAL LAW, MAY 7, 1956, AS AMENDED FEBRUARY 14, 1964

PART I: ELECTORAL SYSTEM

### Article 1: Composition of the Bundestag and Basic Electoral Principles

1. The Bundestag consists of 518 representatives, unless provided otherwise by this law. These will be determined by Germans eligible to vote in a general, direct, free, equal, and secret election according to the basic principles of proportional representation.

2. Of the representatives, 259 are elected on the basis of district (or constituency) nominations [*Kreiswahlvorschläge*] in the election districts, and the remainder are chosen on the basis of *Land* nominations [*Landesvorschläge*].

·    ·    ·

### Article 3: Establishment of Constituencies

1. The federal president appoints a standing commission on constituencies. It consists of the president of the federal bureau of statistics, one judge of the Federal Administrative Court, and five other members.

2. It is the responsibility of the commission to note changes in the size of the population of the electoral territory and to submit, during the first year after the Bundestag elections, a report to the federal government proposing changes in the size of the constituencies. The federal government shall submit this report to the Bundestag without delay and shall publish it in the *Federal Law Gazette*.

3. Each constituency must consist of a contiguous area. Whenever possible, *Land* boundaries must not, and city and county boundaries should not, be violated by constituency boundaries. The population of any constituency must not vary more than 33.3 per cent from the average population of all constituencies.

### Article 4: Votes

Every voter shall cast two votes: the first for a candidate in his constituency, the second for a candidate from the *Land* list [*Länderliste*] of the party of his choice.

FROM *FLG*, I (1956), pp. 383–407. Amended by the law for the incorporation of the Saarland, December 23, 1956 (*FLG*, I [1956], p. 1011); further amended on February 2, 1964 (*FLG*, I [1964], p. 61); and by article 9 of the law detailing the procedure for territorial changes of the *Länder* according to article 29 of the Basic Law (*FLG*, I, [1964], p. 65).

## Article 5: Voting in the Constituencies

One member shall be elected from each constituency. The candidate receiving the largest number of votes shall be elected. In case of a tie, election shall be decided by a lot to be drawn by the election supervisor in the constituency.

## Article 6: Voting on the "Land" Lists

1. The allocation of seats on the basis of *Land* lists shall be decided by the number of second votes cast for each *Land* list. However, the second vote cast by a voter who gave his first vote to a successful candidate in his constituency who was nominated according to article 21, paragraph 3, of this law or who voted for a party that was not allowed to submit a *Land* list shall not be counted for this purpose. From the total number of members, the number of successful candidates shall be subtracted as well as the number of candidates elected but nominated by parties ineligible according to paragraph 4 below. The remaining members shall be apportioned among the *Land* lists, and their second votes shall be counted on the basis of the d'Hondt system[1] of proportional representation. In the event of a tie for the allocation of the last seat, the decision shall be made by a lot to be drawn by the federal election supervisor.

2. From the number of members allotted to each *Land* list, the number of seats won by a party on the basis of constituency elections in the *Land* shall be subtracted. The remaining seats will be filled from the *Land* lists in the numerical order in which candidates appeared on the list. Candidates elected in a constituency are ineligible for election from a *Land* list. In the event that a *Land* list is entitled to more seats than there were candidates listed, such seats shall remain vacant.

3. A party shall retain all seats in a constituency that were won by election, even if the party's total number of seats should then exceed the number to which the party is entitled according to paragraph 1 above. In that event, the over-all total of seats will be increased by the difference, but no new allocation under paragraph 1 above shall be made.

4. Only those parties shall be eligible for the apportionment of seats from the *Land* lists that have received at least 5 per cent of all valid second votes cast in the electoral territory or that have won seats in at least three constituencies. The first sentence of this paragraph shall not apply to lists submitted by national minority parties.

.    .    .

PART IV: PREPARATION OF THE ELECTION

## Article 17: Election Day

The federal president shall determine the day of the general election. Election day must fall on a Sunday or on a legal holiday.

[1] The method of the "large average" that over-represents the largest party.

### Article 18: Voting Register and Voter's Certificate

1. Local authorities shall keep a register of all eligible voters in each electoral district. The voting register shall be displayed for public inspection between the twenty-first and the fourteenth day preceding the election.

2. An eligible voter who is unable to vote in the election district where he is registered or who has not been registered for reasons beyond his control shall, upon application, be issued a voter's certificate.

### Article 19: Nominations

1. Nominations can be made by parties and by eligible voters according to article 21 below.

2. Parties not represented by at least five members in the outgoing Bundestag or *Landtag* may present nominations only if they have announced their participation in the election of the federal election supervisor by the forty-seventh day before the election at the latest and if the federal election committee has determined their character as a party. . . .

4. A party may nominate only one candidate in each constituency and only one *Land* list in each *Land*.

.  .  .

### Article 22: Selection of Candidates

In order to become the party's candidate for a constituency nomination, a person must have been elected by secret ballot, either by a convention of party members who are eligible voters in the constituency or by a convention of delegates who have been elected by such party members.

2. A convention of elected party delegates meeting regularly under party rules in order to designate candidates for forthcoming elections may nominate a candidate, provided the convention did not meet more than one year before election day.

.  .  .

### Article 28: "Land" Lists

.  .  .

2. *Land* lists must bear the name of the party. . . .

4. A candidate may be nominated in one *Land* and on one list only. A *Land* list may show only candidates who have given their written consent to the nomination; such consent is irrevocable. . . .

### Article 31: Ballots

.  .  .

2. The ballot shall contain for election in the constituencies the names of the admitted candidates and the party's name or identifying motto; for voting on the *Land* lists, the identification of the party and the names of the first five candidates on the certified *Land* lists. . . .

PART V: CONDUCT OF THE ELECTION

### Article 33: Inadmissible Electioneering

Any attempt to influence voters by speech, sound, writing, or posters in the polling place is prohibited.

### Article 34: Preservation of Secrecy of the Ballot

1. Arrangements shall be made for the voter to mark his ballot secretly and to place it in the envelope. The ballot boxes, into which the envelopes are deposited, shall be constructed to assure the secrecy of the ballot. . . .

### Article 35: The Act of Voting

1. Voting shall be done with official ballots placed in official envelopes. . . .

PART VIII: ATTAINMENT AND LOSS OF MEMBERSHIP IN THE BUNDESTAG

### Article 45: Attainment of Membership

An elected candidate becomes a member of the Bundestag after his election supervisor has been informed of his acceptance but not before dissolution of the last elected Bundestag.

### Article 46: Loss of Membership

1. A member shall lose his seat if: (1) his election is declared invalid; (2) a new determination is made of the results of the election; (3) a condition necessary for his eligibility has been forfeited; (4) a criminal court has dispossessed him of his rights to be elected to public office. . . .

### Article 48: Appointment of Successive Candidates from Party Lists, and By-Elections

1. If an elected candidate dies or refuses acceptance of his election or if a member dies or is otherwise eliminated from the Bundestag after the election, his vacant seat will be filled from the *Land* list of his party.

### Article 49: Consequences of the Unconstitutionality of a Party

If a party or a subsidiary organization of that party has been declared unconstitutional by the Federal Constitutional Court according to article 21 of the Basic Law, the members of the Bundestag who are also members of that party or of its subsidiary organization at the commencement of court proceedings, or at the time of the verdict, shall lose their seats; non-elected candidates lose their claims as successors on the party list.

## 2. FEDERAL REPUBLIC

ART. 41   1. The scrutiny of elections is the responsibility of the Bundestag. It also decides whether a deputy has lost his seat in the Bundestag. [See 4:8:48(2).]

2. Against the decision of the Bundestag, an appeal can be made to the Federal Constitutional Court.

3. Details will be regulated by federal law.

### 3. WEIMAR

ART. 31 The Reichstag shall establish a court for examining elections. This court also decides the question whether a representative has lost his membership.

### 4. EMPIRE

ART. 27 The Reichstag shall examine the legality of the election of its members and decide thereon. It shall regulate its own procedure and discipline through its order of business and elect its president, vice-presidents, and secretaries. [See 2:10:20.]

## LEGISLATIVE TERM

### 5. FEDERAL REPUBLIC

ART. 39 1. The Bundestag is elected for a four-year term. Its legislative term ends four years after its first meeting or on its dissolution. The new election takes place during the last three months of the term or within sixty days after dissolution. [See 5:20:115h(2).]

2. The Bundestag assembles within thirty days after the election but not before the end of the term of the previous Bundestag.

3. The Bundestag determines the termination and resumption of its meetings. The president of the Bundestag may convene it at an earlier date. He must do so if one-third of the members or the federal president or the federal chancellor so demand.

### 6. WEIMAR

ART. 23 1. The Reichstag is elected for four years. New elections must be held, at the latest, on the sixtieth day after the expiration of this term.

ART. 24 The Reichstag convenes each year on the first Wednesday of November at the seat of the federal government. The president of the Reichstag must summon it earlier when the federal president or at least one-third of the members of the Reichstag shall so demand. The Reichstag decides upon the closing of the session and the date of reassembling. [See 2:15:25.]

### 7. EMPIRE

ART. 12 The emperor shall have the right to convene the Bundesrat and the Reichstag and to open, adjourn, and close them.

ART. 13    The Bundesrat and the Reichstag shall be convened annually, and the Bundesrat may be called together for the preparation of business without the Reichstag; the latter, however, shall not be convened without the Bundesrat.

.    .    .

ART. 24    1. The Reichstag shall be elected for five years.[1] [See 2:16: 24–25.]

.    .    .

ART. 26    Without the consent of the Reichstag, an adjournment of that body shall not exceed the period of thirty days and shall not be repeated during the same session.

## FEDERAL DIET: RULES OF PROCEDURE

### 8. FEDERAL REPUBLIC

ART. 40    1. The Bundestag elects its president, vice-president, and secretaries. It draws up its rules of procedure. [See 4:11.]

2. The president exercises the proprietary and police powers in the Bundestag building. No search or seizure may take place in the premises of the Bundestag without his permission.

.    .    .

ART. 42.    1. The meetings of the Bundestag are public. Upon a motion of one-tenth of its members or upon a motion of the federal government, the public may, by a two-thirds majority vote, be excluded. The decision on the motion is taken at a meeting not open to the public.

2. Decisions of the Bundestag require a majority of votes cast, unless this Basic Law provides otherwise. For the elections to be made by the Bundestag, the rules of procedure may provide exceptions.

3. True and accurate reports of the public meetings of the Bundestag and of its committees shall not give rise to any liability.

ART. 43    1. The Bundestag and its committees may demand the presence of any member of the federal government. [See 5:6:65.]

2. The members of the Bundesrat and of the federal government as well as persons commissioned by them have access to all meetings of the Bundestag and its committees. They must be heard at any time.

ART. 44    1. The Bundestag has the right and, upon the motion of one-fourth of its members, the duty to set up a committee of investigation to take the requisite evidence at public hearings. The public may be excluded.

2. The rules of criminal procedure shall apply *mutatis mutandis* to the taking of evidence. The secrecy of the mail, posts, and telecommunications remains unaffected.

[1] Changed to three years on March 19, 1888.

3. Courts and administrative authorities are bound to render legal and administrative assistance. [See 6:1:92.]

4. The decisions of the committees of investigation are not subject to judicial consideration. The courts are free to evaluate and judge the facts on which the investigation is based.

ART. 45   1. The Bundestag appoints a standing committee, which shall safeguard the rights of the Bundestag as against the federal government in the interval between two legislative terms. The standing committee also has the powers of a committee of investigation.

2. Wider powers, such as the right to legislate, to elect the federal chancellor, and to impeach the federal president, are not within the province of the standing committee. [See 2:14:63(1); 5:1:61(1).]

ART. 45a   1. The Bundestag shall appoint a committee on foreign affairs and a committee on defense. Both committees shall function also in the intervals between any two legislative terms.

2. The committee on defense shall also have the rights of a committee of investigation. Upon the motion of one-fourth of its members, it shall have the duty to make a specific matter the subject of investigation.

3. Article 44, paragraph 1, shall not be applied in matters of defense.[1] [See 5:20:45b.]

ART. 46   1. A deputy may not at any time be prosecuted in the courts or subjected to disciplinary action or otherwise called to account outside the Bundestag on account of a vote cast or an utterance made by him in the Bundestag or one of its committees. This does not apply to defamatory insults.

2. A deputy may be called to account or arrested for a punishable offense only by permission of the Bundestag, unless he is apprehended in the commission of the offense or during the course of the following day.

3. The permission of the Bundestag is also necessary for any other restriction of the personal freedom of a deputy or for the initiation of proceedings against a deputy under article 18. [See 6:12:18.]

4. Any criminal proceedings and any proceedings under article 18 against a deputy, any detention, and any other restriction of his personal freedom shall be suspended upon the request of the Bundestag. [See 5:1:60(4).]

ART. 47   Deputies may refuse to give evidence concerning persons who have confided facts to them in their capacity as deputies or to whom they have confided facts in such capacity, as well as concerning these facts themselves. To the extent that this right to refuse to give evidence exists, no seizure of documents may take place.

ART. 48   1. Any person seeking election to the Bundestag is entitled to the leave necessary for his election campaign.

2. No one may be prevented from accepting and exercising the office of deputy. He may not be dismissed from employment, with or without notice, on this ground.

3. Deputies are entitled to compensation adequate to ensure their in-

[1] As amended by federal law of March 19, 1956. See *FLG*, I (1956), p. 111.

dependence. They are entitled to the free use of all state owned transport. Details will be regulated by a federal law.

## 9. WEIMAR

ART. 26   The Reichstag elects its president, his substitutes, and its clerks. It establishes its own order of business. [See 2:15:25.]

ART. 27   Between two sessions or election periods, the president and his substitutes from the last session continue to perform their official duties.

ART. 28   The president enforces the regulations and exercises the police authority in the Reichstag building. The administration of the house is placed under him; he authorizes the receipts and expenditures of the house according to the provisions of the federal budget and represents the federation in all legal affairs and suits connected with his administration.

ART. 29   The proceedings of the Reichstag are public. Upon the motion of fifty members, the public may be excluded by a two-thirds majority.

ART. 30   True records of the transactions of the public sessions of the Reichstag, of a *Land* Diet, or of their committees remain free from all liability. [See 4:3:31.]

.    .    .

ART. 32   A simple majority is sufficient for a decision of the Reichstag, insofar as the constitution does not require another proportion of votes. For the elections to be made by the Reichstag, the order of business may make exceptions. The quorum needed for action is regulated by the order of business.

ART. 33   The Reichstag and its committees can demand the presence of the federal chancellor and of any federal minister. [See 5:7:55.] The federal chancellor, the federal ministers, and the agents appointed by these have the right of entry to the sessions of the Reichstag and its committees. The *Länder* are entitled to send authorized agents to these sessions to explain the point of view of their governments upon the matters under consideration. Upon their demand, the *Länder* representatives must be heard during the discussion and the representatives of the federal government even outside of the order of the day. They are subject to the power of the chairman to keep order.

ART. 34   The Reichstag has the right and, upon the motion of one-fifth of its members, the duty to establish investigating committees. These committees take up in public sessions the matters that they or the persons who brought the motions consider necessary. The public can be excluded by a two-thirds majority vote of the investigating committee.

ART. 35   The Reichstag appoints a standing committee for foreign affairs, which can act even outside the sessions of the Reichstag after the close of the election period or after the dissolution of the Reichstag until the convening of the new Reichstag. The sessions of this committee are not public, unless the committee votes them so by a two-thirds majority.

The Reichstag also establishes a standing committee to safeguard the rights of the representatives of the people as against the national cabinet for the time outside of the sessions, after the close of an election period, or after the dissolution of the Reichstag, until the convening of the new Reichstag.[1] These committees have the rights of investigating committees.

ART. 36  No member of the Reichstag or of a *Land* Diet may at any time be prosecuted in court or by official discipline for his vote or for any expressions employed in carrying out his functions; nor can he otherwise be held responsible outside of the assembly.

ART. 37  No member of the Reichstag or of a *Land* Diet, without the consent of the house to which the delegate belongs, can be compelled to undergo a criminal investigation or be arrested, unless such member is apprehended while committing the act or, at the latest, in the course of the following day.

Similar consent is required for any other limitation upon personal liberty that interferes with the performance of the duties of a delegate.

Any criminal process against a member of the Reichstag or of a *Land* Diet and any imprisonment or other restraint upon his personal liberty, upon the demand of the house to which the delegate belongs, is to be suspended for the duration of the session.

ART. 38  The members of the Reichstag and of the *Land* Diets are entitled to refuse to give evidence concerning persons who have entrusted them with information in their capacity as deputies or to whom they have given information in exercising their official functions, as well as concerning these facts themselves. In respect of the seizure of documents, they have the same status as persons who enjoy a legal right to refuse to give evidence.

ART. 39  Public officers and members of the armed forces need no leave in order to perform their official duties as members of the Reichstag or of a *Land* Diet. If they are candidates for a seat in these bodies, they are to be granted the requisite leave to prepare for their election. [See 5:22:133.]

ART. 40  The members of the Reichstag possess the right to free transportation on all German railways as well as to compensation according to the provisions of federal law.

## 10. EMPIRE

ART. 1  Each member of the Bundesrat shall have the right to appear in the Reichstag and must be heard there at any time he shall so request, in order to represent the views of his government, even if such views have not been adopted by the majority of the Bundesrat. No one shall at the same time be a member of the Bundesrat and of the Reichstag.

.   .   .

---

[1] The last part of this sentence was added by an amendment on December 15, 1923. See *FLG*, I (1923), p. 1185.

ART. 21   No leave of absence shall be required for public officials to enter the Reichstag. When a member of the Reichstag accepts a salaried office of the Empire, a salaried office in one of the states [*Staaten*] of the federation, or any office of the Empire or of a state involving higher rank or salary, he shall forfeit his seat and his vote in the Reichstag and may recover his place in the same only by a new election. [See 4:4.]

ART. 22   The proceedings of the Reichstag shall be public. No one shall be held responsible for truthful reports of the proceedings of the public sessions of the Reichstag. [See 4:4; 4:7:26; 4:21:23.]

. . .

ART. 28   The Reichstag shall take action by absolute majority to render any action valid, the presence of a majority of the statutory number of members is required.

ART. 29   The members of the Reichstag are the representatives of the people as a whole and shall not be bound by orders or instructions.

ART. 30   No member of the Reichstag shall at any time suffer legal or disciplinary prosecution on account of his vote or on account of utterances made while performing his functions; nor shall he be held responsible in any other way outside the Reichstag.

ART. 31   Without the consent of the Reichstag, none of its members shall be tried or arrested during the session for any penal offense, unless he be taken in the commission of the offense or during the course of the following day.

At the request of the Reichstag all criminal proceedings instituted against one of its members and any detentions for judicial inquiry or cases shall be suspended during its session.

ART. 32   The members of the Reichstag shall receive no salaries from the government. They shall receive an indemnification in accordance with the provisions of law.[1]

## 11. FEDERAL REPUBLIC, BUNDESTAG, STANDING ORDERS, JANUARY 1, 1952

ART. 1   1. The first sitting of the Bundestag shall be convened by the president still in the chair of the Bundestag. This sitting shall take place not later than the thirtieth day following the elections but not before the end of the term of the previous Bundestag. . . .

4. After the presence of a quorum has been established, the house shall proceed with the election of its president, vice-presidents, and secretaries.

FROM Hans Trossmann, *The German Bundestag* (Darmstadt; Neue Darmstädter Verlagsanstalt, 1966), pp. 77–130. Adopted by the Bundestag on December 6, 1951, in accordance with article 40 of the Basic Law. Amended by a decision of the Bundestag on December 13, 1961.

[1] As altered May 21, 1906. A law of that date provided for free railway transportation of deputies as well as for an annual compensation of 3,000 marks.

ART. 2   1. The Bundestag shall elect by secret and separate ballots the president and the vice-presidents for the duration of the legislative term. . . .

ART. 5   The presidium shall consist of the president and the vice-presidents.

ART. 6   The internal committee of the house shall consist of the president, the vice-presidents, one party whip from each parliamentary group, and the secretaries. The members of this committee may be represented at its meetings by members of the Council of Elders [*Ältestenrat*]. . . .

ART. 7   1. The president shall represent the Bundestag and conduct its business. He shall ensure the dignity and the rights of the Bundestag, promote its work, conduct the debates equitably and impartially, and maintain order in the house. He may attend, in an advisory capacity, all meetings of the committees. . . .

ART. 10   1. The parliamentary parties are associations of Bundestag members belonging to the same party. The number of members required to constitute a group shall be determined by a decision of the Bundestag. . . .[1]

ART. 12   The composition of the internal committee of the house and of the committees, as well as the distribution of committee chairmanships, shall be determined in accordance with the strength of each parliamentary group. The same shall apply where elections are to be held by the Bundestag.

ART. 13   The Council of Elders shall consist of the president, the vice-presidents, and other members of the Bundestag, whose names shall be communicated in writing to the president by the parties. The numerical strength of the Council of Elders shall be determined by the Bundestag.

ART. 14   1. It shall be the duty of the Council of Elders to support the president in conducting the business of the Bundestag and, in particular, to ensure that there is agreement between the parliamentary groups as regards both the Bundestag agenda and the appointment of committee chairmen and deputy chairmen. It is not a decision-making body.

2. Should it be decided to depart from the agenda agreed to by the Council of Elders, the president of the Bundestag and the parliamentary groups shall be informed thereof, beforehand, if at all possible. . . .

ART. 24   The president shall open, conduct, and close the sittings. Before the closure of each sitting, the president, on a decision of the Bundestag, shall inform the house of the date of the next sitting and of the agenda, if the latter has been completed. The agenda shall be communicated to the deputies in due course. . . .

ART. 30   1. The president shall declare the closure of a debate after all the speakers on the list have taken the floor or if nobody else requests leave to speak.

2. The Bundestag may interrupt or close debates. Any request for adjournment or closure requires the support of no less than thirty deputies

[1] By resolution of the Bundestag, December 19, 1957, fifteen members are necessary to form a parliamentary party.

present. Any demand for closure shall take precedence over a demand for adjournment. However, in case of a debate on a bill, a demand for closure may only be made if at least one deputy has taken the floor in addition to the mover or the rapporteur. . . .

ART. 32   1. No member may have the floor unless invited to do so by the president. . . . Members who wish to speak on the point at issue should, as a rule, submit a written demand to the secretary responsible for drawing up the list of speakers. When deputies wish to refer to the rules of procedure and to make personal observations, they try to catch the attention of the president.

2. As regards matters relating to immunity, the deputy concerned may not be given the floor on matters of substance pertaining to immunity.

ART. 33   1. The president shall lay down the order of the speakers. Any decisions he may take in this connection must ensure that debates proceed objectively and rationally and that due consideration is given to party opinions and to the respective strength of the parliamentary groups.

2. During debates on motions, the first speaker cannot belong to the same parliamentary group as the mover. Both the mover and the rapporteur may request the floor at the beginning and at the end of a debate. The rapporteur shall have the right to speak at any time.

3. In the committees, the floor shall be given to a speaker according to the order in which it has been requested. . . .

ART. 37   In principle, speakers shall not read their speeches. They may, however, use notes. The use of prepared speeches shall constitute an exception to the rule, and such speeches may be read only with the permission of the president. . . .

ART. 42   In the event of a serious breach of the rules of procedure, the president may suspend a deputy for the duration of a sitting without having called him to order beforehand. Before the closure of the sitting, the president must state the number of sittings from which the deputy is to be excluded. The maximum number of sittings from which a deputy may be excluded shall be thirty.

ART. 43   The deputy shall have the right until the next sitting to protest in writing against the call to order or the suspension. This objection shall be placed on the agenda for the relevant sitting. The Bundestag shall decide on this matter without debate. Such an objection shall not have the effect of postponing the call to order of the suspension.

ART. 44   In the event of disturbances in the Bundestag that jeopardize the progress of the debates, the president may suspend a sitting for a certain period or even close it. If he cannot succeed in making himself heard, he shall leave the chair. In this way, the sitting is automatically interrupted. It shall be up to the president to ask the deputies to resume the sitting. . . .

ART. 46   Any deputy may request the presence of any member of the federal government. Such a demand must be supported by at least thirty deputies present. The Bundestag shall decide on such a demand by a simple majority. . . .

ART. 54 Votes shall be taken by the raising of hands or by members rising from their seats. During a final vote following a third reading, the vote shall be taken by members rising from their seats. Unless otherwise provided for in the Basic Law or in these rules of procedure, decisions shall be taken by a simple majority vote. A tie shall mean a negative vote. Every deputy has the right to abstain from voting. . . .

ART. 56 In the event that the chairmen [*Sitzungsvorstand*] do not agree on the result of a vote, verification shall be requested. If, after such verification, no agreement has been reached, the votes must be counted. After authorization by the chairmen the votes shall be counted in the following manner. After the deputies have left the chamber at the request of the president, all but three doors are closed. Two secretaries shall stand at each of the three doors. After a signal of the president, the deputies shall reenter the chamber through doors marked "yes," "no," or "abstention" and shall be counted aloud by the secretaries when passing through the doors. The president shall then give a signal to indicate that the count is ended. Deputies who enter the hall after the signal has been given shall not be counted. The president and the assisting secretaries shall vote publicly. The president shall then announce the result of the vote.

ART. 57 A roll call vote may be requested up to the time the vote count is to be taken. It shall take place if no less than fifty members present support it. . . .

ART. 60 1. Committees are organs of the Bundestag. Their composition shall be related to the strength of the respective parliamentary groups. The number of members of each committee shall be determined by the Bundestag.

2. The committees must carry out their tasks as expeditiously as possible. As preparing bodies for the decisions of the Bundestag, the committees shall have the right and, indeed, the duty within the scope of their activities, to recommend certain decisions to the Bundestag.

3. Unless otherwise provided in these rules of procedure or by a decision of the Bundestag, committees may only deal with subjects referred to them. . . .

ART. 62 The Bundestag may set up special committees for the purpose of dealing with particular questions.

ART. 63 1. At the request of at least one-quarter of its members, the Bundestag must set up a committee of investigation without first presenting the motion to establish the committee to another committee. The motion must indicate the matter to be investigated. . . .

ART. 68 1. The Bundestag shall determine a system for determining the composition of committees in accordance with article 12 and for the determination of the number of members to be appointed.

2. The federal parliamentary party shall nominate the members of the committees and their deputies. . . .

ART. 69 1. The committees shall appoint their chairmen and deputy chairmen in accordance with agreements reached in the Council of Elders. The Bundestag shall be informed thereof.

ART. 70   The committees may appoint one or more rapporteurs for certain subjects. Subject to the decision of these committees, the rapporteurs of the standing committees shall be appointed by the chairmen. . . .

ART. 72   The ministries concerned and the Bundesrat shall be notified of the place, date, and agenda of any committee meeting.

ART. 73   1. Committee debates shall not be open to the public.

2. Committees may decide that any of their meetings not open to the public may be preceded by public meetings. At such public meetings, the representatives of the various interest groups, witnesses and experts, the press, and any other person may be invited to attend if there is enough room available. . . .

ART. 74   1. Reports submitted by the committees to the Bundestag on bills and basic questions of considerable importance must, as a rule, be made in writing and must be included in the stenographic report. In other cases, verbal reports shall be submitted.

2. The reports must not only represent the views and the proposals of the responsible [*federführend*] committee but must also present the opinions of the minority in the committee and of any other committee not allowed to place motions before the house.

ART. 75   1. The federal government and the Bundesrat shall present their proposals in writing to the Bundestag (article 76 *et seq.*).

2. With the exception of motions presented under article 103, motions may only be presented by deputies (article 75 *et seq.*).

3. Interpellations addressed to the federal government must be signed by at least thirty deputies (articles 105–9).

4. Written questions addressed to the federal government must be signed by a number of deputies that at least corresponds to the strength of the respective federal parliamentary parties (article 110).

5. Verbal questions may be asked by any deputy during the question time (article 111). . . .

ART. 77.   1. Bills, budget bills, treaties with foreign states, and similar agreements that regulate the political relations of the federation or relate to matters of federal legislation under article 59 of the Basic Law shall be given three readings. All other proposals and motions shall only be given one reading. . . .

ART. 79   1. At the end of the first reading, the bill may be referred to a committee. Only in special cases may a bill be referred simultaneously to several committees: in such a case, the decision shall rest with the committee responsible for the bill.

2. No other vote shall take place during the first reading.

ART. 80   1. As a rule, the second reading shall begin on the second day after the termination of the first reading and, if prior discussions have taken place in committee, the second reading shall begin not earlier than the second day after the committee report has been circulated. As a rule, a general debate can take place only if the Bundestag decides on such debate.

2. In case of a debate on clauses to be included, each provision shall be examined separately and in the order in which it appears in the bill. The

debate shall end with an examination of the introduction to and the title of, the bill. At the end of the debate, a vote shall be taken on each clause. . . .

ART. 81   1. Amendments to bills and resolutions may be proposed so long as the debate on the question to which the amendment refers has not been terminated. Such proposals must be submitted in writing. They shall be read if they have not been printed and circulated beforehand. . . .

ART. 84   . . . 2. Decisions taken during the second reading shall form the basis of the third reading.

3. In the event that all parts of a bill have been rejected during the second reading, no further reading or vote shall take place.

ART. 85   . . . The third reading shall begin with a general debate on the main principles of the bill. This debate shall be followed by discussions of those provisions for which amendments have been proposed during the third reading. . . .

ART. 117   1. A stenographic report shall be prepared for each sitting.

2. The stenographic reports shall be circulated to all deputies.

3. All other records of Bundestag business, such as tape recordings, shall be filed in accordance with the instructions of the presidium. . . .

### 12. FEDERAL REPUBLIC, BUNDESTAG, RULES ON THE QUESTION PERIOD, JUNE 29, 1959

1. Every member shall be entitled to address short oral questions to the federal government. The questions shall be submitted to the president in triplicate (through the office filing motions). . . .

3. Each plenary session shall begin with a question period. . . .

4. The question time may not exceed sixty minutes. . . .

6. Questions must be brief and must permit brief answers.

7. A question may contain only one concrete point. It may not be subdivided into several subsidiary questions. . . .

9. Questions must be submitted in time for submission to the federal government three days before the question period in which an answer is to be given. . . . As an exception, the president may authorize urgent questions of obvious public interest to be raised during the question period, provided they are submitted not later than noon of the previous day. . . .

11. The president shall determine the order in which the questions are discussed.

12. Questions not answered during the question period of any week shall be answered by the federal government in writing. . . .

14. When the question has been answered verbally, a deputy shall have the right to ask two supplementary questions. Supplementary questions may not be subdivided into several parts. . . .

FROM Bundestag, Standing Orders (September, 1965), pp. 74–76; Hans Trossmann, *The German Bundestag* (Darmstadt: Neue Darmstädter Verlagsanstalt, 1966), pp. 131–33.

15. The president may allow supplementary questions by other members of the house. He must be notified of such questions before the question period. The orderly progress of the question period must not be jeopardized thereby. . . .

### 13. FEDERAL REPUBLIC, BUNDESTAG, RULES ON DISCUSSION OF QUESTIONS OF GENERAL INTEREST, 1965

#### DISCUSSION ON MOTION
1. Members of the Bundestag numerically strong enough to form a federal parliamentary party can introduce a motion to discuss a topic of general interest. The motion must be presented to the president in writing. . . .

#### DISCUSSION ON REQUEST
After the federal government's reply to such a motion, a discussion takes place if, immediately after the question period, at least thirty members present in the house so desire.

#### DURATION OF THE DISCUSSION AND ORDER OF SPEAKING
1. The discussion is limited to one hour; this does not include the time taken up by members or representatives of the federal government or of the Bundesrat.
2. No speaker may speak for more than five minutes. Statements or speeches may not be read. . . .

FROM Hans Trossman, *The German Bundestag* (Darmstadt: Neue Darmstädter Verlagsanstalt, 1966), pp. 151–52. These rules were adopted by the Bundestag on January 27, 1965; they became known as the rules on the *Aktuelle Stunde*.

## FEDERAL COUNCIL: RULES OF PROCEDURE

### 14. FEDERAL REPUBLIC

ART. 50 [See 2:11:50.]

ART. 51 1. The Bundesrat consists of members of the *Länder* governments that appoint and recall them. Other members of such governments may act as substitutes.

2. Each *Land* has at least three votes; *Länder* with more than 2 million inhabitants have four; *Länder* with more than 6 million inhabitants have five votes.

3. Each *Land* may delegate as many members as it has votes. The votes of each *Land* may be cast only as a block and only by members present or by their substitutes.

ART. 52 1. The Bundesrat elects its president for one year.

2. The president convenes the Bundesrat. He must convene it if the members of at least two *Länder* or the federal government so demand.

3. The Bundesrat takes its decisions by at least a majority of its votes. It

draws up its rules of procedure. Its meetings are public. The public may be excluded.

4. Other members of or persons commissioned by the *Länder* governments may serve on the committees of the Bundesrat.

ART. 53   The members of the federal government have the right and, on demand, the duty to take part in the debates of the Bundesrat and of its committees. They must be heard at any time. The Bundesrat must be kept informed by the federal government of the conduct of affairs. [See 2:20:91(2); 4:17:19; 5:1:57.]

## 15. WEIMAR

ART. 60   [See 2:12:60.]

ART. 61   1. Each *Land* has at least one vote in the Reichsrat. In the larger *Länder*, one vote shall be assigned for every million inhabitants.[1]

2. No single *Land* shall have more than two-fifths of the total number of votes. . . .

ART. 63   The *Länder* shall be represented in the Reichsrat by members of their governments. However, half of the Prussian vote shall be cast by the Prussian provincial administrations.

ART. 64   The federal government must convoke the Reichsrat upon the demand of one-third of its members.

ART. 65   The chairmanship in the Reichsrat is held by a member of the federal government. The members of the federal government have the right and, if requested, the duty to participate in the deliberations of the Reichsrat and of its committees. During the deliberations, they must be heard at any time upon their request.

ART. 66   The federal government and any member of the Reichsrat are entitled to place motions before the Reichsrat. The Reichsrat regulates the conduct of its business by an order of business. The plenary sessions of the Reichsrat are public. In accordance with provisions of the order of business, the public may be excluded from the discussion of individual subjects.

A vote is decided by a simple majority of those voting.

ART. 67   The Reichsrat is to be kept currently informed by the federal ministry in respect to the conduct of federal affairs. The appropriate committees of the Reichsrat shall be invited by the federal ministerial departments to the discussion of important matters.

## 16. EMPIRE

ART. 6   [See 2:13:6.]

ART. 7   The Bundesrat shall take action upon: (1) the measures to be proposed to the Reichstag and the resolutions passed by the same; (2) the general administrative provisions and arrangements necessary for the execution of the federal laws . . .; (3) the defects that may be discovered

[1] Amended by law, March 24, 1921, to every 700,000 inhabitants. See *FLG*, I (1921), p. 440.

in the execution of the federal laws or of the provisions and arrangements heretofore mentioned.

Each member of the federation has the right to make propositions and introduce motions. . . . Decisions shall be reached by simple majority, with the exceptions provided for in articles 5, 37, and 78. Votes not represented or not instructed shall not be counted. . . .

ART. 8   The Bundesrat shall appoint from its members permanent committees. . . . In each of these committees, there shall be representatives of at least four states [*Staaten*] of the federation in addition to the presidium (Prussia). . . . In the committee on the army . . . Bavaria shall have a permanent seat. . . . A committee on foreign affairs, over which Bavaria shall preside, shall also be appointed in the Bundesrat. . . .

ART. 9   [See 4:10:9.]

ART. 10   The emperor shall afford the customary diplomatic protection to the members of the Bundesrat.

.   .   .

ART. 12 AND 13   [See 4:7:12,13.]

ART. 14   The Bundesrat shall be convened whenever a meeting is demanded by one-third of the total number of votes.

ART. 15   [See 2:16:15.]

## 17. FEDERAL REPUBLIC, BUNDESRAT, STANDING ORDERS, JULY 1, 1966

### Article 1: Members

The governments of the *Länder* report to the president of the Bundesrat the names of the Bundesrat members, the date of their appointment as Bundesrat members and as members of the *Länder* governments as well as the expiration date of their membership.

### Article 2: Incompatibility

Bundesrat members may not simultaneously be members of the Bundestag. If a member of the Bundesrat is elected to the Bundestag, he must report to the president of the Bundesrat within an appropriate time which of the offices he will resign from. . . .

### Article 5: Election of President and Vice-President

The Bundesrat elects, without discussion, from among its members a president and three vice-presidents. Their term of office is one year. . . .

### Article 6: Position of the President

The president represents the F.R.G. in all matters of the Federal Constitutional Court. He is the highest authority for the civil servants of the Federal Constitutional Court. . . .

### Article 11: Committees

1. The Bundesrat forms permanent committees. It can set up additional committees for special matters.

FROM *FLG*, I (1966), pp. 437–42.

2. The *Länder* must be represented in every committee by a member of the Bundesrat or by one member of their governments or his delegate.

### Article 15: Convocation and Promulgation

1. The president has to convene the Bundesrat immediately if one *Land* or the federal government so demands.

2. The president prepares the sessions. For the preparation of the sessions the motions to be discussed are placed on a preliminary agenda.

3. The preliminary agenda, the motions, and the notes and recommendations of the committees must be forwarded to the *Länder* representatives as early as possible.

### Article 19: The Right to ask Questions

1. During the session, every member of the Bundesrat can ask the federal government or its members questions concerning items on the agenda.

2. Additionally, every *Land* can ask the federal government questions not related to an item on the agenda. These questions must be written and sent to the president not later than two weeks before the session in which they shall be discussed. The president forwards them to the federal government and places them on the agenda. . . .

### Article 25: Reporting

1. The committees must give oral reports on important matters under discussion during the Bundesrat session.

2. These reports not only must give objective information about the committee discussions but also must be restricted to results of political importance. . . .

### Article 26: Motions and Recommendations

1. Every *Land* has the right to present motions to the Bundesrat. . . . If a committee recommends that the Bundesrat modify or reject such a motion, it must also present the reason for the recommendations. . . .

### Article 29: Voting

Votes are cast by raising hands. If a *Land* so requests, a vote can be taken by calling upon each *Land* separately. The *Länder* are called upon in alphabetical order. . . .

### Article 30: Voting Rules

According to articles 76–78 of the Basic Law [see 4:18:76–78], the questions voted on in a legislative procedure must be so formulated as to leave no doubt whether the Bundesrat has decided by majority vote to: (1) submit a bill to the Bundestag (article 76, paragraph 1, of the Basic Law); (2) offer an opinion on a bill of the federal government and to describe the nature of this opinion (article 76, paragraph 2, of the Basic Law); (3) vote for a bill accepted by the Bundestag (article 78 of the Basic Law); (4) demand the establishment of a mediating committee as a result of Bundestag support for the bill (article 77, paragraph 1, of the Basic Law); (5) veto a bill supported by the Bundestag or recall it (article 77, paragraph 3, and article 78 of the Basic Law). . . .

### Article 37: Meeting Place, Publicity, List of Participants in the Meetings
1. The committees meet at the seat of the Bundesrat.
2. The sessions of the committees are not public. Negotiations are confidential, unless the committee decides otherwise. . . .

### Article 38: Convocation, Chairmanship, Agenda
1. The chairman convenes the committee. He must convene it immediately if a member of the committee so demands. The chairman prepares the sessions of the committee and presides over them.
2. The agenda must be forwarded to the representatives of the *Länder* as early as possible and not later than six days before the session begins. If this deadline cannot be observed, the agenda must be forwarded to the representatives of the *Länder* and simultaneously, by telegram, to the members of the committee.

### Article 39: Deliberation
1. The committees prepare the resolutions to be voted on by the Bundesrat.
2. The president can order the committees to submit expert opinions.

### Article 42: Conclusions
1. A quorum is constituted in the committees if more than half of the *Länder* representatives are present.
2. Every *Land* has one vote in the committees.
3. The committees pass resolutions by a simple majority.

### Article 43: Procedure of Inquiry
If the chairman thinks the oral discussion of a motion is not necessary, he can ask for the opinion of the committee members by means of an inquiry. The inquiry must be made early enough so that, upon the request of a *Land*, a session can still be convened in time. . . .

## LEGISLATIVE PROCESS

### 18. FEDERAL REPUBLIC

ART. 76  1. Bills are introduced in the Bundestag by the federal government, by members of the Bundestag or by the Bundesrat. [See 5:20:115c–f, 115h–l.]
2. Bills of the federal government shall be submitted first to the Bundesrat. The Bundesrat is entitled to state its position on these bills within three weeks.
3. Bills of the Bundesrat shall be submitted to the Bundestag by the federal government. In doing so, the federal government must state its own views. [See 5:20:115a(1).]
ART. 77  1. Federal laws are adopted by the Bundestag. Upon their adoption, they shall, without delay, be transmitted to the Bundesrat by the president of the Bundestag.
2. The Bundesrat may, within two weeks of the receipt of the adopted

bill, demand that a committee for joint consideration of bills, composed of members of the Bundestag and the Bundesrat, be convened. The composition and the procedure of this committee are regulated by rules of procedure adopted by the Bundestag and require the consent of the Bundesrat. The members of the Bundesrat on this committee are not bound by instructions. If the consent of the Bundesrat is required for a law, the demand for convening this committee may also be made by the Bundestag or by the federal government. Should the committee propose any amendment to the adopted bill, the Bundestag must again vote on the bill. [See 4:14:53; 5:20:115d(1).]

3. Insofar as the consent of the Bundesrat is not required for a law, the Bundesrat may, if the proceedings under paragraph 2 are completed, enter a protest within one week against a law adopted by the Bundestag. This period begins, in the case of paragraph 2, last sentence, on the receipt of the bill as readopted by the Bundestag; in all other cases, on the conclusion of the proceedings of the committee provided for in paragraph 2.

4. If the protest is adopted by a majority of the votes of the Bundesrat, it can be rejected by a decision of the majority of the members of the Bundestag. If the Bundestag adopted the protest by a majority of at least two-thirds of its votes, the rejection by the Bundestag requires a majority of two-thirds, including at least the majority of the members of the Bundestag.

ART. 78   A law adopted by the Bundestag is deemed to have been passed if the Bundesrat consents to it, does not make a demand pursuant to article 77, paragraph 2, does not enter a protest within the time limit stated in article 77, paragraph 3, or withdraws such protest, or if the protest is overridden by the Bundestag. [See 5:20:115d(1).]

ART. 82   Laws passed in accordance with the provisions of this Basic Law will, after countersignature, be signed by the federal president and promulgated in the *Federal Law Gazette*. Ordinances having the force of law will be signed by the agency that issues them and, unless otherwise provided by law, will be promulgated in the *Federal Law Gazette*. [See 5:20:115a(2),115d(1).]

2. Every law and every ordinance having the force of law should specify its effective date. In the absence of such a provision, it becomes effective on the fourteenth day after the end of the day on which the *Federal Law Gazette* was published.


### 19. THIRD REICH, ENABLING ACT TO COMBAT THE NATIONAL CRISIS, MARCH 24, 1933

The Reichstag has enacted the following law which, with the consent of the Reichsrat and after the determination that the requirements for laws changing the constitution have been complied with, is hereby promulgated:

FROM *FLG*, I (1933), pp. 141–48. This act was known in Germany as the *Gesetz zur Behebung der Not von Volk und Reich*. The Reichstag extended it twice: on January 30, 1937, and on January 30, 1939. Hitler extended it by decree on May 10, 1943.

ART. 1   Federal laws can be enacted by the federal government as well as in accordance with the procedure established in the constitution. . . .

ART. 2   The federal laws enacted by the federal government may deviate from the constitution insofar as they do not affect the positions of the Reichstag and of the Reichsrat. The powers of the president remain undisturbed.

.     .     .

ART. 4   Treaties of the federation with foreign states that concern matters of federal legislation do not require the consent of the bodies participating in legislation. The federal government is empowered to issue the necessary provisions for the execution of these treaties.

ART. 5   This law becomes effective on the day of its publication. It becomes invalid on April 1, 1937; it further becomes invalid when the present federal government is replaced by another government.

## 20. WEIMAR

ART. 68   Bills are brought in by the federal government from the Reichstag. Federal laws are enacted by the Reichstag.

ART. 69   The bringing in of proposals for laws by the federal government requires the consent of the Reichsrat. If an agreement is not reached between the Reichsrat and the Reichstag, the federal government may nevertheless bring in the proposal but, in so doing, must state the dissenting position of the Reichsrat.

If the Reichsrat decides upon a proposition of law to which the government does not agree, the latter must bring the bill before the Reichstag, with an explanation of its own viewpoint.

ART. 70   The federal president must prepare the laws that have been passed in accordance with the constitution, and, within the period of a month, he must publish them in the *Federal Law Gazette*.

ART. 71   Federal laws, unless they provide otherwise, go into effect on the fourteenth day after the end of the day on which the *Federal Law Gazette* was published in the federal capital.

ART. 72   The publication of a federal law is to be postponed for two months if one-third of the Reichstag so demands. Laws declared urgent by the Reichstag and the Reichsrat may be published by the federal president notwithstanding this demand.

ART. 73   A law of the Reichstag must be submitted to popular referendum before its proclamation, if the federal president, within one month of its passage, so decides. . . .

A popular referendum must also be held if one-tenth of those entitled to vote desire that a law be issued. . . .

ART. 74   The Reichsrat has the right to object to laws passed by the Reichstag. The objection must be announced to the federal government within two weeks after the final determination by the Reichstag, and within two more weeks, at the latest, the reasons must be supplied.

In case of objection, the law is submitted to the Reichstag for another vote. If the Reichstag and the Reichsrat cannot reach an agreement, the federal president may order a popular referendum on the subject of disagreement within three months. If the president does not use this right, the law does not go into effect. If the Reichstag has overruled the objection of the Reichsrat by a two-thirds majority, the president must publish the law within three months in the form decided upon by the Reichstag, or he must order a popular referendum.

ART. 75   An enactment of the Reichstag can be anulled by popular referendum only if a majority of the qualified voters participate in the vote.

## 21. Empire

ART. 5   The legislative power of the Empire shall be exercised by the Bundesrat and the Reichstag. A majority of the votes of both bodies shall be necessary and sufficient for the passage of a law. . . .

ART. 16   In accordance with the resolutions of the Bundesrat, the necessary bills shall be submitted to the Reichstag in the name of the emperor, and they shall be advocated in the Reichstag by members of the Bundesrat. . . .

ART. 23   The Reichstag shall have the right to propose laws within the competence of the Empire and to refer petitions addressed to it to the Bundesrat or to the chancellor or to the emperor.

## 22. Federal Republic, Bundestag and Bundesrat, Joint Standing Orders, April 19, 1951

For the implementation of article 77 of the Basic Law [see 4:18:77], the Bundestag, with the consent of the Bundesrat, has enacted the following standing orders of the conference committee:

ART. 1   The Bundestag and the Bundesrat shall each delegate eleven[1] members to the permanent conference committee. . . .

ART. 5   The members of the federal government shall have the right and, upon a resolution of the committee, the obligation to attend committee meetings. . . .

ART. 7   . . . 3. A compromise proposal can be adopted only if at least eight members each from the Bundestag and the Bundesrat are present. . . .

ART. 8   The committee shall take its decisions by a majority vote of the members present. . . .

ART. 10   1. A compromise proposal to amend or to reject a bill adopted by the Bundestag shall be put on the agenda of the Bundestag at once. A member designated by the committee shall present a report to the Bundestag and to the Bundesrat respectively.

FROM *FLG*, II (1951), pp. 103–4.

[1] As amended, February 11, 1957. *FLG*, II (1957), p. 31.

2. The Bundestag shall vote only on the compromise proposal. Explanatory statements may be presented before the vote. No other substantive motion shall be permitted. . . .

ART. 11 If a recommendation confirming a law is enacted by the Bundestag, further action by the Bundestag shall not be necessary. . . .

ART. 12 1. If a recommendation is not adopted during a second meeting devoted to the same matter, any member may move the termination of the proceedings.

2. If no majority can be obtained for a recommendation at a subsequent meeting, the proceedings shall be terminated.

3. There shall be no other way of closing the proceedings in the absence of a recommendation.

## JURISDICTION

### 23. FEDERAL REPUBLIC

ART. 70 [See 2:4:70.]

ART. 71 On matters within the exclusive legislative powers of the federation, the *Länder* have authority to legislate only if, and to the extent that, a federal law explicitly authorizes them to do so. . . .

ART. 72 1. On matters within the concurrent legislative powers, the *Länder* have authority to legislate as long as, and to the extent that, the federation does not use its legislative power.

2. The federation has the right to legislate on these matters to the extent that a need for a federal rule exists because: (1) a matter cannot be effectively dealt with by the legislation of the individual *Länder*; (2) dealing with a matter by *Land* law might prejudice the interests of other *Länder* or of the entire community; or (3) the maintenance of legal or economic unity, especially the maintenance of uniformity of living conditions beyond the territory of a *Land*, necessitates it.

ART. 73[1] The federation has the exclusive power to legislate on: (1) foreign affairs as well as defense, including the protection of the civilian population [see 6:12:17a]; (2) citizenship in the federation [see 6:12:16(1)]; (3) freedom of movement, passport matters, immigration, emigration, and extradition [see 6:12:11(1); 6:12:16(2)]; (4) currency, money and coinage, weights and measures, as well as computation of time; (5) the unity of the customs and commercial territory, treaties on commerce and navigation, the freedom of movement of goods and the exchange of goods and payments with foreign countries, including customs and other frontier protection; (6) federal railroads and air traffic; (7) postal and telecommunication services [see 6:12:10]; (8) the legal status of persons employed by the federation and by federal bodies-corporate under public law; (9) industrial property rights, copyrights, and publication rights; (10) cooperation of the federation and

[1] As amended by federal law on March 26, 1954 (see *FLG*, I [1954], p. 45) and by the federal emergency law of 1968.

the *Länder* in matters of criminal police and of protection of the constitution, establishment of a federal office of the criminal police, as well as international control of crime; (11) statistics for federal purposes [see 5:10:87].

ART. 74[1]   Concurrent legislative powers extend to the following matters: (1) civil law, criminal law, and execution of sentences, the system of judicature, the procedure of the courts, the legal profession, notaries, and legal advice [*Rechtsberatung*]; (2) registration of births, deaths, and marriages; (3) the law of association and assembly [see 6:12:9(1)]; (4) the law relating to residence and establishment of aliens; . . . (6) the affairs of refugees and expellees; (7) public welfare; (8) citizenship in the *Länder*; (9) war damage and reparations; . . . (11) the law relating to economic matters (mining, industry, supply of power, crafts, trades, commerce, banking and stock exchanges, private insurance); (11a) the production and utilization of nuclear energy for peaceful purposes, the construction and operation of installations serving these purposes, protection against dangers arising from the release of nuclear energy or from ionizing rays, and removal of radioactive material;[2] (12) labor law, including the legal organization of enterprises, protection of workers, employment exchanges and agencies, as well as social insurance, including unemployment insurance; (13) the promotion of scientific research; (14) the law regarding expropriation, to the extent that matters enumerated in articles 73 and 74 are concerned; (15) transfer of land, natural resources, and means of production into public ownership or other forms of publicly controlled economy; (16) prevention of the abuse of economic power; (17) promotion of agricultural and forest production, safeguarding the supply of food, the import and export of agricultural and forest products, deep sea and coastal fishing, and preservation of the coasts; (18) real estate transactions, land law, and matters concerning agricultural leases, housing, settlements, and homesteads; . . . (21) ocean and coastal shipping as well as aids to navigation, inland shipping, meteorological services, sea waterways, and inland waterways used for general traffic; (22) road traffic, motor transport, and construction and maintenance of long distance highways; (23) railroads other than federal railroads, except mountain railroads.

ART. 75   Subject to the conditions of article 72, the federation has the right to enact general rules concerning: (1) the legal status of persons in the public service of the *Länder*, communities, and other bodies-corporate under public law; (2) the general legal status of the press and motion pictures; (3) hunting, protection of nature, and care of the countryside; (4) land distribution, regional planning, and water conservation; (5) matters relating to the registration of changes of residence or domicile [*Meldewesen*] and to identity cards.

.   .   .

---

[1] As amended by federal law on December 23, 1956. See *FLG*, I (1956), p. 813.
[2] Inserted by federal law on June 16, 1965. See *FLG*, I (1965), p. 513.

ART. 80 1. The federal government, a federal minister, or the *Land* governments may be authorized by a law to issue ordinances having the force of law. The content, purpose, and scope of the powers conferred must be set forth in the law. The legal basis must be stated in the ordinance. If a law provides that a power may be further delegated, an ordinance having the force of law is necessary in order to delegate the power.

2. The consent of the Bundesrat is required, unless otherwise provided by federal legislation, for ordinances having the force of law and issued by the federal government or by a federal minister concerning basic rules for the use of facilities of the federal railroads and of postal and telecommunication services, or charges therefor, or concerning the construction and operation of railroads, as well as for ordinances having the force of law and issued on the basis of federal laws that require the consent of the Bundesrat or that are executed by the *Länder* as agents of the federation or as matters of their own concern.

ART. 80a[1] 1. Where this Basic Law or a federal law on defense, including the protection of the civilian population, stipulates that legal provisions may only be applied in accordance with this article, their application shall, except when a state of defense exists, be admissible only after the Bundestag has determined that a state of tension [*Spannungsfall*] exists or if it has specifically approved such application. In respect of the cases mentioned in article 12a, paragraph 5, sentence 1, and paragraph 6, sentence 2, such determination of a state of tension and such specific approval shall require a two-thirds majority of the votes cast.

2. Any measures taken by virtue of legal provisions enacted under this article shall be revoked whenever the Bundestag so requests.

3. Notwithstanding the provisions of this article, the application of such legal provisions shall also be admissible by virtue of, and in accordance with, a decision taken with the consent of the federal government by an international organ within the framework of a treaty of alliance. Any measures taken pursuant to this paragraph shall be revoked whenever the Bundestag so requests by a majority of its members.

## 24. WEIMAR

ART. 5 [See 2:6:5.]

ART. 6 The federation has exclusive legislative power over: (1) relationships with foreign countries; (2) colonial affairs; (3) citizenship, freedom of travel, immigration, emigration, and extradition [see 6:13:110,112]; (4) military organization; (5) coinage; (6) customs, as well as the unification of the customs and trade area, and freedom of commerce; (7) the post and telegraph system, including the telephone system [see 5:11:88(1); 6:13:117].

ART. 7 The federation has legislative power over: (1) civil law; (2)

[1] Inserted by the federal emergency law of 1968, this is the only provision of the constitution that refers to the state of tension. See also the introduction to chapter 2.

criminal law; (3) judicial procedure, including the execution of penalties and official aid among authorities; . . . (6) regulation of the press, association, and assembly; . . . (9) labor law, insurance, and the protection of laborers and employees, as well as labor offices; . . . (12) the right of expropriation; (13) the socialization of natural resources and economic undertakings, as well as the production, manufacture. distribution, and price regulation of economic goods for the general economy; (14) commerce, weights and measures, the issuing of paper money, the banking system, and the exchange system; (16) traffic in foodstuffs and luxuries as well as objects of everyday necessity; (17) industry and mining; (18) insurance; (19) ocean navigation, deep sea and coastal fishing; (20) railways; . . . [see 5:11:89]; (21) theaters and cinemas.

· · ·

ART. 9   Insofar as a need exists for the issuing of uniform provisions, the federation has legislative power over: (1) public welfare; (2) the protection of public order and safety.

ART. 10   The federation can, by legislation, establish fundamental principles for: (1) the rights and duties of religious organizations; (2) the educational system, including higher schools and scientific libraries; (3) the law of officers of all public corporations; (4) real estate law, the division of property, the settlement and homestead system, restrictions on real estate, housing, and distribution of population; (5) the disposal of the dead.

· · ·

ART. 77   The federal government issues the general administrative provisions necessary for the execution of the federal laws, insofar as the laws do not otherwise provide. The consent of the Reichsrat is required if the execution of the federal laws belongs to the *Land* authorities.

## 25. EMPIRE

ART. 4   The following matters shall be under the supervision of the Empire and subject to imperial legislation: (1) regulations concerning the freedom of migration, matters of domicile and settlement, citizenship, passports, surveillance of foreigners, exercise of a profession; . . . (2) legislation concerning customs duties, commerce, and such taxes as are to be applied to the uses of the Empire; (3) regulation of weights and measures, coinage, and the establishment of the principles for the issue of funded and unfunded paper money; (4) general banking regulations; (5) patents for inventions; (6) the protection of intellectual property; (7) the organization of a general system of protection for German trade in foreign countries, of German navigation, and of the German flag on the high seas, and the establishment of a common consular representation by the Empire; (8) railway matters . . . [see 5:12:41,42]; (10) postal and telegraph affairs . . .

[see 5:12:48,50]; (13) general legislation on the whole domain of civil law, criminal law, and judicial procedure; (14) the imperial military and naval affairs; (15) police regulation of medical and veterinary matters; (16) regulations concerning the press and the right of association.

## FISCAL JURISDICTION

### 26. FEDERAL REPUBLIC

ART. 105   1. The federation has the exclusive power to legislate on customs and fiscal monopolies. [See 5:20:115c–f,115i,115k.]

2. The federation has concurrent power to legislate on: (1) excise taxes and taxes on transactions, with the exception of taxes with localized application, in particular the taxes on the acquisition of real estate, on increments in value, and for fire protection; (2) taxes on income, on property, on inheritances, and on donations; (3) taxes on real estate and businesses, with the exception of the fixing of the tax rates, if it claims the taxes in whole or in part to cover federal expenditure or if the conditions laid down in article 72, paragraph 2, exist. [See 4:23:72(2).]

3. Federal laws relating to taxes the yield of which accrues in whole or in part to the *Länder* or the communities (community associations) require the consent of the Bundesrat.

ART. 106[1]   1. The yield of fiscal monopolies and receipts from the following taxes shall accrue to the federation: (1) customs duties; (2) such excise taxes as do not accrue to the *Länder* in accordance with paragraph 2; (3) turnover tax; (4) transportation tax; (5) nonrecurrent capital levies and equalization taxes imposed for the purpose of implementing the equalization of burdens legislations; (6) Berlin emergency-aid tax; (7) supplementary levies on income and corporation taxes.

2. Receipts from the following taxes shall accrue to the *Länder*: (1) property; (2) inheritance; (3) motor vehicle; (4) such taxes on transactions as do not accrue to the federation in accordance with paragraph 1; (5) beer; (6) levies on gambling establishments; (7) taxes on real estate and businesses; (8) taxes with localized application.

3. Receipts from income tax and corporation tax shall accrue, until March 31, 1958, to the federation and to the *Länder* in a ratio of $33\frac{1}{3}$ per cent to $66\frac{2}{3}$ per cent and from April 1, 1958, to the federation and the *Länder* in a ratio of 35 per cent to 65 per cent.

4. The ratio of apportionment of the income and corporation taxes in paragraph 3 should be modified by a federal law requiring the consent of the Bundesrat whenever the development of the relation of revenues to expenditures in the federation differs from that in the *Länder* and whenever the budgetary needs of the federation or those of the *Länder* exceed the estimated revenues by a margin substantial enough to call for a corresponding

[1] As amended by federal law on December 23, 1955, and on December 24, 1965. See *FLG*, I (1955), p. 817 and *FLG*, I (1956), p. 1077.

adjustment of the ratio of apportionment in favor of either the federation or the *Länder*. . . .

ART. 107[6] . . . 2. A federal law requiring the consent of the Bundesrat shall ensure a reasonable financial equalization between financially strong *Länder* and financially weak *Länder*, due account being taken of the financial capacity and requirements of communities (community associations). Such law shall provide for equalization grants to be paid to financially weak *Länder* from equalization contributions made by financially strong *Länder*; it shall furthermore specify the conditions governing equalization claims and equalization liabilities as well as the criteria for determining the amounts of equalization payments. Such law may also provide for grants to be made by the federation from federal funds to financially weak *Länder* in order to complement the coverage of their general financial requirements (complemental grants).

ART. 108   1. Customs duties, fiscal monopolies, excise taxes subject to concurrent legislative powers, transportation tax, turnover tax, and nonrecurrent capital levies shall be administered by federal revenue authorities. The organization of these authorities and the procedure to be applied to them will be regulated by federal law. . . .

3. All other taxes shall be administered by *Land* revenue authorities. . . . [See 2:4:70; 4:23:71–75.]

ART. 109[2]   1. The federation and the *Länder* shall be autonomous and independent of each other in their fiscal administration.

2. The federation and the *Länder* shall take due account in their fiscal administration of the requirements of over-all economic equilibrium.

3. By means of federal legislation requiring the consent of the Bundesrat, principles may be established governing both responsiveness of the fiscal administration to economic trends and pluri-annual financial planning.

4. With a view to warding off disturbances of the over-all economic equilibrium, federal legislation requiring the consent of the Bundesrat may be enacted providing for: (1) maximum amounts, terms, and timing of loans to be raised by public administrative entities, whether territorial [*Gebietskörperschaften*] or functional [*Zweckverbände*], and (2) an obligation on the part of the federation and the *Länder* to maintain interest-free deposits in the German Federal Bank [reserves for counterbalancing economic trends].

Authorizations to enact pertinent ordinances having the force of law may be issued only to the federal government. Such ordinances shall require the consent of the Bundesrat. They shall be repealed insofar as the Bundestag may demand; details shall be regulated by federal legislation.[3]

ART. 110   1. All revenues and expenditures of the federation must be estimated for each fiscal year and included in the budget.

2. The budget shall be established by a law before the beginning of the

[1] As amended by federal law of December 23, 1955. See *FLG*, I (1955), p. 817.
[2] As amended by federal law on June 6, 1967. See *FLG*, I (1967), p. 581.
[3] See Federal Law for the Furtherance and Growth of the Economy, June 8, 1967, in *FLG*, I (1967), pp. 582–89.

fiscal year. It must be balanced as regards revenue and expenditure. Expenditures will as a rule be authorized for one year; in special cases, they may be authorized for a longer period. Otherwise, no provisions may be inserted in the federal budget law that extend beyond the fiscal year or do not relate to the revenues and expenditures of the federation or its administration.

3. The assets and liabilities shall be set forth in an appendix to the budget. . . .

ART. 111  1. If, by the end of the fiscal year, the budget for the following year has not been established by law, the federal government may, until such a law comes into force, make all payments necessary to (1) maintain institutions existing by law and carry out measures authorized by law; (2) meet the legal obligations of the federation; (3) continue building projects, procurements, and other services or continue the grant of subsidies for these purposes, provided amounts have already been authorized in the budget of a previous year.

2. Insofar as revenues provided by special legislation and derived from taxes or duties or other charges or sources or the working capital reserves do not cover the expenditures set forth in paragraph 1, the federal government may borrow the funds necessary for the conduct of current operations up to a maximum of one-fourth of the total amount of the previous budget.

ART. 112  Expenditures in excess of budgetary appropriations and extra-budgetary ordinary expenditures require the consent of the federal minister of finance. The consent may be given only if an unforeseen and compelling necessity exists.

ART. 113  Decisions of the Bundestag and of the Bundesrat that increase the budget expenditure proposed by the federal government or involve new expenditure or will cause new expenditure in the future require the consent of the federal government.

ART. 114  1. The federal minister of finance must submit annually to the Bundestag and to the Bundesrat an account of all revenues and expenditure as well as assets and liabilities. . . .

ART. 115  Funds may be obtained by borrowing only in case of extraordinary need and, as a rule, only for expenditure for productive purposes and only pursuant to a federal law. . . .

## 27. WEIMAR

ART. 11  By legislation, the federation can establish fundamental principles in respect to the permissibility and method of levying state taxes, insofar as these are needed to guard against: (1) injury to the income or the commercial relationships of the federation; (2) double taxation; (3) burdening the use of public means of communication and public establishments with fees that are excessive or impede traffic; (4) tax burdens upon imported goods in comparison with domestic products and in traffic between the individual *Länder* and parts of the *Länder*, or (5) export premiums. . . .

ART. 85   All receipts and expenditures of the federation must be estimated for each fiscal year and placed in the budget. The budget will be fixed by law before the beginning of the fiscal year. The appropriations as a rule are granted for one year; in special cases, they may also be granted for a longer period. Otherwise, provisions are not permitted in the federal budget law that extend beyond the fiscal year or do not concern the receipts and expeditures of the federation or its administration.

Without the consent of the Reichsrat, the Reichstag cannot increase appropriations in the budget bill or insert new ones. The consent of the Reichsrat can be dispensed with according to the provisions of article 74. [See 4:20:74.]

ART. 86   The federal minister of finance accounts to the Reichsrat and the Reichstag in the following fiscal year for the application of all national receipts, so that the federal government may be discharged from responsibility. The examination of accounts is regulated by federal law.


## 28. EMPIRE

ART. 35   The federation shall have the exclusive power to legislate on everything related to customs; to the taxation of salt and tobacco produced in the federal territory, domestic brandy and beer, and sugar and syrup prepared from beets or other domestic products. . . .

ART. 36   The administration and collection of customs duties and of the taxes on articles of consumption (article 35) shall be left to each member of the federation for its own territory, so far as these functions have heretofore been exercised by each member. . . .

ART. 38   The revenues from customs and from the other taxes designated in article 35, so far as the latter are subject to federal legislation, shall go to the treasury of the federation. . . .

ART. 69   All receipts and expenditures of the federation shall be estimated for each year and included in the budget. The latter shall be determined by law before the beginning of the fiscal year. . . .

ART. 70   For the defrayal of all common expenses, the joint revenues derived from customs duties, from common taxes, the railway, postal and telegraph systems, and from the other branches of the administration shall be used. Insofar as the expenditures are not covered by such receipts, they shall be met by contributions from the member states in proportion to their population; such contributions shall be determined by the federal chancellor. . . .

ART. 72   For the purpose of discharge, an annual report of the expenditure of all the revenues of the federation shall be presented by the federal chancellor to the Bundesrat and the Reichstag for their approval.

# 5. *Executive and Administration*

# INTRODUCTION

The executive branch of the German government is and has always been complicated in structure and powers in three respects: First, the relation between president and premier, i.e., between the head of state on the one hand, and the head of government on the other; second, the relation between executive and legislature; third, the relation between the federal government and member states, i.e., because of the federal structure of German government. Since the introduction of republican government in the Weimar years, executive power has been divided between two offices; the presidency and the chancellorship. Under the Weimar Constitution, the federal president was given broad powers; in particular, he had the power to dissolve the Reichstag and to exercise broad emergency powers (article 48). His independent status was underlined by the fact that he was popularly elected for a term of seven years. The extremely broad interpretation of his powers and, in the last years of the Weimar Republic, their abuse were major factors in the downfall of the Weimar regime. In consequence, the Basic Law of the Federal Republic of Germany conferred upon the federal president only limited powers, many of which are of a more or less ceremonial nature. For most of his acts, the president needs the countersignature of the chancellor or of a minister. He is elected for a five-year term by a federal convention, which consists of the members of the Bundestag and an equal number of members elected by the *Landtage.*

Much more power is vested in the federal chancellor. During the Weimar period, true to the principles of parliamentary government, the chancellor and his ministers were at all times dependent on the majority backing of the Reichstag, and they had to resign if they no longer had its confidence. Under the Basic Law, the federal chancellor can be dismissed only if a majority of the Bundestag elects a successor by the same vote by which it expresses its lack of confidence in the incumbent; this is known as the "constructive vote of nonconfidence" (article 67). Moreover, parliament has no power to dismiss cabinet ministers. The chancellor, once elected by the Bundestag, is free to form and re-form his cabinet; he may appoint and dismiss his ministers at will.

In the *Länder*, the relation between the legislature and the executive varies according to the constitution of the *Land*. Some *Länder*, such as North Rhine–Westphalia, recognize the constructive vote of nonconfidence; other *Länder* practice a more or less pure parliamentary system.

The federal government transacts its business under its own standing orders (document 8). Ministers conduct the business of their departments independently and under their own responsibility. The chancellor determines the general principles of his government's policy, and certain matters such as passing on a bill before it is submitted to the Bundestag are handled and, if necessary, voted upon by the cabinet as a group. Each minister has at least one ministerial aide—called a state secretary (*Staatssekretär*)—who is his political assistant.[1] The chancellor has his own office, the chancellery. It is headed by a state secretary, who is sometimes given ministerial rank and who is responsible for the coordination of cabinet business. If the state secretary possesses the confidence of the chancellor, he emerges as an extremely influential officer. The status of the ministers is regulated by the Federal Ministers Law of 1953 (document 9).

The problem of determining the special powers of the executive in an emergency situation has long troubled Germany. In the Empire years, martial law could be proclaimed by the emperor, acting jointly with the Bundesrat. In the Weimar period, article 48 conferred vast emergency powers upon the federal president. The Nazi regime exercised unlimited emergency powers. By contrast, the Bonn Constitution initially provided only for the exceptional and limited case of "legislative emergencies" (article 81). Under this provision, the government, with the consent of the Bundesrat, can enact bills not passed by the Bundestag. The Emergency Law of 1968, amending the Bonn Constitution, creates new powers for the executive and, in some cases, for a newly established parliamentary body; these have been described above (see Introduction to chapter 2).

Like emergency powers, the status and control of the military has been a difficult political and constitutional problem in Germany. During the Empire period, the emperor was the supreme commander of the armed forces and, in this capacity, he was not responsible to parliament or to any other organ. In the Weimar era, parliamentary control of the armed forces (*Reichswehr*), as permitted by the Versailles Treaty, was in principle vested in the Reichstag and in the minister of defense, who was responsible to the Reichstag. But under the federal president, who was the supreme commander, the armed forces gained a rather independent position in the course of time. The Bonn constitution has tried to reaffirm civilian control over the federal armed forces (*Bundeswehr*) by naming the federal minister of defense supreme commander in time of peace. In time of war, according to emergency legislation dealing with the "state of defense," command devolves upon the federal chancellor. This legislation regulates in detail the functions of various government organs once a state of defense has been proclaimed (document 20).

One of the most controversial decisions of the Bundestag in recent years was the appointment, in 1956, of a parliamentary military commissioner, to serve as a link between the military and the parliament and to be specifically responsible for safeguarding the basic rights of the members of the armed forces (document 24). While the idea of appointing the com-

---

[1] Under a law enacted in 1967, a new post of "parliamentary undersecretary" was created to provide, somewhat on the British pattern, for representation of the respective minister before parliament.

missioner was generally lauded, controversies have arisen about the extent of the commissioner's authority vis-à-vis the Bundestag, and several commissioners, appointed consecutively, have resigned.

One of the most constant and characteristic features of German government has been the existence of a career civil service (*Beamtentum*). The political leaders of the government, particularly the ministers, have always staffed their departments with career officials who execute and, at times, even initiate policies. Ministerial bureaucracy as well as the civil service system in general have deep roots in German history. The system, which developed in the German states, especially in Prussia, prior to unification in 1871, gave the public service a status different from that of other social groups and professions. Members of the civil service enjoyed such privileges as life-time tenure, retirement pensions, and pensions for surviving widows and minors. In return for such privileges, the civil servant was expected to devote his life to his profession. The same was true under the Weimar Constitution, and the Basic Law also guarantees similar constitutional protection to the civil servant. The details of service are regulated by a federal law for federal officials (document 19) and by state laws for the *Land* officials. These laws establish four categories of higher and lower civil service, with different educational and recruitment requirements, different rules for promotion, and so forth. In contrast to other countries, grade and high school teachers as well as professors, judges, prosecutors, and other categories of public employees are considered civil servants.

The law prohibits strikes by German civil servants. They can, however, form their own professional organizations, usually not connected with the trade unions. German civil servants can be active politically; they may be elected to the Bundestag or to a *Landtag*. In fact, they abound in both parliaments. A civil servant can be dismissed only for cause.

Under the Nazi regime, a civil servant could be dismissed if there were doubts about his political reliability (documents 14, 15, and 16). After 1945, many supporters of the Nazi regime were de-Nazified—that is, they were suspended from office; however, most of them were soon reinstated. Final federal legislation on de-Nazification exempted only former members of the Gestapo and people in a few other limited categories from reinstatement.

In the German Democratic Republic, the traditional civil service system was entirely abolished. Employees of the government there have a status no different from that of other workers and employees.

Numerically speaking, most German civil servants are members of a *Land*, not federal, administration, because German administration lay traditionally more in the hands of the *Länder* than in the hands of the federal government. Federal administration was limited in the Empire and extended mostly to diplomacy, the navy, and customs. It tended to increase in the Weimar period, adding, for example, federal financial administration. Federal administration was most extensive under Nazi centralism. In the main, the *Länder* predominate in the Bonn system.

Whenever the *Länder* execute federal laws, the federal government has certain powers of supervision and enforcement. Since the *Länder* carry the greatest burden for the administration and execution of the laws, the question of financial relations with the federal government has created severe problems. Traditionally, German federal constitutions have regulated the distribution between the federation and the *Länder* of income from taxes, customs, and so on. Under the Bonn Constitution, receipts from income and corporation taxes are shared by the federation and the *Länder* according to a specific ratio (see chapter 4). Mail and railroads have traditionally been controlled by the federal government and have been run, with some degree of autonomy, by federal ministries. By contrast, radio and television are organized as autonomous public corporations on the *Land* level.

The survey of constitutional provisions under Bonn, Weimar, and the Empire, and, occasionally, the Nazi regime is divided into five sections. The first deals with the position of the emperor and the federal president as top representatives of the nation. The second discusses the position of the government, that is, of the chancellor and the ministers. The third section presents the rules on federal administration, especially the execution of federal laws, and on federal administrative agencies. The fourth section contains constitutional provisions for the civil service. The fifth singles out the rules for the federal armed forces and for military affairs.

# DOCUMENTS

## FEDERAL PRESIDENT

### 1. Federal Republic

ART. 54   1. The federal president is elected without debate by the federal convention [*Bundesversammlung*]. Every German is eligible who is entitled to vote for the Bundestag candidates and who has attained the age of forty. [See 2:1:20(2).]

2. The term of office of the federal president is five years. Re-election for a consecutive term is permitted only once. [See 5:20:115h(1).]

3. The federal convention consists of the members of the Bundestag and an equal number of members elected by the representative assemblies of the *Länder*, according to the rules of proportional representation. . . .

6. The person receiving the votes of the majority of the members of the federal convention is elected. If a majority is not obtained by any candidate in two ballots, the candidate who receives the largest number of votes in an additional ballot is elected.

7. Details will be regulated by federal law. [See 5:5.]

ART. 55   1. The federal president may not be a member of the government or of a legislative body of the federation or of a *Land*.

2. The federal president may not hold any other salaried office nor engage in a trade or occupation, nor practice a profession nor belong to the management or the board of directors of an enterprise carried on for profit.

ART. 56. On assuming his office, the federal president takes the following oath before the assembled members of the Bundestag and the Bundesrat: "I swear that I will dedicate my efforts to the well-being of the German people, enhance its benefits, ward harm from it, uphold and defend the Basic Law and the laws of the federation, fulfill my duties conscientiously, and do justice to all. So help me God." The oath may also be taken without religious affirmation.

ART. 57 If the federal president is prevented from exercising his powers or if his office falls prematurely vacant, his powers will be exercised by the president of the Bundesrat. [See 5:20:115h(1).]

ART. 58 Orders and decrees of the federal president require for their validity the countersignature of the federal chancellor or the appropriate federal minister. This does not apply to the appointment and dismissal of the federal chancellor, the dissolution of the Bundestag under article 63 and the request under article 69, paragraph 3. [See 2:14:63; 5:6:69(3).]

ART. 59 1. The federal president represents the federation in its international relations. He concludes treaties with foreign states on behalf of the federation. He accredits and receives envoys. [See 8:1:32.]

2. Treaties that regulate the political relations of the federation or relate to matters of federal legislation require the consent or participation in the form of a federal law of the bodies competent in any specific case for such federal legislation. For administrative agreements, the provisions concerning the federal administration apply *mutatis mutandis.*

ART. 60[1] 1. The federal president appoints and dismisses the federal judges, the federal civil servants, the officers and noncommissioned officers, unless otherwise provided for by law.

2. He exercises the power of pardon on behalf of the federation in individual cases.

3. He may delegate these powers to other authorities.

4. Article 46, paragraphs 2–4, apply *mutatis mutandis* to the federal president. [See 4:5:39(3); 4:8:46(2–4).]

ART. 61 1. The Bundestag or the Bundesrat may impeach the federal president before the Federal Constitutional Court for willful violation of the Basic Law or any other federal law. The motion for impeachement must be brought forward by at least one-fourth of the members of the Bundestag or one-fourth of the votes of the Bundesrat. The decision to impeach requires a majority of two-thirds of the members of the Bundestag or of two-thirds of the votes of the Bundesrat. The prosecution is conducted by a person commissioned by the impeaching body. [See 4:8:45(2).]

2. If the Federal Constitutional Court finds the federal president guilty of a willful violation of the Basic Law or of another federal law, it may declare him to have forfeited his office. After impeachment, it may issue an

[1] As amended by federal law on March 19, 1956. See *FLG,* I (1956), p. 111.

interim order preventing the federal president from exercising the powers of his office.

## 2. THIRD REICH, LAW CONCERNING THE HEAD OF THE GERMAN REICH, AUGUST 1, 1934

The federal government has decided to proclaim the following law.

1. The office of the federal president is united with that of the federal chancellor. In consequence, the former powers of the federal president pass to the Führer and federal chancellor, Adolf Hitler. He appoints his deputy.

2. This law becomes effective from the moment of the death of Federal President von Hindenburg.[1]

FROM *FLG*, I (1934), p. 747.

## 3. WEIMAR

ART. 41    The federal president is elected by the whole German people. Every German who has completed his thirty-fifth year is eligible. Details will be regulated by federal law.

ART. 42    Upon assuming office, the federal president takes the following oath before the Reichstag: "I swear that I will devote my powers to the welfare of the German people, will develop its advantages. will guard it against dangers, will uphold the constitution and the laws of the federation, will fulfill my duties conscientiously, and will practice justice toward everyone." The addition of a religious sanction is permitted.

ART. 43.    1. The term of office of the federal president is seven years. Re-election is permitted.

2. Before the completion of the term, the federal president may be removed by popular vote upon the motion of the Reichstag. The decision of the Reichstag requires a two-thirds majority. Through the decision, the federal president is suspended from the further exercise of his functions. A rejection by popular vote of the motion for removal counts as a new election and is followed by a dissolution of the Reichstag.

3. The federal president cannot be criminally prosecuted without the consent of the Reichstag.

ART. 44    The federal president cannot, at the same time, be a member of the Reichstag.

ART. 45    The federal president represents the federation in international law. In the name of the federation, he concludes alliances and other treaties with foreign powers. He accredits and receives ambassadors. The declaration of war and the conclusion of peace take place through federal laws. Treaties and agreements with foreign states that concern matters of federal legislation require the consent of the Reichstag. [See 8:4:78.]

[1] President von Hindenburg died on August 2, 1934.

ART. 46    The federal president appoints and dismisses the federal civil servants and officers, insofar as no other provision is made by law. He can permit the right of appointment and dismissal to be exercised by other authorities.

ART. 48    [See 2:6:48(1); 2:22:48(2).]

ART. 49    The federal president exercises the right of pardon for the federation. Federal amnesties require a federal law.

ART. 50    All orders and decrees of the federal president, including those relating to the armed forces, must, in order to be valid, be countersigned by the federal chancellor or by the federal minister. Responsibility is assumed by countersignature. . . .

ART. 51    In case the federal president is prevented from performing his duties, he is represented at first by the federal chancellor. If the disability appears likely to endure for some time, the representation is to be regulated by a federal law. The same applies in the case of a premature vacancy of the presidency, until new elections have been held.

.    .    .

ART. 59    The Reichstag is authorized to impeach the federal president, the federal chancellor, and the federal ministers before the High Court of State of the German federation for having violated the national constitution or a national law. The motion for bringing impeachment must be signed by at least 100 members of the Reichstag and requires the consent of the majority prescribed for constitutional amendments. The details are to be regulated by the federal law regarding the High Court of State.

## 4. EMPIRE

ART. 11    1. To the king of Prussia shall belong the presidency of the federation, and he shall have the title of German emperor. It shall be the duty of the emperor to represent the Empire [*Deutsches Reich*] among the nations, to declare war and conclude peace in the name of the Empire, to enter into alliances and other treaties with foreign countries, to accredit ambassadors and to receive them.

2. For a declaration of war in the name of the Empire, the consent of the Bundesrat is required, unless an attack is made upon the federal territory or its coasts.

3. So far as treaties with foreign countries relate to matters that, according to article 4, are to be regulated by federal legislation, the consent of the Bundesrat shall be required for their conclusion, and the approval of the Reichstag shall be necessary to render them valid. [See 4:25:4.]

.    .    .

ART. 17    It shall be the duty of the emperor to prepare and publish the laws of the Empire and to supervise their execution. The decrees and ordinances of the emperor shall be issued in the name of the Empire and shall require for their validity the countersignature of the imperial chancellor, who thereby assumes responsibility for them.

ART. 18   1. The emperor shall appoint the federal officials, cause them to take the oath for the federation, and dismiss them when necessary. . . .

### 5. FEDERAL REPUBLIC, PRESIDENTIAL ELECTION LAW, APRIL 25, 1959

ART. 1   The president of the Bundestag shall determine the place and date of the convening of the federal convention. . . .

ART. 4   1. The *Länder* legislatures shall elect the number of members to which their *Land* is entitled according to nominating lists. . . .

2. Each member of the *Land* legislature shall have one vote.

3. If several nominating lists are submitted, seats shall be apportioned according to the number accruing to each on the basis of the d'Hondt system of the highest average.

.     .     .

ART. 9   1. Any member of the federal convention may make written nominations to the president of the Bundestag for the election of a federal president. New nominations may be made for the second and third ballots. . . .

ART. 10   The term of office of the federal president shall begin with the expiration of the term of his predecessor, but not before the receipt by the president of the Bundestag of his statement of acceptance.

FROM *FLG*, I (1959), p. 230.

### *FEDERAL GOVERNMENT*

### 6. FEDERAL REPUBLIC

ARTS. 62, 63   [See 2:14:62–63.]

ART. 64   1. [See 2:14:64.]

2. The federal chancellor and the federal ministers, on assuming office, take before the Bundestag the oath provided in article 56. [See 5:1:56; 5:20:115b.]

ART. 65.   The federal chancellor determines and is responsible for general policy. Within the limits of this general policy, each federal minister conducts the business of his department autonomously and on his own responsibility. The federal government decides on differences of opinion between the federal ministers. . . . [See 4:8:43.]

ART. 66   The federal chancellor and the federal ministers may not hold any other salaried office nor engage in a trade or occupation nor practice a profession nor belong to the management or, without the consent of the Bundestag, to the board of directors of an enterprise carried on for profit.

.     .     .

ART. 69   1. The federal chancellor appoints a federal minister as his deputy.

2. The tenure of office of the federal chancellor or a federal minister ends in any event on the first meeting of a new Bundestag; the tenure of office of a federal minister ends also on any other termination of the tenure of office of the federal chancellor. [See 2:4:67,68; 2:8:53a.]

3. At the request of the federal president, the federal chancellor, or at the request of the federal chancellor or of the federal president, a federal minister shall be bound to continue to transact the affairs of his office until the appointment of a successor.

## 7. WEIMAR

ARTS. 52, 53, 54   [See 2:15:52–54.]

ART. 55   The federal chancellor presides over the government and conducts its business according to an order of business adopted by the federal government with the consent of the federal president.

ART. 56   The federal chancellor determines the general policy of the federation and is responsible to the Reichstag. Within this general policy, each federal minister conducts independently the office entrusted to him and is held individually responsible to the Reichstag.

ART. 57   The federal ministers must lay before the federal government for discussion and decision all bills for laws and any other matters for which this is prescribed by the constitution or by statute as well as differences of opinion over questions that affect the spheres of competence of several federal ministers.

ART. 58   The federal government makes its decisions by a majority vote. In case of a tie, the chairman casts the deciding vote. [See 4:20:68,69.]

## 8. FEDERAL REPUBLIC, FEDERAL GOVERNMENT, STANDING ORDERS, MAY 11, 1951

ART. 1   1. The federal chancellor shall determine general policies in domestic and foreign affairs. These policies shall be binding upon the federal ministers and shall be carried out by them in their respective spheres of competence and on their own responsibility. In cases of doubt, a decision of the federal chancellor shall be obtained.

2. The federal chancellor shall have the right and the duty to see that these policies are followed.

ART. 2   In addition to determining general policy, the federal chancellor shall also make efforts toward harmonizing the operations of the federal government.

ART. 3   The federal chancellor shall receive from the departments of

ENACTED in accordance with article 65 of the Basic Law, with the consent of the federal president and the Bundestag.

the various federal ministers information on measures and plans that are significant for the determination of general policy and for the conduct of the business of the federal government.

ART. 4 Whenever a federal minister deems an extension or change of federal policy necessary, he shall inform the federal chancellor, giving his reasons and requesting the chancellor's decision.

ART. 5 The federal chancellor shall keep the federal president informed of his policies and of the work of the various federal ministers by transmitting to him essential records on matters of particular significance or, if necessary, by reporting in person.

ART. 6 The federal chancellor shall direct the operations of the federal government. . . .

ART. 7 1. The state secretary of the federal chancellery shall also act as a state secretary of the federal government. . . .

ART. 9 The general outlines of the spheres of competence of the various federal ministers shall be determined by the federal chancellor. If overlapping and differences of opinion arise among several federal ministers, the federal government shall decide the issue by a resolution. . . .

ART. 12 Statements by a federal minister that are made in, or intended for, the public must be in accord with the general policies laid down by the federal chancellor.

ART. 13 1. Each federal minister shall notify the federal chancellor whenever he shall leave the seat of the federal government for longer than one day. . . .

2. Acceptance of invitations for visits abroad shall be contingent on the consent of the federal chancellor.

ART. 14 In the event that a federal minister is disabled, he shall be represented in the government by the federal minister designated for this purpose, and he shall be represented as head of a superior federal agency by the state secretary or, in the event of his disability, by an official designated by his ministry.

ART. 15 1. The federal government shall be furnished, for its considerations and decisions, with all matters of general importance in the country's domestic, foreign, economic, social, financial, or cultural policy, particularly with: (1) all legislative bills; (2) all drafts of orders of the federal government; (3) drafts of other orders, if they are of particular political importance; (4) statements by the Bundestag of its position on bills submitted by the federal government; (5) all matters in which the Basic Law or these standing orders so require; (6) differences of opinion among various federal ministries. . . .

ART. 17 1. Differences of opinion among federal ministers shall be submitted to the federal government only after the federal ministers involved or, in the event of their disability, their deputies have personally made an unsuccessful attempt to reach an agreement.

2. Before the matter is discussed by the government, the federal chancellor may first discuss it with the federal ministers involved in a ministerial conference over which he presides. . . .

ART. 20   1. As a rule, the federal government shall reach its decisions in a joint meeting.

2. If oral discussion of a matter is not required, the state secretary of the federal chancellery shall obtain the written approval of the members of the federal government. If doubts exist about the necessity of an oral deliberation, the state secretary shall obtain the decision of the federal chancellor. . . .

ART. 21   . . . 3. The transmittal of government bills shall be made in sufficient time to allow a review of the matter prior to the deliberations. . . .

ART. 22   1. Meetings of the federal government shall be presided over by the federal chancellor or, in the event of his disability, by the deputy chancellor.

.   .   .

3. The meetings of the federal government shall be confidential. Particularly, publication of the remarks of various federal ministers, of voting results, and of the contents of the minutes shall not be permitted without special authorization of the federal chancellor. . . .

ART. 24   1. The federal government shall constitute a quorum if one-half of the federal ministers, including the chairman, are present.

2. The federal government shall render its decisions by majority vote. In case of a tie, the chairman shall cast the deciding vote. . . .

ART. 28   1. Bills approved by the federal government shall be transmitted to the lawmaking organs by the federal chancellor, and they shall be handled by the federal minister having jurisdiction over the matter.

2. The handling must be undertaken uniformly, even if the individual federal ministers hold different views. Federal ministers shall not be permitted to act against the views of the federal government. . . .

ART. 29   1. Laws shall be presented to the federal president for action only after the federal chancellor and the appropriate federal minister have countersigned them. In the event that the law affects the sphere of competence of several federal ministers, these ministers shall, as a rule, also sign the engrossed copy.

9. FEDERAL REPUBLIC, FEDERAL MINISTERS' LAW, APRIL 1, 1953

ART. 4   A member of the federal government cannot simultaneously be a member of a *Land* cabinet.

ART. 5   1. Members of the federal government cannot, in addition to their office, occupy any other salaried position nor undertake any business or profession. Neither can they belong during their term of office to the management, board of trustees, or board of directors of a profit-making enterprise, nor can they act as a paid arbiter nor render out-of-court expert opinions. The Bundestag may allow exceptions for membership on a board of trustees or of directors. . . .

ART. 6   1. Even after termination of their tenure, the members of the

FROM *FLG*, I (1953), p. 407.

federal government shall be obliged to maintain secrecy regarding matters learned by virtue of their office. This does not apply to notifications received as part of regular office business nor to facts that are publicly known or that no longer require secrecy. . . .

ART. 9 1. The tenure of the members of the federal government terminates after: (1) the Bundestag, in accordance with article 67 of the Basic Law, has expressed its lack of confidence in the federal chancellor and has discharged him; (2) a new Bundestag has convened; or (3) the office of federal chancellor has terminated for other reasons.

2. The tenure of individual federal ministers also terminates after their discharge. Federal ministers can be discharged at any time and can ask for their discharge at any time.

. . .

ART. 15 1. Beginning with the date of his discharge, a former member of the federal government receives a life-time pension provided that : (1) he was fifty-five years old when he left his office; (2) he was a member of the federal government for at least four years or was, at the time of his appointment as a cabinet member, a civil servant, a judge, a retired civil servant, a retired judge, a *Land* minister, a former *Land* minister entitled to a pension and having served for a total of ten years, including at least one year as a member of the federal government, in public service.

## ADMINISTRATION: THE EXECUTION OF LAW

### 10. FEDERAL REPUBLIC

ART. 35 1. All federal and *Land* authorities render each other mutual legal and administrative assistance. [See 2:4:30.]

. . .

ART. 83 [See 2:4:83.]

ART. 84 1. If the *Länder* execute federal laws as matters of their own concern, they provide for the establishment of authorities and the regulation of administrative procedures insofar as federal laws consented to by the Bundesrat do not otherwise provide.

2. The federal government may, with the consent of the Bundesrat, issue general administrative rules. [See 5:20:87b(2).]

3. The federal government exercises supervision to ensure that the *Länder* execute federal laws in accordance with applicable law. For this purpose, the federal government may send commissioners to the highest *Land* authorities and, with their consent or, if this consent is refused, with the consent of the Bundesrat, also to subordinate authorities.

4. Should any shortcomings that the federal government has found to exist in the execution of federal laws in the *Länder* not be corrected, the

Bundesrat decides, on the application of the federal government or the *Land*, whether the *Land* has acted unlawfully. The decision of the Bundesrat may be challenged in the Federal Constitutional Court. [See 6:1:92.]

5. For the execution of federal laws, the federal government may, by federal law requiring the consent of the Bundesrat, be authorized to issue individual instructions for particular cases. They must be addressed to the highest *Land* authorities, unless the federal government considers the matter urgent.

ART. 85   1. Where the *Länder* execute federal laws as agents of the federation, the establishment of the authorities remains the concern of the *Länder* insofar as federal laws consented to by the Bundesrat do not provide otherwise. [See 2:4:28(2),70(2),83.]

2. The federal government may, with the consent of the Bundesrat, issue general administrative rules. It may regulate the uniform training of civil servants and salaried government employees. The heads of authorities at the intermediate level shall be appointed with its agreement. [See 5:13:33(5).]

3. The *Land* authorities are subject to the instructions of the appropriate highest federal authorities. The instructions shall be addressed to the highest *Land* authorities, unless the federal government considers the matter urgent. Execution of the instructions shall be ensured by the highest *Land* authorities.

4. Federal supervision extends to the conformity with the law and the appropriateness of the execution. The federal government may, for this purpose, require the submission of reports and documents and send commissioners to all authorities.

ART. 86   Where the federation executes laws by federal administrative agencies or by federal bodies-corporate or by institutions under public law, the federal government issues, insofar as the law contains no special provision, the general administrative rules. It provides for the establishment of authorities insofar as the law concerned does not otherwise provide. [See 5:20:87b(1).]

ART. 87   1. The foreign service, the federal finance administration, the federal railroads, the federal postal service, and, in accordance with the provisions of article 89, the administration of the federal waterways and of shipping are conducted as matters of federal administration with their own subordinate administrative structure. Federal frontier protection authorities and central offices for police information and communications for the compilation of data with a view to protecting the constitution and for the criminal police may be established by federal legislation. . . . [See 4:23:73.]

ART. 89   1. The federation is the owner of the former Reich waterways.

2. The federation administers the federal waterways through its own authorities.

ART. 90   1. The federation is the owner of the former federal motor roads and federal highways. . . .

ART. 91   [See 2:20:91.]

## 11. Weimar

ART. 14   [See 2:6:14.]

ART. 15   The federal cabinet exercises supervision in matters in which the federation possesses the right of legislation. Insofar as the federal laws are to be carried out by the *Land* authorities, the federal government can issue general instructions. In order to supervise the execution of federal laws, it is empowered to send agents to the central authorities of the *Länder* and, with their consent, to the lower authorities. Upon the demand of the Reichsrat, the state governments are obliged to correct faults that have arisen in connection with the execution of federal laws. In case of differences of opinion, the Reichsrat as well as the *Land* government may seek the decision of the High Court of State, provided that no other court is specified by federal law.

. . .

ART. 88   1. The post and telegraph system, including the telephone system, is exclusively a function of the federation. [See 4:24:6(7).]

. . .

4. The federal government, with the consent of the Reichsrat, establishes a council for advisory cooperation in matters of the mail, telegraph, and telephone communication and rates. Only the federation concludes agreements in respect to intercourse with foreign countries.

ART. 89   It is a duty of the federation to assume the ownership of the railways serving general traffic and to administer them as a unified undertaking. [See 4:24:7(20).]

. . .

ART. 97   It is a duty of the federation to take into its ownership and administration the waterways serving general traffic.

## 12. Empire

ART. 41   Railways considered necessary for the defense of Germany or in the interest of general commerce may by force of federal law be built at the expense of the federation. . . .

ART. 42   The governments of the *Länder* bind themselves . . . to manage the German railways as one system. . . . [See 4:25:4(8).]

ART. 48   The postal and telegraph system shall be organized and managed uniformly. . . .

ART. 50   The emperor shall have supreme supervision over the administration of post and telegraph. . . . [See 4:25:4(10).]

## ADMINISTRATION: CIVIL SERVICE

### 13. FEDERAL REPUBLIC

ART. 33   1. Every German has in every *Land* the same civic rights and duties.

2. Every German is equally eligible for any public office according to his aptitude, qualifications, and professional achievements.

3. Enjoyment of civil and civic rights, eligibility for public office, and rights acquired in the public service are independent of religious denomination. No one may suffer disadvantage by reason of his adherence or nonadherence to a denomination or ideology.

4. The exercise of state authority as a permanent function shall as a rule be entrusted to members of the public service whose status, service, and loyalty are governed by public law.

5. The law of the public service shall be regulated with due regard to the traditional principles of the permanent civil service. [See 5:10:85(2).]

ART. 34   If any person, in the exercise of a public office entrusted to him, violates his official obligations to a third party, liability rests in principle on the state or the public authority that employs him. In the case of willful intent or gross carelessness, the right of recourse is reserved. With respect to the claim for compensation or the right of recourse, the jurisdiction of the ordinary courts must not be excluded.

. . .

ART. 36   1. Civil servants employed in the highest federal authorities shall be drawn from all *Länder* in appropriate proportion. Persons employed in other federal agencies should, as a rule, be drawn from the *Land* in which they serve. . . .

ART. 131   Federal legislation shall regulate the legal status of persons, including refugees and expellees, who, on May 8, 1945, were employed in the public service, have left the service for reasons other than those arising from civil service regulations or collective agreement rules, and have not until now been employed or are employed in a position not corresponding to their former one. . . .

ART. 132   1. Civil servants and judges who, when this Basic Law comes into force, are appointed for life, may, within six months after the first meeting of the Bundestag, be placed on the retired list or waiting list or be transferred to another office with lower remuneration if they lack the personal or professional aptitude for their office. . . . [See 6:1:96a(4).]

### 14. Third Reich, Law for the Restoration of the Professional Civil Service, April 7, 1933

ART. 1  1. For the restoration of a federal civil service and for the simplification of the administration, officials may be discharged according to the following regulations. . . .

ART. 3  1. Officials who are not of Aryan descent,[1] are to be retired. . . .

2. Paragraph 1, does not apply to officials who have been in service since August 1, 1914, or who fought in World War I at the front for the German Reich or for its allies or whose fathers or sons were killed in World War I. . . .

ART. 4  Officials who, because of their previous political activity,[2] do not offer the guarantee that they will exert themselves for the nation without reservations, may be discharged. For three months after their dismissal, they will receive their full former salary. As of the fourth month after their dismissal, they receive three-fourths of their pensions . . . and corresponding annuities for their heirs.

From *FLG*, I (1933), p. 175.

### 15. Third Reich, Law Changing the Regulations in Regard to Public Officers, June 30, 1933

#### chapter 2

ART. 1a  1. Only such persons can be appointed federal officials who possess the required education or customary training for their careers or have special qualifications for their office and guarantee that they will support the nation at all times and without reservation.

2. Women can be appointed as lifetime federal officials only if they are at least thirty-six years old.

3. Anyone not of Aryan descent or married to a person not of Aryan descent cannot be appointed a federal official. Federal officials of Aryan descent who marry a person not of Aryan descent must be discharged. The question of who is not of Aryan descent will be decided by regulations decreed by the minister of the interior.

4. If urgent requirements of the federal administration so necessitate, the highest national officials can make exceptions in individual cases. . . .

From *FLG*, I (1933), p. 433.

[1] A non-Aryan is one who is descended from non-Aryan, particularly Jewish, parents or grandparents. It suffices if one parent or one grandparent is non-Aryan. This is especially presumed if one parent or one grandparent has professed the Jewish religion. [Eds. note: The footnotes to this law are part of its text.]

[2] Those who have participated in Communistic activities are to be discharged even if they no longer belong to the Communist Party, or its auxiliary or collateral organizations.

### 16. Third Reich, Law Concerning the Oath of Allegiance for Civil Servants and for the Armed Forces, Berlin, August 20, 1934

ART. 2    1. The oath of allegiance of the civil servants reads as follows: "I swear that I will be loyal and obedient to the Führer of the German Reich and people, Adolf Hitler, will uphold the laws, and will fulfill my duties, conscientiously, so help me God."

From *FLG*, I (1934), p. 785.

### 17. Weimar

ART. 128    All citizens must be admitted to public offices without distinction and in accordance with the provisions of the laws and in correspondence with their capabilities and achievements. All provisions against women as public officers are set aside. The fundamental principles of the civil service must be regulated by federal law.

ART. 129    Civil servants are appointed for life, unless the law provides otherwise. Pensions and care for surviving dependents are regulated by law. The duly acquired rights of civil servants are inviolable. The legal route remains open for the claims of civil servants to property rights. Civil servants can be suspended from office, placed in temporary or permanent retirement, or transferred to another position with a smaller salary only under conditions and procedures provided by law.

ART. 130    Civil servants are servants of the entire public and not of a party. All civil servants are guaranteed freedom of political opinion and of association. According to the detailed provisions of the federal law, civil servants enjoy special representation as civil servants.

ART. 131    If an officer, in exercising the public authority entrusted to him, violates his official obligation toward a third party, the state or the public body the officer serves is held responsible. The right to redress in respect to the officer is reserved. The ordinary legal route cannot be excluded. [See 6:18:143.]

### 18. Empire

ART. 18    1. [See 5:4:18(1).]

2. State officials who shall be appointed to a federal office shall enjoy the same rights in the federation as in their native state, provided that no other legal provisions were made before they entered the service of the federation.

### 19. Federal Republic, Federal Civil Service Law, November, 1965

ART. 1    This law shall apply to federal civil servants [*Bundesbeamte*], unless specifically stated otherwise.

.    .    .

From *FLG*, I (1965), pp. 1776–1808.

ART. 4   Appointment as a civil servant shall be permitted only for the exercise of sovereign functions and such functions as, for reasons of state and public security, cannot be assigned to private persons.

ART. 5   1. Civil servants can be appointed for: (1) life, if the appointees shall be assigned permanently for the discharge of functions specified in article 4; or (2) a probationary period, if the appointee is required to serve a probationary term before being employed as a lifetime civil servant. . . .

ART. 7   1. Only those persons may be appointed as civil servants who: (1) are Germans within the meaning of article 116 of the Basic Law [see 6:12:116]; (2) offer assurance that they will at all times support the free democratic basic order within the meaning of the Basic Law; (3) possess the prescribed or, in its absence, the customary, preparation for a civil service career or have acquired the necessary competence through general or professional experience within or outside the public service. . . .

ART. 8   1. Candidates are selected by public competition [*Stellenausschreibung*]. Their selection shall be made on the basis of aptitude, competence, and professional performance, without regard to sex, origin, race, creed, religious or political beliefs, place of birth, or relationships. . . .

ART. 16   For careers in the ordinary service [*einfacher Dienst*], the minimum requirements shall be: (1) successful attendance in elementary school [*Volksschule*] or a corresponding education and (2) preparatory service.

ART. 17   For careers in the intermediate service [*gehobener Dienst*], the minimum requirements shall be: (1) successful attendance in an intermediate school [*Mittelschule*] or a corresponding education, (2) preparatory service of three years and passing of an intermediate service examination.

.   .   .

ART. 19   1. For careers in the higher service [*höherer Dienst*], the minimum requirements shall be: (1) completed studies at a university, a technical institute, or an equivalent institution of higher learning; (2) passing of the first state examination or, if customary, a university or institute examination; (3) preparatory service of three years; and (4) passing of the second state examination.

2. For purposes of paragraph 1(1), studies in private and public law and in economics, finance, and the social sciences shall be considered an equivalent.

.   .   .

ART. 23   Promotions shall be made in accordance with the principles stated in article 8, paragraph 1, second sentence.

ART. 24   Civil service salary increases must represent the regular progression of a career. . . . Exceptions shall be decided upon by the federal personnel committee.

ART. 25   Transfer from a lower to the next higher career shall not be possible without meeting the entrance requirements. For such transfers, an examination shall be required; the career regulations may provide for exceptions.

ART. 26    Unless provided otherwise by law, a civil servant may be transferred . . . if he so requests or if a service vacancy exists. Transfer into another position without the civil servant's permission shall be allowed only if the new position is identical with or equivalent to his present position and carries at least the same basic salary. . . .

ART. 32    1. Nontenure civil servants may be dismissed at any time. . . .

ART. 36    1. The federal president may put the following servants on the temporary list at any time, even though they are civil servants for life: (1) state secretaries and ministerial directors; (2) other higher civil servants in the foreign service [in the higher salary brackets]; (3) higher civil servants in the federal office for the protection of the constitution and in the federal intelligence service [in the higher salary brackets]; (4) the federal press officer and his deputy; (5) the federal attorneys-general of the Federal Appeals Court and of the Federal Administrative Court.

.    .    .

ART. 41    1. Lifetime civil servants shall be retired at the end of the month in which they reach the age of sixty-five. Different age limits may be established by law for specific groups of civil servants. . . .

ART. 52    1. Civil servants shall serve the entire people and not a party. They shall discharge their duties impartially and justly and consider the welfare of the general public in their official actions.

2. Civil servants must support the free democratic basic order within the meaning of the Basic Law and must work toward its preservation.

ART. 53    In their political activities, civil servants must maintain such moderation and restraint as are required by their position in society and by their official duties.

ART. 54    Civil servants must be dedicated to their profession. They shall fulfill their duties selflessly and conscientiously. Their behavior in and outside their service must justify the respect and confidence that their profession requires.

ART. 55    Civil servants must advise and support their superiors. They shall be required to execute their superiors' orders and to follow general instructions, except in cases where a civil servant is by virtue of a special statutory provision not bound by instructions and subject only to the law.

ART. 56    1. Civil servants shall bear full personal responsibility for the legality of their official acts.

2. Doubts about the legality of official orders shall be voiced to their immediate superior without delay. If an order is affirmed and the civil servant's doubts about the legality of the order persist, he shall turn to the next higher superior. If the latter confirms the order, the civil servant must execute it unless the order is punishable or the ordered behavior violates the dignity of man; in this case, the civil servant shall be relieved of his personal responsibility. . . .

ART. 95    For the uniform administration of the civil service regulations, a federal personnel committee shall be established, which shall exercise its functions independently and under its own responsibility within the limits set by law.

## ARMED FORCES AND THE STATE OF DEFENSE

### 20. FEDERAL REPUBLIC

ART. 45b[1]   A military commissioner of the Bundestag shall be appointed to safeguard the basic rights and to assist the Bundestag in exercising parliamentary control. Details shall be regulated by a federal law. [See 4:8:45a.]

.     .     .

ART. 65a[2]   1. Power of command in respect of the armed forces shall be vested in the federal minister of defense. [See 2:20:115b.]

.     .     .

ART. 87a[3]   1. The federation shall establish armed forces for defense purposes. Their numerical strength and general organizational structure shall be shown in the budget.

2. Apart from defense, the armed forces may only be committed to the extent explicitly permitted by this Basic Law.

3. While a state of defense or a state of tension exists, the armed forces shall have the power to protect civilian objects and discharge functions of traffic control insofar as this is necessary for the performance of their mission of defense. Moreover, the armed forces may, when a state of defense or a state of tension exists, be entrusted with the protection of civilian objects in support of police measures; in this event the armed forces shall cooperate with the competent authorities.

4. In order to ward off any imminent danger to the existence or to the free democratic basic order of the federation or of a *Land*, the federal government may, if conditions as envisaged in article 91, paragraph 2, obtain, and the police forces and the federal border police are inadequate, commit the armed forces to support the police and the federal border police in the protection of civilian objects and in combating organized and militarily armed insurgents. Any such committal of armed forces must be discontinued whenever the Bundestag or the Bundesrat so requests. [See 2:20:91.]

ART. 87b[4]   1. The federal armed forces administration shall be conducted as a federal administration with its own administrative substructure. Its function shall be to administer personnel matters and directly to

---

[1] As amended by federal law of March 19, 1956. See *FLG*, I (1956), p. 111.
[2] As amended by federal emergency law of 1968.
[3] As amended by federal emergency law of 1968.
[4] As amended by federal emergency law of 1968.

meet the material requirements of the armed forces. Tasks connected with benefits to invalids or with construction work shall not be assigned to the federal armed forces administration except by federal legislation, which shall require the consent of the Bundesrat. Such consent shall also be required for any legislative provisions empowering the federal armed forces administration to interfere with rights of third parties; this shall, however, not apply in the case of laws concerning personnel. [See 5:10:86; 6:1:96a(2,4); 6:12:17a; 6:17:12(2–3); 8:1:26(2).]

2. Moreover, federal laws concerning defense including recruitment for military service and protection of the civilian population may, with the consent of the Bundesrat, provide that they shall be carried out, wholly or in part, either by means of direct federal administration having its own administrative substructure or by the *Länder* acting as agents of the federation. If such laws are executed by the *Länder* acting as agents of the federation, they may, with the consent of the Bundesrat, provide that the powers vested in the federal government or appropriate highest federal authorities by virtue of article 85 shall be transferred wholly or in part to higher federal authorities; in such an event it may be enacted that these authorities shall not require the consent of the Bundesrat in issuing general administrative rules as referred to in article 85, paragraph 2, sentence 1. [See 5:1:85(2).]

ART. 115a[1] 1. The determination that the federal territory is being attacked by armed force or that such an attack is directly imminent (state of defense) shall be made by the Bundestag with the consent of the Bundesrat. Such determination shall be made at the request of the federal government and shall require a two-thirds majority of the votes cast and comprising at least the majority of the members of the Bundestag. [See 4:18:76(3).]

2. If the situation imperatively calls for immediate action and if insurmountable obstacles prevent the timely meeting of the Bundestag or if there is no quorum in the Bundestag, the Joint Committee shall make this determination with a two-thirds majority of the votes cast and comprising at least the majority of its members. [See 2:8:53a.]

3. The determination shall be promulgated in the *Federal Law Gazette* by the federal president pursuant to article 82. If this cannot be done in time, the promulgation shall be effected in another manner; it shall subsequently be printed in the *Federal Law Gazette* as soon as circumstances permit. [See 5:18:82(1).]

4. If the federal territory is being attacked by armed force and if the competent organs of the federation are not in a position at once to make the determination provided for in article 115a, paragraph 1, sentence 1, such determination shall be deemed to have been made and to have been promulgated at the time the attack began. The federal president shall announce such time as soon as circumstances permit.

5. When the determination of the existence of a state of defense has been

[1] Inserted by federal law of June 24, 1968. *FLG*, I (1968), p. 111.

promulgated and if the federal territory is being attacked by armed force, the federal president may, with the consent of the Bundestag, issue internationally valid declarations regarding the existence of such state of defense. Subject to the conditions mentioned in paragraph 2 of this article, the Joint Committee shall thereupon deputize for the Bundestag. [See 4:39.]

ART. 115b    Upon the promulgation of a state of defense, the power of command over the armed forces shall pass to the federal chancellor. [See 5:6:64(2).]

ART. 115c    1. The federation shall have the right to exercise concurrent legislation, also in matters belonging to the legislative competence of the *Länder*, by enacting laws to be applied upon the occurrence of a state of defense. Such laws shall require the consent of the Bundesrat. [See 4:18:76,77.]

2. Federal legislation to be applied upon the occurrence of a state of defense to the extent required by conditions obtaining while such state of defense exists, may make provision for: (1) preliminary compensation to be made in the event of expropriations, thus derogating from the second sentence of paragraph 3 of article 14 [see 6:17:14]; (2) deprivations of liberty for a period not exceeding four days, if no judge has been able to act within the period applying in normal times, thus derogating from the third sentence of paragraph 2 and the first sentence of paragraph 3 of article 104 [see 6:1:104(2)].

3. Federal legislation to be applied upon the occurrence of a state of defense to the extent required for warding off an existing or directly imminent attack may, subject to the approval of the Bundesrat, regulate the administration and the financial system of the federation and the *Länder* in derogation of section VIII [Execution of Federal Laws and the Federal Administration] and articles 106–15, provided that the viability of the *Länder*, communes, and associations of communes is safeguarded, including in particular such matters as relate to their finances. [See 5:26:106–15.]

4. Federal laws enacted pursuant to paragraph 1 or subparagraph 1 of paragraph 2 of this article may, for the purpose of preparing for their execution, be applied even prior to the occurrence of a state of defense.

ART. 115d    1. While a state of defense exists, the provisions of paragraphs 2 and 3 of this article shall apply in respect of federal legislation, notwithstanding the provisions of paragraph 2 of article 76, the second sentence of paragraph 1 and paragraphs 2–4 of article 77, article 78, and paragraph 1 of article 82. [See 4:18:76(1),77(1–2,4),78,82.]

2. Bills submitted as urgent by the federal government shall be forwarded to the Bundesrat at the same time as they are submitted to the Bundestag. The Bundestag and the Bundesrat shall debate such bills in common without delay. Insofar as the consent of the Bundesrat is necessary, the majority of its votes shall be required for any such bill to become a law. Details shall be regulated by rules of procedure adopted by the Bundestag and requiring the consent of the Bundesrat. [See 4:11,14.]

3. The second sentence of paragraph 3 of article 115a shall apply *mutatis mutandis* in respect of the promulgation of such laws.

ART. 115e 1. If, while a state of defense exists, the Joint Committee determines with a two-thirds majority of the votes cast and comprising at least the majority of its members, that insurmountable obstacles prevent the timely meeting of the Bundestag or that there is no quorum in the Bundestag, the Joint Committee shall have the status of both the Bundestag and the Bundesrat and shall exercise their rights as one body. [See 2:8:53a.]

2. The Joint Committee may not enact any law to amend this Basic Law or to deprive it of effect or application either in whole or in part. The Joint Committee shall not be authorized to enact laws by virtue of paragraph 1 of article 24 or paragraph 1 of article 29. [See 2:4:29; 8:1:24(1).]

ART. 115f 1. While a state of defense exists, the federal government may, insofar as circumstances necessitate: (1) commit the federal border police throughout the federal territory and (2) issue instructions not only to federal administrative authorities but also to *Land* governments and, if it deems the matter urgent, to *Land* authorities and may delegate this power to members of *Land* governments to be designated by it.

2. The Bundestag, the Bundesrat, and the Joint Committee shall be informed without delay of the measures taken in accordance with paragraph 1 of this article.

ART. 115g The constitutional status and the exercise of the constitutional functions of the Federal Constitutional Court and its judges must not be impaired. The law on the Federal Constitutional Court may not be amended by a law enacted by the Joint Committee except insofar as such amendment is required, also in the opinion of the Federal Constitutional Court, to maintain the capability of the court to function. Pending the enactment of such a law, the Federal Constitutional Court may take such measures as are necessary to maintain the capability of the court to carry out its work. Any decisions by the Federal Constitutional Court in pursuance of the second and third sentences of this article shall require a two-thirds majority of the judges present. [See 6:1:97.]

ART. 115h 1. Any legislative terms of the Bundestag or of *Land* diets due to expire while a state of defense exists shall end six months after the termination of such state of defense. A term of office of the federal president due to expire while a state of defense exists and the exercise of his functions by the president of the Bundesrat in case of the premature vacancy of the federal president's office shall end nine months after the termination of such state of defense. The term of office of a member of the Federal Constitutional Court due to expire while a state of defense exists shall end six months after the termination of such state of defense.

2. Should the necessity arise for the Joint Committee to elect a new federal chancellor, the committee shall do so with the majority of its members; the federal president shall nominate a candidate to the Joint Committee. The Joint Committee can express its lack of confidence in the federal chancellor only by electing a successor with a two-thirds majority of its members. [See 2:8:53a.]

3. The Bundestag cannot be dissolved while a state of defense exists. [See 4:5:39(1).]

ART. 115i    1. If the competent federal organs are incapable of taking the measures necessary to ward off the danger and if the situation imperatively calls for immediate independent action in individual parts of the federal territory, the *Land* governments or the authorities or commissioners designated by them shall be authorized to take, within their respective spheres of competence, the measures provided for in paragraph 1 of article 115f.

2. Any measures taken in accordance with paragraph 1 of this article may be revoked at any time by the federal government or, in the case of *Land* authorities and subordinate federal authorities, by *Land* prime ministers. [See 2:4:70.]

. . .

ART. 115k    1. Laws enacted in accordance with articles 115c, 115e, and 115g, as well as ordinances having the force of law issued by virtue of such laws, shall, for the duration of their applicability, suspend legislation contrary to such laws or ordinances. This shall not apply to earlier legislation enacted by virtue of articles 115c, 115e, and 115g.

2. Laws adopted by the Joint Committee and ordinances having the force of law issued by virtue of such laws shall cease to have effect not later than six months after the termination of a state of defense.

3. Laws containing provisions in derogation of articles 106 and 107 shall apply no longer than the end of the second fiscal year following upon the termination of the state of defense. After such termination of the state of defense they may, with the consent of the Bundesrat, be amended by federal legislation so as to arrive at the settlement provided for in section X [Finance]. [See 4:26:105,106.]

ART. 115l    1. The Bundestag, with the consent of the Bundesrat, may at any time repeal laws enacted by the Joint Committee. The Bundesrat may request the Bundestag to make a decision in any such matter. Any measures taken by the Joint Committee or the federal government to ward off a danger shall be repealed if the Bundestag and the Bundesrat so decide.

2. The Bundestag, with the consent of the Bundesrat, may at any time declare the state of defense terminated by a decision to be promulgated by the federal president. The Bundesrat may request the Bundestag to make a decision in such matter. The state of defense must without delay be declared terminated when the prerequisites for the determination thereof no longer exist.

3. The conclusion of peace shall be the subject of a federal law.

21. THIRD REICH, LAW CONCERNING THE OATH OF ALLEGIANCE FOR CIVIL SERVANTS AND FOR THE ARMED FORCES, BERLIN, AUGUST 20, 1934

ART. 2    1. [See 5:16:2(1).]

2. The oath . . . for the soldiers of the armed forces is as follows:

FROM *FLG*, I (1934), p. 785.

"I swear by God this holy oath: I will render unconditional obedience to the Führer of the German Reich and people, Adolf Hitler, the supreme commander of the armed forces, and will be ready, as a brave soldier, to stake my life at any time for this oath."

## 22. WEIMAR

ART. 47   The federal president exercises supreme command over all the armed forces of the federation. [See 2:6:48(1); 2:22:48(2).]

. . .

ART. 79   The defense of the federation is a federal function. The organization of the defense forces of the German people will be regulated uniformly by a federal law; due consideration will be given to the peculiarities of the citizens of the various *Länder*.

. . .

ART. 133   . . . 2. Military service is regulated by the provisions of the federal military law. This law also provides how far individual fundamental rights are limited for members of the armed forces in the fulfillment of their duties and the maintenance of discipline. [See 4:9:39.]

. . .

ART. 176   All public officers and members of the armed forces must take an oath upon the constitution. The details are to be provided by ordinance of the federal president.

## 23. EMPIRE

ART. 53   The navy of the Empire shall be united under the supreme command of the emperor. The emperor is charged with its organization and construction; he shall appoint officers and employees of the navy, and they and the seamen shall take an oath of obedience to him.

. . .

ART. 57   Every German is liable to military duty, and, in the discharge of this duty, no substitute shall be accepted.

. . .

ART. 59   Every German capable of bearing arms shall belong to the standing army for seven years, as a rule from the end of his twentieth to the beginning of his twenty-eighth year; during the next five years, he shall belong to the national guard [*Landwehr*] of first summons and then to the national guard of second summons until the thirty-first day of March of the year in which he reaches the age of thirty-nine. During the period of service in the standing army, the members of the cavalry and of the mounted field artillery are required to serve the first three years in unbroken active service; all other forces are required to give the first two years in active service.

. . .

ART. 63  1. The total land force of the Empire shall form one army under the command of the emperor in war and in peace. . . .

ART. 64  All German troops are bound to render unconditional obedience to the commands of the emperor. This obligation shall be included in the military oath. The commander-in-chief of a contingent, all officers commanding troops of more than one contingent, and all commanders of fortresses shall be appointed by the emperor. The officers appointed by the emperor shall take the military oath to him. The appointment of generals and of officers performing the duties of generals in a contingent shall, in every case, be subject to the approval of the emperor.

## 24. FEDERAL REPUBLIC, LAW CONCERNING THE PARLIAMENTARY MILITARY COMMISSIONER OF THE BUNDESTAG, JUNE 26, 1957

ART. 1  The military commissioner must fulfill the duties as stated in article 45b of the Basic Law. [See 5:20:45b.]

ART. 2  1. Upon the order of the Bundestag or of the defense committee of the Bundestag, the military commissioner must investigate certain matters. The defense committee can give this order only if it does not itself investigate the matter. If so ordered, the military commissioner must make a special report on the result of his investigation.

2. The military commissioner starts an investigation (exercising his own judgment in terms of his duty) if, by exercising his right as defined in article 3, paragraph 1, he is informed by members of the Bundestag of complaints of soldiers or if he is notified in any other way of conditions that seem to imply a violation of the basic rights of the soldiers or of the basic principles of internal leadership. He informs the Bundestag of the result of his investigation, either by a special report on the case or as a part of his general report.

ART. 3  In fulfilling the tasks delegated to him, the military commissioner has the following rights.

1. He can ask the federal minister of defense and all officers and persons under him for information and for permission to inspect the records. These rights may be denied to him only if cogent reasons of secrecy so dictate. The decision to deny his rights is made by the federal minister or by his deputy. The minister or his deputy must defend this decision before the Bundestag.

2. He can delegate the settlement of a matter to the department responsible for it.

FROM *FLG*, I (1957), pp. 652–54.

3. He is entitled to bring a matter before the department responsible for instituting criminal or disciplinary procedures.

4. He is entitled to visit all troop headquarters, administrative officers, and their establishments at any time and without prior notice.

5. He has the right to request from the federal minister of defense comprehensive reports on the exercise of the disciplinary power in the federal armed forces and, from the federal and the various *Land* ministers of justice, statistical reports on the execution of criminal law so far as the federal armed forces or their members are concerned with it.

6. He is entitled to attend criminal and disciplinary proceedings connected with his duties, and he is entitled to attend legal proceedings of law courts, even if they are closed meetings. He has the same right to inspect the records as the defense lawyer does.

ART. 4   The administrative authorities of the federation, of the *Länder*, and of the municipalities must cooperate with the military commissioner in making the necessary inquiries.

ART. 5   1. The Bundestag and the defense committee of the Bundestag can issue general guidelines for the work of the military commissioner.

2. The military commissioner does not receive specific instructions, except as stated in article 2, paragraph 2.

ART. 6   The Bundestag and the defense committee of the Bundestag may request the presence of the military commissioner at any time.

ART. 7   Every soldier has the right to appeal individually and directly to the military commissioner, without observing official channels. A soldier may not be officially reprimanded or placed at a disadvantage because he appealed to the military commissioner.

ART. 8   Anonymous petitions and complaints will not be accepted.

ART. 9   If the military commissioner examines a case that resulted from a complaint, he can use his own judgment whether to reveal the subject of the complaint and the name of the complainant. He shall make no announcement if the complainant so requests, provided legal provisions do not demand otherwise.

ART. 10   1. Even after the expiration of his term of office, the military commissioner is obliged not to reveal secret knowledge acquired in his official capacity. This does not apply to official or public information.

2. A retired military commissioner cannot make statements on secret matters in or outside a law court without prior permission. Permission is given by the president of the Bundestag acting with the consent of the federal defense committee of the Bundestag.

3. He is exempt from this regulation if he fulfills his lawful obligation to report activities that must be punished and if the basic free and democratic order is endangered.

. . .

ART. 13   The Bundestag elects the military commissioner by secret ballot and by a majority vote of its members. The defense committee of the Bundestag, the parliamentary parties, and the deputies authorized by the standing orders of the Bundestag can make nominations; there is no debate prior to the election.

ART. 14   1. Any German who can vote during Bundestag elections and has passed his thirty-fifth birthday can be a candidate for the office of military commissioner. He must have served in the army for at least one year.

2. The term of office is five years; he can be re-elected.

3. The military commissioner may not hold any other salaried office; he may not have any business or job, nor may he belong to the management or the board of directors of a profit-making enterprise, nor can he be a member of the government or of any other federal or *Land* legislative body.

4. Upon taking office, the military commissioner must take an oath before the Bundestag. The text of the oath is given in article 56 of the Basic Law. [See 5:1:56.]

5. The military commissioner is exempt from military service for the duration of his term of office.

.    .    .

ART. 16   The military commissioner has his headquarters in the Bundestag. He is subject to the control of the president of the Bundestag.

# 6. Legal System and Basic Rights

## INTRODUCTION

### THE LEGAL SYSTEM

Codification of German civil and criminal law and procedure began in 1871 on the basis of article 4, paragraph 13, of the Empire's constitution. These codes, which were basically in effect until recently in both Germanys, have been amended considerably in recent years by the German Democratic Republic and replaced in part by the new East German penal code and portions of other laws promulgated on June 24, 1968. This "socialist" legislation foreshadows an entirely new legal system in East Germany that adds legal disunity to political partition.

Specialized fields such as labor law and commercial law are usually likewise regulated by federal legislation throughout the nation, i.e., West Germany, and uniformity of law thus prevails.

On the other hand, except during the Nazi period (document 2), the administration of justice has, for the most part, been the responsibility of the *Länder*. Only the high courts of final appeal are federal. The organization of the courts is regulated by federal law, specifically, by the Judiciary Act of 1950 (document 5).

Three levels of criminal and civil courts (local, district, and regional) were established in the *Länder*. The highest court in the Federal Republic of Germany is the Federal Supreme Court at Karlsruhe, which serves as the court of last resort. In addition to ordinary jurisdiction, the German administration of justice has developed a number of special court systems, such as labor courts, tax courts, and administrative courts; the last-mentioned decide cases that involve disputes between citizens and public agencies. This system of administrative jurisdiction recognizes two levels of *Land* courts and one superior federal administrative tribunal.

Of special importance in the judicial system is the Federal Constitutional Court at Karlsruhe; this court is an outgrowth of the Bonn Constitution and the Federal Constitutional Court Act of 1951 (document 9). It has far-reaching and varied jurisdiction. It has the power of judicial review, previously unknown in Germany; it acts upon the constitutional complaints of West German citizens; it decides cases of so-called organ conflicts—for instance conflicts between the federation and a *Land* or between the cabinet and a parliamentary party of the Bundestag. It can outlaw political parties for cause. Members of the Federal Constitutional Court are elected in part by the Bundestag and in part by the Bundesrat; in each case, election is by qualified majorities.

The judges of all other federal courts are also elected (document 6). However, the bulk of the judiciary—that is, the judges, in the *Länder*—is appointed by the respective *Land* ministries of justice, although their professional status is regulated by federal law. The judges as well as the *Land* prosecutors are members of the civil service and enjoy all rights and prerogatives of a civil servant. The professional independence of the judges is legally guaranteed; they are career officials with special educational and professional requirements. Disciplinary measures against judges such as dismissal and lesser punishments can be taken only by special disciplinary courts.

Certain basic rules concerning judicial matters—especially those relating to citizens' rights—are contained in the Basic Law. These include rules prohibiting capital punishment, providing for *habeas corpus*, and forbidding both *ex post facto* penal law and double jeopardy. Detailed rules concerning procedure, the rights of the defendants in criminal trial, and so forth, are contained in ordinary statutes such as the federal code on criminal procedure.

In the GDR, matters relating to courts and administration of justice have now been codified in one comprehensive Justice Ordinance of 1963. There are three levels of courts, with the Supreme Court constituting the top level. Judges are elected by the diets of the different levels. They have no life tenure and are relatively easily dismissed. The Supreme Court has powers of supervision and direction.

Nazi criminality confronted German justice with vast and difficult tasks. When jurisdiction after World War II reverted from the occupying powers to German authorities, the prosecution of Nazi crimes was at first haphazard. Later, a coordinating office for preliminary investigation and the preparation of indictments was established by the joint action of the *Länder* ministries of justice. This action led to an increasing number of trials, especially of persons responsible for criminal actions in concentration camps. Since no legislation was ever enacted for the definition and prosecution of such crimes, most of these criminals have by now come under the general statute of limitations. Such would have been the case even for first degree murder (1965 was the date at which liability would have lapsed) if the statute had not been extended twice by special action of the Bundestag.


## BASIC RIGHTS

German society, always highly structured, has been characterized for almost a century by two contradictory features. The first has been deep class divisions based not only on the economic division between the working and middle classes but also on an equally sharp contrast between the few with higher education and the majority of the people, who have only an elementary education. Thus, the educational system in Germany has been of prime importance for the structure of German society. The second feature is the early growth of the social welfare state, which has staved off revolutionary extremism on the part of the workers, who, for the most part, have been satisfied with a reformist welfare capitalism. From the Weimar period on, German constitutions have reflected these features. Both the Weimar and the Bonn constitutions include among their "fundamental rights and duties" (Weimar) and "basic rights" (Bonn) provisions dealing with schools and education, state and religion, property and expropriation, trade unions and collective bargaining. These provisions are presented in the fourth section of this chapter. Also included is the law on codetermination, which gives labor a share in management and has provided a generally acceptable alternative to previous demands for nationalization of industries (document 19). The 1963 version of the basic program of the German Trade Union Federation (DGB) shows that the extension of codetermination to all major enterprises remains one of the chief objectives of German labor.

With the exception of the Nazi period, education has been under the jurisdiction of the *Länder*, which have consistently been faced with two major problems: whether to organize public primary schools along denominational (Catholic and Protestant) lines as requested chiefly by the Catholic Church or along interdenominational lines, and second, how to bridge the gap formed by the two-tier system, which provides higher education for an elite and vocational training for the mass. The demands of a highly developed industrial country render broader access to higher education not only a requirement of social fairness but, increasingly, one of economic necessity.

This chapter presents, first, a synopsis of the constitutional rules for the courts and the judiciary and the respective implementing laws. Second, it presents rules on constitutional jurisdiction and the law on the Federal Constitutional Court. The third section provides a synopsis of the basic personal and political rights of citizens. A bill of rights was included in both the Weimar and the Bonn constitutions, with some significant changes and innovations in the latter. Prior to 1919, a few such rights were guaranteed in the constitutions of the individual states but none in the federal constitution. This section also includes portions of the Nürnberg Judgment of 1946, which illustrates the complete disregard of the Nazi regime for the rights both of Germans and of the people of occupied territories (document 15) and the preamble to the Restitution Law of the Federal Republic of Germany (document 16), which illustrates the intention to make up, at least in some way, for the injury inflicted. A final section (documents 17–19) presents a synopsis of social rights, i.e., rights and other provisions in the area of religion and churches, family, education and schools, economic structure, and labor.

# DOCUMENTS

## JUDICIARY: ADMINISTRATION AND PROCEDURE

### 1. FEDERAL REPUBLIC

ART. 92[1]   The judicial authority is vested in the judges; it is exercised by the Federal Constitutional Court, by the federal courts provided for in this Basic Law, and by the courts of the *Länder*. [See 2:1:20(2); 4:8:44(3–4); 5:1:60(1); 5:10:84(4).]

. . .

ART. 95   1. For the purposes of ordinary, administrative, fiscal, labor, and social jurisdiction, the federation shall establish as highest courts of justice the Federal Court of Justice, the Federal Administrative Court, the Federal Fiscal Court, the Federal Labor Court, and the Federal Social Court.

2. The judges of each of these courts shall be selected jointly by the competent federal minister and a committee for the selection of judges consisting of the competent *Land* ministers and an equal number of members elected by the Bundestag.

3. In order to preserve uniformity of jurisdiction, a joint panel [*Senat*] of the courts specified in paragraph 1 of this article shall be set up. Details shall be regulated by a federal law.

ART. 96[2]   1. The federation may establish a federal court for matters concerning industrial property rights.

2. The federation may establish military criminal courts for the armed forces as federal courts. They shall exercise criminal jurisdiction while a state of defense exists and otherwise only over members of the armed forces serving abroad or on board warships. Details shall be regulated by a federal law. These courts shall be within the competence of the federal minister of justice. Their full-time judges must be persons qualified to exercise the functions of a judge.

3. The highest court of justice for appeals from the courts mentioned in paragraphs 1 and 2 of this article shall be the Federal Court of Justice.

4. The federation may establish federal disciplinary courts for disci-

---

[1] Articles 92 and 95 as amended by federal law on June 18, 1968, and by the federal Law to Provide the Conformity of the Judgments of the Federal Superior Courts, June 19, 1968. See *FLG*, I (1968), pp. 657, 661–63.

[2] The original article 96 was repealed by federal law on June 18, 1968. The present article 96 is the former article 96a as inserted by federal law on March 19, 1956 (see *FLG*, I [1956], p. 111), and amended by federal laws on March 6, 1961 (see *FLG*, I [1961], p. 141), and June 18, 1968 (*FLG*, I [1968], p. 658).

plinary proceedings against federal civil servants and federal judges, as well as federal service courts for disciplinary proceedings against soldiers and for proceedings in pursuance of complaints by soldiers.

ART. 97   1. The judges are independent and subject only to the law. [See 5:20:115g.]

2. Judges appointed permanently on a full-time basis to an established post cannot against their will be dismissed or permanently transferred to another post or retired before the expiration of their term of office, except by virtue of a judicial decision and only on the grounds and in the form provided for by law. Legislation may set age limits for the retirement of judges appointed for life. In the event of changes in the structure of the courts or their areas of jurisdiction, judges may be transferred to another court or removed from their office, provided they retain their full salary.

ART. 98   1. The legal status of the federal judges shall be regulated by a special federal law. [See 6:7.]

2. If a federal judge, in his official capacity or unofficially, infringes upon the principles of this Basic Law or the constitutional order of a *Land*, the Federal Constitutional Court may decide by a two-thirds majority, upon the request of the Bundestag, that the judge be transferred to another office or placed on the retired list. In a case of intentional infringement, his dismissal may be ordered.

3. The legal status of the judges in the *Länder* shall be regulated by special *Land* laws. The federation may enact general rules. . . . [See 6:8:99,100.]

ART. 101   1. Extraordinary courts are inadmissible. No one may be removed from his lawful jurisdiction.

2. Courts for special fields may be established only by a law.

ART. 102   Capital punishment is abolished.

ART. 103   1. In the courts, everyone is entitled to a hearing in accordance with the law.

2. An act can be punished only if it was an offense against the law before the act was committed.

3. No one may be punished for the same act more than once in pursuance of general penal legislation.

ART. 104   1. The freedom of the individual may be restricted only on the basis of a formal law and only with due regard to the forms prescribed therein. Detained persons may not be subjected to mental or to physical ill treatment.

2. Only judges may decide on permissibility or continuation of any deprivation of liberty. Where such deprivation is not based on the order of a judge, a judicial decision must be obtained without delay. The police may hold no one on their own authority in their own custody longer than the end of the day of apprehension. Details shall be regulated by legislation.

3. Any person detained on suspicion of having committed a punishable offense must be brought before a judge, at the latest on the day following the day of apprehension; the judge shall inform him of the reasons for the detention, examine him, and give him an opportunity to raise objections.

The judge must without delay either issue a warrant of arrest setting forth the reasons therefor or order his release from detention.

4. A relative or a person enjoying the confidence of the person detained must be notified without delay of any judicial decision ordering or continuing his deprivation of liberty.

## 2. THIRD REICH, LAW FOR THE TRANSFER OF THE ADMINISTRATION OF JUSTICE TO THE REICH, FEBRUARY 16, 1934

ART. 1    All courts administer law in the name of the German people.

ART. 2    In addition to exercising the right of pardon, the federal president is empowered to quash pending criminal actions. Amnesties may be ordered only by federal law.

ART. 3    According to the requirements of existing legal provisions, a person qualifying as a judge must be admitted to the bar in each *Land*.

ART. 4    Notarial documents have the same validity throughout the Reich....

ART. 5    The federal minister of justice is empowered to issue all regulations necessary to bring about the transfer of the judiciary to the Reich.

FROM *FLG*, I (1934), pp. 331–36.

## 3. THIRD REICH, LAW CHANGING THE PROVISIONS OF CRIMINAL LAW AND PROCEDURE, APRIL 24, 1934

ART. 1    . . . 80. Whoever undertakes by force or by threat of force to annex to a foreign state territory belonging to the Reich, in whole or in part, or to separate any part of the Reich territory from the Reich will be punished with death. Anyone who undertakes by force or by threat of force to change the constitution of the Reich will receive a similar punishment.

81. Whoever undertakes to deprive the federal president or the federal chancellor or any other member of the federal government of his constitutional power or to compel or hinder by force or by threat of force or by a crime or by assault the exercise of his constitutional authority, entirely or in any particular manner, will be punished with death or with life imprisonment or with imprisonment of not less than five years.

·    ·    ·

ART. 3    1. For the adjudication of cases of high treason or of treason against the country, a People's Court [*Volksgerichtshof*] is set up. In the principal proceedings, the People's Court reaches decisions by five members, in other cases by three members, the chairman being included in both cases. The chairman and one other member must qualify as a judge. Several sections may be formed. The prosecuting official is the chief federal prosecutor.

2. The members of the People's Court and their deputies are named for

FROM *FLG*, I (1934), pp. 331–56.

a period of five years by the federal chancellor upon the proposal of the minister of justice.

3. The People's Court has the right to investigate and to decide in first and last instance cases of high treason, . . . of treason against the country, . . . and of attacks against the federal president.

### 4. WEIMAR

ART. 102    Judges are independent and are subject only to the law. [See 5:2:46.]

ART. 103    Ordinary jurisdiction is exercised by the federal court and the courts of the *Länder.*

ART. 104    The judges of the regular courts are appointed for life. Against their will, they may not be removed, temporarily or permanently, from office or transferred to another position or placed in retirement, except by virtue of a judicial decision and only on the grounds and through the forms prescribed by the laws. Legislation may establish age limits; when reaching these, a judge shall retire. . . .

ART. 105    Extraordinary courts are illegal. No one may be denied his rightful jurisdiction. The legal provisions concerning courts martial are not affected hereby. Military courts of honor are abolished.

ART. 106    Military jurisdiction is abolished, except in time of war and on board warships. Details are regulated by federal law.

ART. 107    According to standards set by law, administrative courts must be established in the federation and in the *Länder* for the protection of individuals against ordinances and orders of the administrative authorities. [See 6:10:108.]

### 5. FEDERAL REPUBLIC, JUDICIARY ACT, SEPTEMBER 20, 1950

ART. 1    Judicial power shall be exercised by independent courts subject only to the law.

·    ·    ·

### PART 2: JURISDICTION

ART. 12    Jurisdiction over ordinary litigation shall be exercised by district courts [*Amtsgerichte*], county courts [*Landgerichte*], and the federal appeals court [the Federal Superior Court for ordinary jurisdiction]. . . .

ART. 22    Each district court shall be presided over by one judge.

ART. 23    The jurisdiction of district courts over civil law controversies shall include, insofar as they have not been assigned to county courts: (1) controversies over property claims whose sum or monetary value does not exceed 1,000 DM and (2) disputes involving landlord and tenant, public accommodations and travel, support claims, bankruptcy proceedings, and so forth irrespective of the value of the object.

ART. 24   1. In criminal cases, district courts shall have jurisdiction over: (1) misdemeanors; (2) offenses [*Vergehen*], provided that the public prosecutor does not file charges before the county court because of the special significance of the case or provided that jurisdiction is not vested in the county court pursuant to article 74a or in the Federal Supreme Court pursuant to article 134; (3) crimes [*Verbrechen*], provided that the jurisdiction is not vested in the assize court or in the Federal Supreme Court, that no penalty of more than two years in the penitentiary and no security detention [*Sicherungsverwahrung*] order is to be expected, or that the public prosecutor does not file charges before the county court because of the special significance of the case.

2. A district court may pronounce neither a penalty of imprisonment in a penitentiary of more than two years nor a security detention. . . .

ART. 28   Lay judge courts shall be created in the district courts for hearing and deciding on criminal cases falling under the jurisdiction of district courts; they are not to be decided by a district court judge alone.

ART. 29   Lay judge courts shall be composed of a district judge as chairman and two lay judges [*Schöffen*]. . . .

ART. 59   County courts shall be composed of a president and the required number of directors and members. . . .

ART. 60   Civil and criminal senates shall be established at the county courts. . . .

ART. 74   1. The criminal senates shall have jurisdiction . . . over all crimes not assigned to district courts, assize courts, or the Federal Appeals Court. . . .

2. The criminal senates shall also have jurisdiction over proceedings and decisions relating to appeals against verdicts by district court judges and lay court judges. . . .

ART. 75   1. In proceedings other than trials, the criminal senates shall decide by three members, including the presiding judge.

2. For trials, the criminal senates shall be composed as follows: of the presiding judge and two lay judges (minor criminal senate), if an appeal against a district court verdict is involved, and of three judges, including the presiding judge, and two lay judges (major criminal senate) in all other cases. . . .

ART. 79   For the trial and decision of criminal cases, assize courts shall be established in the county courts as required.

ART. 80   Assize courts shall have jurisdiction over crimes such as rape resulting in death, murder, manslaughter, major robbery, serious cases of arson, and various crimes resulting in death. . . .

ART. 81   Assize courts shall be composed of three judges, including the presiding judge, and six jurymen [*Geschworene*].

ART. 82   The judges and jurymen shall decide jointly the questions of guilt and punishment. During the trial, the jurymen exercise the same judicial office as lay judges. . . .

ART. 115   Superior courts shall be composed of a president and of the required number of senate presidents and councillors.

ART. 116   Civil and criminal senates shall be established at the superior courts. . . .

ART. 119   The superior courts shall be competent to act and render decisions in the following civil cases: (1) appeals against final judgments of district courts and (2) appeals against decisions of county courts.

ART. 120   The superior courts shall be competent to act and render decisions in first and last instance in criminal cases referred to it under appropriate procedures. . . .

ART. 122   1. The senates of the superior courts shall decide by agreement of three judges, including the presiding judge, unless the procedural codes provide that a single judge shall decide instead of a senate.

2. The criminal senates shall be composed of five judges, including the presiding judge, in trials of first instance.

ART. 123   The Federal Appeals Court shall have its seat at Karlsruhe.

ART. 124   The Federal Appeals Court shall be composed of a president and the requisite number of senate presidents.

ART. 125   1. The judges of the Federal Appeals Court shall be chosen by the federal minister of justice together with the judicial election committee and shall be appointed by the federal president.

2. Only persons of at least thirty-five years of age shall be eligible for the Federal Appeals Court. . . .

ART. 130   Civil and criminal senates shall be established at the Federal Appeals Court. . . .

ART. 133   In civil cases, the Federal Appeals Court shall be competent to act and render decisions on: (1) the revision of final judgments of superior courts . . . and (2) appeals against certain decisions of the superior courts. . . .

ART. 134   In criminal cases, the Federal Appeals Court shall be competent to investigate and decide in first and last instance proceedings that involve high treason and constitutional treason [*Hochverrat* and *Verfassungsverrat*], . . . treason [*Landesverrat*], . . . attempts at assassination of foreign statesmen, . . . duress of parliament [*Parlamentsnötigung*], . . . genocide. . . .

ART. 139   1. A decision of the senates of the Federal Appeals Court shall be made by five members, including the presiding judge.

2. A decision of the criminal senate in first instance other than the trial shall be made by three members, including the presiding judge. . . .

ART. 141   A public prosecution shall be established at each court.

ART. 142   The public prosecution's functions shall be exercised: (1) by a federal prosecutor-general and one or several federal prosecutors at the Federal Appeals Court, (2) by one or several public prosecutors at the superior and county courts, (3) by one or several public prosecutors [*Amtsanwälte*] at the district courts. . . .

ART. 150   The public prosecution shall conduct its official business independently of the courts.

### 6. FEDERAL REPUBLIC, JUDICIAL ELECTION LAW, AUGUST 25, 1950

ART. 1   The judges of the Federal Supreme Court and of the high federal courts shall be chosen by the appropriate federal minister jointly with the judicial election committee; they shall be appointed by the federal president. . . .

ART. 2   The judicial election committee shall be composed of an equal number of ex officio and elected members.

ART. 3   Ex officio members of the committee electing judges to a high federal court shall be the *Land* ministers who have jurisdiction over the lower *Land* courts of which the federal court in question is the court of appeal. . . .

ART. 5   The elected members and their deputies shall be chosen by the Bundestag according to the rules of proportional representation. . . .

ART. 12   1. The judicial election committee shall decide by secret ballot and by a majority of the votes cast. . . .

FROM *FLG*, I (1950), pp. 368–69.

### 7. FEDERAL REPUBLIC, JUDGES ACT, SEPTEMBER 8, 1961

ART. 5   1. Qualifications for judicial office entail passing two examinations.

2. The first examination must be preceded by legal studies of at least three and one-half years at a university. . . .

3. Probationary service of at least three and one-half years must be rendered between the first and second examinations. This time must be spent as follows: (1) twenty-four months in regular courts, serving with the public prosecution and with solicitors and lawyers; (2) six months in other courts, including two months in labor courts; (3) six months in administrative agencies. . . .

ART. 7   Any law professor holding tenure at a university within the jurisdiction of this act shall qualify for judicial office.

ART. 8   Only the following may be appointed to judicial office: (1) Germans within the meaning of article 116 of the Basic Law [see 6:12:116]; (2) those offering assurance that they will at all times support the free democratic basic order within the meaning of the Basic Law; (3) those having qualified for judicial office (articles 5–7).

ART. 9   Persons who have acquired the qualifications for judicial office and have served in a judicial office for at least three years may be appointed judges for life. . . .

ART. 21   . . . 3. Judges appointed for life or for a term may without written consent be dismissed only on the basis of a final judicial decision. . . .

ART. 24   If a German court within the jurisdiction of this act renders a verdict against a judge involving . . . imprisonment or loss of civil rights

FROM *FLG*, I (1961), pp. 1665–83.

. . . the judicial office shall be terminated without further judicial decision. . . .

ART. 25 The judges shall be independent and subject only to the laws. . . .

ART. 27 Judges for life and judges for a term must be assigned a judicial position at a specific court. . . .

ART. 30 Judges for life or judges for a term may, without their written consent, be transferred to another office or may be deprived of their office only: (1) pursuant to impeachment proceedings (article 98, paragraphs 2 and 5) of the Basic Law [see 6:1:98]; (2) pursuant to a formal disciplinary proceeding; (3) in the interest of the administration of justice (article 31); (4) pursuant to changes in court organization (article 32). . . .

ART. 31 Judges for life or judges for a term may be transferred to another judicial office with the same basic salary or to temporary or permanent retirement, if facts outside their judicial activities urgently require such measures for the protection of the administration of justice. . . .

ART. 39 Judges must conduct themselves in and outside their office as well as in political activities in such a manner that confidence in their independence is not threatened. . . .

ART. 48 Judges for life serving at the high federal courts shall be retired at the end of the month in which they reach their sixty-eighth year; all other judges shall be retired at the end of the month in which they reach their sixty-fifth year. . . .

ART. 61 1. A special senate of the Federal Supreme Court shall be established as the disciplinary court for federal judges. . . .

## JUDICIARY: THE FEDERAL CONSTITUTIONAL COURT

### 8. FEDERAL REPUBLIC

ART. 93 1. The Federal Constitutional Court shall decide: (1) on the interpretation of this Basic Law in the event of disputes concerning the extent of the rights and duties of a highest federal organ or of other parties concerned that have been endowed with rights of their own by this Basic Law or by rules of procedure of a highest federal organ; (2) in case of differences of opinion or doubts on the formal and material compatibility of federal law or *Land* law with this Basic Law or on the compatibility of *Land* law with other federal law, at the request of the federal government, of a *Land* government, or of one-third of the Bundestag members; (3) in the case of differences of opinion on the rights and duties of the federation and the *Länder*, particularly in the execution of federal law by the *Länder* and in the exercise of federal supervision; (4) in the case of other disputes involving public law between the federation and the *Länder*, between different *Länder*, or within a *Land*, unless recourse to another court exists; (5) in the other cases provided for in this Basic Law.

2. The Federal Constitutional Court shall also act in such cases as are otherwise assigned to it by federal law.

ART. 94   1. The Federal Constitutional Court shall consist of federal judges and other members. Half of the members of the Federal Constitutional Court shall be elected by the Bundestag and half by the Bundesrat. They may not belong to the Bundestag, the Bundesrat, the federal government, or the corresponding *Land* organs.

2. Its constitution and procedure shall be regulated by a federal law, which shall specify in what cases its decisions have the force of law.

.     .     .

ART. 99[1]   The decision on constitutional disputes within a *Land* may be assigned by *Land* legislation to the Federal Constitutional Court and the decision of last instance in matters involving the application of *Land* law to the higher courts of justice referred to in article 95, paragraph 1. [See 6:1:95(1).]

ART. 100   1. If a court considers a law unconstitutional, the validity of which is relevant to its decision, the proceedings shall be stayed, and a decision shall be obtained from the *Land* court competent for constitutional disputes if the matter concerns the violation of the constitution of a *Land* or from the Federal Constitutional Court if the matter concerns a violation of this Basic Law. This shall also apply if the matter concerns the violation of this Basic Law by *Land* law or if it concerns the incompatibility of a *Land* law with a federal law.

2. If, in the course of litigation, doubt exists whether a rule of public international law is an integral part of federal law and whether such rule directly creates rights and duties for the individual (article 25) [see 6:1:25], the court shall obtain the decision of the Federal Constitutional Court.

3. If the constitutional court of a *Land*, in interpreting this Basic Law, intends to deviate from a decision of the Federal Constitutional Court or of the constitutional court of another *Land*, it must obtain a decision of the Federal Constitutional Court.

9. FEDERAL REPUBLIC, FEDERAL CONSTITUTIONAL COURT LAW,
MARCH 12, 1951, AS AMENDED TO JUNE, 1959

PART I: CONSTITUTION AND JURISDICTION OF THE FEDERAL
CONSTITUTIONAL COURT

ART. 1   1. The Federal Constitutional Court shall be a judicial tribunal independent and autonomous in relation to all other constitutional organs.

2. The seat of the Federal Constitutional Court shall be determined by law.

ART. 2   1. The Federal Constitutional Court shall consist of two senates.

2. Eight judges shall be elected to each senate.

ART. 3   1. Judges must be forty years old to be eligible for election to

FROM *FLG*, I (1951), pp. 243–54; (1956), p. 662; and (1959), p. 297.

[1] As amended by federal law on June 18, 1968. See *FLG*, I (1968), p. 658.

the Federal Constitutional Court and must give written expression of their willingness to become a member of the Federal Constitutional Court.

2. They must possess the qualifications for judicial office as defined in the federal law on judges. [See 6:7.]

3. They may not be members of the Bundestag, the Bundesrat, the federal government, or of any of the corresponding *Land* organs. Upon their appointment, their membership in such bodies ceases.

4. Any other professional occupation, except that of professor of law at a German institution of higher learning, is incompatible with judicial activity. The position as judge of the Federal Constitutional Court takes precedence over that of a law professor at a German institution of higher learning.

ART. 4  1. Three judges of each senate shall be elected from among the judges of the federal superior courts for the duration of their terms of office at these courts. Only judges who have served at least three years on such a federal court shall be elected.

2. The remaining judges shall be elected for terms of eight years; at the first election one-half shall be elected for a term of four years. Re-election is permitted. . . .

ART. 5  1. One-half of the judges of each senate shall be elected by the Bundestag, the other half by the Bundesrat. Of the judges to be elected for a limited term, three shall be elected by one of the electing organs and two by the other; of the judges to be elected for their term of office in a high federal court, one shall be elected by the one and two by the other elected organ.

ART. 6  1. The judges to be chosen by the Bundestag shall be elected indirectly.

2. According to the rules of proportional representation, the Bundestag elects twelve members as electors. Each federal parliamentary party may submit a list. The number of electors chosen from each list shall be determined by using the d'Hondt system. The electors are chosen in the order of names appearing on the lists.

. . .

5. He who has obtained at least eight votes shall be elected judge.

ART. 7  The judges to be chosen by the Bundesrat shall be elected by a two-thirds majority. . . .

ART. 13  The Federal Constitutional Court decides in the cases laid down in the Basic Law—namely: (1) on the forfeiture of basic rights (article 18 of the Basic Law) [see 6:12:18]; (2) on the unconstitutionality of political parties (article 21, paragraph 1); (3) on appeals against decisions by the Bundestag concerning the validity of an election or the acquisition or loss of a deputy's membership in the Bundestag (article 41, paragraph 2) [see 3:1:21(2)]; (4) on impeachment of the federal president by the Bundestag or the Bundesrat (article 61) [see 5:1:61]; (5) on the interpretation of the Basic Law in cases of disputes concerning the scope of rights and duties of a superior federal organ or of other independent organs according to the Basic Law or to the standing orders of a superior federal organ (article 93, paragraph 1) [see 6:8:93(1)]; (6) in cases of differences of opinion or doubts concerning the formal or material compatibility of federal law or *Land* law with the Basic Law or concerning the compatibility of *Land* law with ordinary federal law, if a motion to do so is submitted by the federal government, by a *Land* government, or by one-third of the members of the Bundestag (article 93, paragraph 1) [see 6:8:93(1)]; (7) in cases of differences of opinion concerning rights and duties of the federation and of the *Länder*, particularly regarding the execution of federal law by the *Länder* and the exercise of federal supervision (article 93, paragraph 1, and article 84, paragraph 4) [see 6:8:93(1); 5:10:84(4)]; . . . (9) on impeachment of federal or *Land* judges (article 98, paragraphs 2, 5) [see 6:1:98(2,5)]; (10) on constitutional disputes within a *Land*, if *Land* legislation assigns this jurisdiction to the Federal Constitutional Court (article 99) [see 6:8:100(1)]; (11) on the compatibility of a federal or *Land* statute with the Basic Law or the compatibility of a *Land* statute or other *Land* law with a federal statute, upon application by a court (article 100, paragraph 1) [see 6:8:100(2)]; (12) if there is doubt whether a rule of international law forms part of federal law and whether it creates direct rights and duties for an individual, upon application by a court (article 100, paragraph 2) . . . [see 6:8:100(2)]; (14) in the event of differences of opinion on the continued validity of a law as federal law (article 126); (15) in other cases assigned to it by federal statute (article 93, paragraph 2) [see 6:8:93(2)].

ART. 14   1. The first senate of the Federal Constitutional Court shall have jurisdiction over judicial review proceedings (article 13, paragraphs 6, 11) concerning the incompatibility of a rule with basic rights or with rights derived from articles 33, 101, 103 and 104 [see 5:13:33; 6:1:101,103, 104] as well as over constitutional complaints, with the exception of complaints based on article 91 or belonging to the area of election law.

2. The second senate of the Federal Constitutional Court shall have jurisdiction in the cases of article 13, paragraphs 1–5, 7–9, 12, 14 and in cases of judicial review proceedings and constitutional complaints not assigned to the first senate.

.        .    .    .

ART. 16   1. If one senate wishes to deviate on a question of law from the legal views contained in a decision of the other senate, the matter shall be decided by the plenum of the Federal Constitutional Court.

.    .    .

ART. 31   1. The decisions of the Federal Constitutional Court are binding for the constitutional organs of the federation and of the *Länder* as well as for all courts and public authorities.

2. In the cases of article 13, paragraphs 6, 11, 12, 14, a decision of the Federal Constitutional Court has the force of law. The same applies if the Court annuls a statute according to article 95, paragraph 3. That part of the decision having the force of law shall be published in the *Federal Law Gazette* by the federal minister of justice.

ART. 32   1. The Federal Constitutional Court may regulate a dispute provisionally by preliminary injunction in order to avoid grave detriment and prevent violence or any other situation that might harm the interest of general welfare.

· · ·

5. The preliminary injunction shall become ineffective after three months. It may be reinstated by a two-thirds majority.

· · ·

PART II: PROCEDURE IN CASES UNDER ARTICLE 13, PARAGRAPH 2

ART. 43   The application for a decision on whether a political party is unconstitutional (article 21, paragraph 2) [see 3:1:21(2)] may be made by the Bundestag, the Bundesrat, or the federal government.

· · ·

ART. 45   The Federal Constitutional Court shall grant the party representative an opportunity to make a statement within a specified period of time and shall then decide whether to reject the application as inadmissible or insufficiently substantiated or whether the proceedings shall take place.

ART. 46   1. If the application is substantiated, the Federal Constitutional Court shall consider the political party unconstitutional.

2. The unconstitutionality may be limited to a legally or organizationally autonomous part of the party.

3. In such instances, the Federal Constitutional Court shall also decree the dissolution of the party or of the autonomous part of the party and shall prohibit the formation of a substitute organization. In addition, the Federal Constitutional Court may also decree the confiscation for philanthropic purposes of the party's or its autonomous part's property in favor of the federation of the *Land*.

· · ·

PART X: PROCEDURE IN CASES UNDER ARTICLE 13, PARAGRAPH 6

ART. 76   An application by the federal government, by a *Land* government, or by one-third of the members of the Bundestag, based on article 93, paragraph 1, shall be admissible only if the applicant considers federal or *Land* law to be: (1) void because of its formal or material incompatibility with the Basic Law or any other federal law or (2) valid after a court, an administrative authority, or an organ of the federation or of a *Land* has failed to apply the law on the ground that it is incompatible with the Basic Law or with any other federal law.

· · ·

ART. 78   If the Federal Constitutional Court comes to the conclusion that a federal or *Land* law is incompatible with the Basic Law or any other federal law, it shall declare that law void. If additional provisions of the same law are for the same reasons incompatible with the Basic Law or any other federal law, the Federal Constitutional Court may declare them also void.

## 10. WEIMAR

ART. 19    Insofar as no other court of the federation has jurisdiction, the Federal Constitutional Tribunal decides constitutional controversies in a *Land* in which no court exists. It also decides legal controversies between *Länder* or between the federation and a *Land*, on the motion of either party. The federal president executes the judgment of the Federal Constitutional Tribunal.

.    .    .

ART. 108    According to the provisions of a federal law, a Federal Constitutional Tribunal must be established.

## 11. EMPIRE

ART. 76    Disputes between several member states [*Staaten*] of the federation, so far as they do not relate to matters of private law and are therefore to be decided by the competent judicial authorities, shall be adjusted by the Bundesrat at the request of one of the parties. In disputes relating to constitutional matters in those states whose constitution does not designate an authority for the settlement of such differences, the Bundesrat shall, at the request of one of the parties, effect an amicable adjustment, and if this cannot be done, the matter shall be settled by federal law.

## *BASIC RIGHTS*

## 12. FEDERAL REPUBLIC

ART. 1    1. The dignity of man is inviolable. To respect it and protect it is the duty of all state authority.

2. The German people therefore acknowledge inviolable and inalienable human rights as the basis of every community, of peace, and of justice in the world.

3. The following basic rights bind the legislature, the executive, and the judiciary as directly enforceable law. [See 4:23:73–75.]

ART. 2    1. Everyone has the right to the free development of his personality insofar as he does not violate the rights of others or offend against the constitutional order or the moral code.

2. Everyone has the right to life and to the inviolability of his person. The freedom of the individual is inviolable. These rights may only be encroached upon pursuant to a law.

ART. 3. 1. All persons are equal before the law.

2. Men and women have equal rights.

3. No one may be prejudiced or favored because of his sex, his parentage, his race, his language, his homeland and origin, his faith, or his religious or political opinions.

ART. 4 1. Freedom of faith and of conscience and freedom of creed, religious or ideological [*weltanschaulich*], shall be inviolable. [See 6:13:136.]

2. The undisturbed practice of religion is guaranteed. [See 6:13:137–39, 141.]

3. No one may be compelled against his conscience to render war service involving the use of arms. Details shall be regulated by a federal law. [See 6:17:12(2).]

ART. 5 1. Everyone has the right freely to express and to disseminate his opinion by speech, writing, and pictures and freely to inform himself from generally accessible sources. Freedom of the press and freedom of reporting by radio and motion pictures are guaranteed. There shall be no censorship.

2. These rights are limited by the provisions of the general laws, by the provisions of law for the protection of youth, and by the right to inviolability of personal honor.

3. Art and science, research and teaching are free. Freedom of teaching does not absolve one from loyalty to the constitution. [See 6:16:7.]

. . .

ART. 8 1. All Germans have the right to assemble peacefully and unarmed without prior notification or permission.

2. With regard to open-air meetings, this right may be restricted by or pursuant to a law.

ART. 9 1.[1] All Germans have the right to form associations and societies.

2. Associations, the objects or activities of which conflict with the criminal laws or are directed against the constitutional order or the concept of international understanding, are prohibited.

3. The right to form associations to safeguard and improve working and economic conditions is guaranteed to everybody and to all trades, occupations, and professions. Agreements that restrict or seek to impair this right are null and void; measures directed to this end are illegal. [See 6:17:12.] Measures taken pursuant to article 12a, paragraphs 2 and 3 of article 35, to paragraph 4 of article 87a, or to article 91 may not be directed against any industrial conflicts engaged in by associations within the meaning of the first sentence of this paragraph in order to safeguard and improve working and economic conditions.

ART. 10[2] 1. Secrecy of the mail and secrecy of posts and telecommunications are inviolable.

2. Restrictions may be ordered only pursuant to a law. Such a law may lay down that the person affected shall not be informed of any such restriction

[1] As amended by federal emergency law of 1968.
[2] As amended by federal emergency law of 1968.

if it serves to protect the free democratic order or the existence or security of the federation or a *Land* and that recourse to the courts shall be replaced by a review of the case by bodies and auxiliary bodies appointed by parliament.

ART. 11   1.[1] All Germans enjoy freedom of movement throughout the federal territory. [See 4:23:73(3).]

2. This right may be restricted only by or pursuant to a law and only in cases in which an adequate basis of existence is lacking and special burdens would arise to the community as a result thereof or in which the restriction is necessary to ward off an imminent danger to the existence of the free democratic order of the federation or a *Land*, to combat the danger of epidemics, to deal with natural catastrophes or particularly grave accidents, to protect young people from neglect, or to prevent crime.

.   .   .

ART. 13   1. The home is inviolable.

2. Searches may be ordered only by a judge or, in the event of danger in delay, by other organs as provided by law; they may be carried out only in the form prescribed by law.

3. Otherwise, this inviolability may be encroached upon or restricted only to ward off a common danger or a mortal danger to individuals, or, pursuant to a law, to prevent imminent danger to public security and order, especially to alleviate the housing shortage, to combat the danger of epidemics, or to protect endangered juveniles.

.   .   .

ART. 16   1. No one may be deprived of his German citizenship. Loss of citizenship may arise only pursuant to a law, and, against the will of the person affected, it may arise only if such person does not thereby become stateless. [See 4:23:73(2).]

2. No German may be extradited to a foreign country. Persons persecuted for political reasons enjoy the right of asylum.

ART. 17   Everyone has the right, individually or jointly with others, to address written requests or complaints to the competent authorities and to the representative assemblies.

ART. 17a   1.[2] Laws concerning military service and substitute service may, by provisions applying to members of the armed forces and of substitute services during their period of military or substitute service, restrict the basic right freely to express and to disseminate opinions by speech, writing, and pictures (article 5, paragraph 1, first half-sentence), the basic right of assembly (article 17) insofar as these laws provide for addressing requests or complaints jointly with others.

2. Laws for defense purposes, including the protection of the civilian population, may provide for the restriction of the basic rights of freedom of movement (article 11) and inviolability of the home (article 13).

[1] As amended by federal emergency law of 1968.
[2] As amended by federal law of March 19, 1956.

ART. 18    Whoever abuses freedom of expression of opinion, in particular freedom of the press (article 5, paragraph 1), freedom of teaching (article 5, paragraph 3), freedom of assembly (article 8), freedom of association (article 9), the secrecy of mail, posts, and telecommunications (article 10), property (article 14), or the right of asylum (article 16, paragraph 2) in order to attack the free democratic basic order forfeits these basic rights. Such forfeiture and the extent thereof shall be pronounced by the Federal Constitutional Court.

ART. 19    1. Insofar as, under this Basic Law, a basic right may be restricted by or pursuant to a law, such a law must apply generally and not solely to an individual case. Furthermore, such a law must name the basic right, indicating the article concerned.

2. In no case may a basic right be infringed upon in its essential content.

3. The basic rights apply also to domestic juristic persons to the extent that the nature of such rights permits.

4. Should any person's right be violated by public authority, recourse to the court shall be open to him. If no other court has jurisdiction, recourse shall be to the ordinary courts. The second sentence of paragraph 2 of article 10 shall not be affected by provisions of the paragraph.

.    .    .

ART. 116    1. Unless otherwise provided by law, a German within the meaning of this Basic Law is a person who possesses German citizenship or who has been admitted to the territory of the German federation, within the frontiers of December 31, 1937, as a refugee or expellee of German stock or as the spouse or descendant of such a person.

2. Former German citizens who, between January 30, 1933, and May 8, 1945, were deprived of their citizenship on political, racial, or religious grounds, and their descendants, shall be regranted German citizenship on application. They are considered as not having been deprived of their German citizenship if they have established their domicile in Germany after May 8, 1945, and have not expressed a contrary intention.

.    .    .

ART. 140    The provisions of articles 136, 137, 138, 139, and 141 of the German constitution of August 11, 1919, are an integral part of this Basic Law. [See 6:13:136–39,141.]

## 13. WEIMAR

ART. 109    All Germans are equal before the law. Men and women have fundamentally the same civil rights and duties. Special privileges or disadvantages of birth or of rank are abolished. Titles of nobility are considered only as a part of the name and may no longer be bestowed. Titles may be bestowed only if they designate an office or a calling; academic degrees are not affected hereby. Orders and decorations may not be bestowed by the state. No German may accept a title or an order from a foreign government. [See 6:18:119.]

ART. 110　Citizenship in the federation and in the *Länder* is acquired and lost according to the provisions of federal law. Every citizen of a *Land* is also a citizen of the federation. Every German has in every *Land* of the federation the same rights and duties as the citizens of that *Land*. [See 4:24:6 (3).]

ART. 111　All Germans enjoy freedom of travel and residence throughout the federation. Everyone has the right to stop and to settle in any place of his choice in the federation, to acquire real estate, and to pursue any means of livelihood. Limitations are established only by federal law.

ART. 112　Every German is permitted to emigrate to a foreign country....

ART. 114　Freedom of the person is inviolable. Any limitation or encroachment upon personal freedom by public authority is permitted only by statutory law. Persons deprived of their freedom must be informed, at the latest on the day following this deprivation, by what authority and on what grounds the deprivation was ordered; they shall immediately be given an opportunity to oppose the loss of their freedom.

ART. 115　The dwelling of every German is his sanctuary, which is inviolable. Exceptions are permitted only by law....

ART. 117　Secrecy of correspondence, of the post, the telegraph, and the telephone are inviolable. Exceptions can be permitted only by federal law. [See 4:24:6(8).]

ART. 118　Within the limits of the general laws, every German has the right to express his opinion freely in words, writing, print, pictures, and in other ways. No relationship of labor or employment may interfere with this right, and no one may take action to injure him if he makes use of this right. There is to be no censorship, but the law may provide otherwise for motion pictures. Legal measures are also permitted to combat obscene and indecent literature and to protect the young in connection with public exhibitions and entertainments.

·　　·　　·

ART. 123　All Germans have the right to assemble peacefully and unarmed without notice or special permission. Federal law may require previous notice for outdoor meetings; these can be forbidden in case of immediate danger to the public safety.

ART. 124　All Germans have the right to form associations or organizations for purposes that do not contravene the criminal laws. This right cannot be limited by preventive regulations. The same provisions apply to religious associations or organizations. According to the provisions of the civil law, every association possesses the right of incorporation. This may not be refused to any association on the ground that its purpose is political, socio-political, or religious.

·　　·　　·

ART. 126 Every German has the right to address written requests or complaints to the proper authorities or to the representatives of the people. This right can be exercised by individuals as well as by groups.

.    .    .

ART. 135 All inhabitants of the federation enjoy full freedom of belief and conscience. The undisturbed practice of religion is guaranteed by the constitution and remains under public protection. The general public laws on this matter remain unaffected hereby.

ART. 136 Civil and political rights and duties are neither dependent upon nor restricted by the practice of religious freedom. The enjoyment of civil and political rights as well as the admission to official posts is independent of religious creed. No one is bound to disclose his religious convictions. The authorities have the right to make inquiries about membership in a religious body only if rights and duties depend on it or if the collection of statistics ordered by law so requires. No one may be compelled to take part in any ecclesiastical act or ceremony or to use any religious form of oath.

ART. 137 There is no state church. Freedom of association is guaranteed to religious bodies. There are no restrictions as to the union of religious bodies in the territory of the federation. Each religious body regulates and administers its affairs independently within the limits of the general laws. It appoints its officials without the cooperation of the *Land* or of the local community. [See 6:18:146,149.] Religious bodies acquire legal rights in accordance with the general regulations of the civil code. Religious bodies remain corporations with public rights insofar as they have been so up to the present. Upon application, equal rights shall be granted to other religious bodies if their constitution and membership offer assurance of permanency. If several public religious bodies merge to form one body this institution also becomes a public corporation. Religious bodies forming public corporations are entitled to levy taxes on the basis of civil tax rolls in accordance with the provisions of *Land* law. Associations that consider the task of promoting a world-philosophy [*Weltanschauung*] shall enjoy the same status as religious bodies. . . .

ART. 138 . . . Religious bodies and institutions are guaranteed ownership and other rights in their institutions, foundations, and other properties devoted to public worship, education, or charity.

ART. 139 Sundays and public holidays shall be legally protected as days of rest from work and for the promotion of spiritual purposes.

.    .    .

ART. 141 Religious bodies shall have the right to enter for religious purposes, into army establishments, hospitals, prisons, or other public institutions if this is necessary for the arrangement of public worship or for the exercise of pastoral duties, but every form of compulsion must be avoided.

ART. 142    Art and science are free, as is the teaching of these subjects. The state guarantees their protection and participates in their cultivation.

.    .    .

ART. 159    Freedom of association in order to promote labor and economic conditions is guaranteed to all persons and professions. Agreements and measures seeking to restrict or inhibit this freedom are illegal. [See 6:18:165.]

## 14. EMPIRE

ART. 3    There shall be a common citizenship for all Germany, and the citizens of each member state [*Staat*] shall be treated as natives in every other state and shall accordingly have the right to become permanent residents, to carry on business, to hold public office, to acquire real estate, to obtain citizenship, and to enjoy all other civil rights under the same conditions as the natives of this state. They shall also receive the same treatment as regards judicial remedies and legal protection. No German shall be restricted in the exercise of these rights by the authorities of his native state or by the authorities of any other state of the federation. [See 4:25:4.]

## 15. INTERNATIONAL MILITARY TRIBUNAL, JUDGMENT RELATING TO WAR CRIMES, NÜRNBERG, OCTOBER 1, 1945

The evidence relating to war crimes has been overwhelming in volume and detail. It is impossible for this judgment to review it adequately or to record the mass of documentary and oral evidence that has been presented. The truth remains that war crimes were committed on a vast scale, never before seen in the history of war. They were perpetrated in all countries occupied by Germany and on the high seas, and they were attended by every conceivable circumstance of cruelty and horror. . . .

Prisoners of war were ill treated, tortured, and murdered, not only in defiance of the well-established rules of international law but also in complete disregard of the elementary dictates of humanity. Civilian populations in occupied territories suffered the same fate. Whole populations were deported to Germany for slave labor in defense works, armament production, and similar tasks connected with the war effort. Hostages were taken in very large numbers from the civilian populations in all occupied countries and shot as suited the German purposes. Public and private property was systematically plundered and pillaged in order to enlarge the resources of Germany at the expense of the rest of Europe. Cities, towns,

FROM Office of U.S. Chief of Counsel for Prosecution of Axis Criminality, *Nazi Conspiracy and Aggression, Opinion and Judgment* (Washington, D.C.: U.S. Gov't. Printing Office, 1947), pp. 56–82.

and villages were wantonly destroyed without military justification or necessity. . . .

The territories occupied by Germany were administered in violation of the laws of war. Evidence of a systematic rule of violence, brutality, and terror is quite overwhelming. . . .

One of the most notorious means of terrorizing the people in occupied territories was the use of concentration camps. They were first established in Germany when the Nazi government seized power. Their original purpose was to imprison, without trial, all persons opposed to the government or in any way obnoxious to German authority. With the aid of a secret police force, this practice was widely extended, and, in the course of time, concentration camps became places of organized and systematic murder where millions of people were destroyed.

In the administration of the occupied territories, concentration camps were used to destroy all opposition groups. Persons arrested by the Gestapo were as a rule sent to concentration camps. In many cases, they were sent to the camps without any care being taken for them, and great numbers died on the way. Those who arrived at the camp were subjected to systematic cruelty. They were given hard physical labor, inadequate food, clothes, and shelter, and they were subjected at all times to the rigors of a soulless regime and to the private whims of individual guards. . . .

Certain concentration camps were equipped with gas chambers to kill all inmates and with furnaces to burn their bodies. Some of them were, in fact, used for the extermination of Jews as part of the "final solution" of the Jewish problem. Most of the non-Jewish inmates were subjected to hard labor and the conditions under which they worked made labor and death almost synonymous. Those inmates who became ill and were unable to work were either killed in the gas chambers or sent to special infirmaries, where they were given inadequate medical treatment, worse food, if possible, than the working inmates, and left to die.

The murder and ill treatment of civilian populations reached its height in the treatment of Soviet and Polish citizens. Approximately four weeks prior to the invasion of Russia, special task forces of the security police and security service, called *Einsatzgruppen*, were formed on the orders of Himmler for the purpose of following the German armies into Russia, to combat partisans and members of resistance groups, and to exterminate Jews, Communist leaders, and other sections of the population. . . .

The Nazi persecution of Jews in Germany before the war, severe and repressive as it was, cannot compare, however, with the policy pursued during the war in the occupied territories. Originally, the policy was similar to that which had been in force in Germany. Jews were required to register, were forced to live in ghettos, to wear the yellow star, and were used as slave laborers. In the summer of 1941, however, plans were made for the "final solution" of the Jewish question in Europe. This "final solution" meant the extermination of the Jews, which, early in 1939 Hitler had threatened to be a consequence of the outbreak of war. A special section in the Gestapo under Adolf Eichmann, the head of section B-4 of the Gestapo, was formed to carry out the policy. . . . Adolf Eichmann . . . estimated that this policy resulted in the killing of 6 million Jews, of which 4 million were killed in extermination camps. . . .

16. Federal Republic, Amendment to the Federal Law Concerning Restitution for the Victims of Nazi Persecution, September 18, 1953

In recognition of the fact that persons who have been persecuted under the totalitarian regime of the National Socialists because of their race, religion, or philosophy of life [*Weltanschauung*] have been treated with injustice and that their resistance against the totalitarian regime of the National Socialists, performed out of convictions, belief, or conscience, has benefited the German people and state, the Bundestag, with the consent of the Bundesrat, has passed the following law. . . .

From *FLG*, I (1953), p. 1387.

## SOCIAL RIGHTS

### 17. Federal Republic

art. 6   1. Marriage and family shall enjoy the special protection of the state.

2. The care and upbringing of children are the natural right of the parents and a duty primarily incumbent on them. The national community shall watch over the performance of this duty.

3. Separation of children from the family against the will of the persons entitled to bring them up may take place only pursuant to a law, if those so entitled fail in their duty or if the children are otherwise threatened with neglect.

4. Every mother shall be entitled to the protection and care of the community.

5. Illegitimate children shall be provided by legislation with the same opportunities for their physical and spiritual development and their position in society as are enjoyed by legitimate children.

art. 7   1. The entire educational system shall be under the supervision of the state.

2. Persons entitled to bring up a child shall have the right to decide whether it shall receive religious instruction.

3. Religious instruction shall form part of the ordinary curriculum in state and municipal schools, except in secular [*bekenntnisfrei*] schools. Without prejudice to the state's right of supervision, religious instruction shall be given in accordance with the tenets of the religious communities. No teacher may be obliged against his will to give religious instruction.

4. The right to establish private schools is guaranteed. Private schools, as a substitute for state or municipal schools, must have the approval of the state and shall be subject to the laws of the *Länder*. This approval must be given if private schools are not to be inferior to the state or municipal schools in their educational aims, in their facilities, and in the professional training of their teaching staff, and if a segregation of pupils, according to the means of the parents, is not to be promoted. Approval must be withheld if the economic and legal position of the teaching staff is not sufficiently assured.

5. A private elementary school shall be admitted only if the educational authority finds that it serves a special pedagogic interest or if, on the application of persons entitled to bring up children, it is to be established as an interdenominational or denominational or ideological school and if a state or municipal elementary school of this type does not already exist in the community [*Gemeinde*].

6. Preparatory schools [*Vorschulen*] shall remain abolished.

. . .

ART. 12[1] 1. All Germans shall have the right freely to choose their trade, occupation or profession, their place of work, and their place of training. The practice of trades, occupations, and professions may be regulated by law. [See 6:12:9.]

2. No one may be compelled to perform a particular work except within the framework of a traditional compulsory public service that applies generally and equally to all. Anyone who refuses on conscientious grounds to render war service involving the use of arms may be required to render an alternative service. The duration of this alternative service shall not exceed the duration of military service. Details shall be regulated by a law that shall not prejudice freedom of conscience and shall provide also for the possibility of an alternative service having no connection with any unit of the armed forces.

3. Forced labor may be imposed only in the event that persons are deprived of their freedom by the sentence of a court. [See 6:12:13.]

ART. 12a 1.[2] Men who have attained the age of eighteen years may be required to serve in the armed forces, in the federal border police, or in a civil defense organization.

2. A person who refuses, on grounds of conscience, to render war service involving the use of arms may be required to render a substitute service. The duration of such substitute service shall not exceed the duration of military service. Details shall be regulated by a law that shall not interfere with the freedom of conscientious decision and must also provide for the possibility of a substitute service not connected with units of the armed forces or of the federal border police.

3. Persons liable to military service who are not required to render

[1] As amended by federal law on March 19, 1956, and the federal emergency law of 1968. See *FLG*, I (1956), p. 111; (1968), p. 709.
[2] Inserted by federal emergency law of 1968. See *FLG*, I (1968), p. 710.

service pursuant to paragraphs 1 or 2 of this article may, when a state of defense [*Verteidigungsfall*] exists, be assigned by or pursuant to a law to specific occupations involving civilian services for defense purposes, including the protection of the civilian population; it shall, however, not be permissible to assign persons to an occupation subject to public law except for the purpose of discharging police functions or such other functions of public administration as can only be discharged by persons employed under public law. Persons may be assigned to occupations—as referred to in the first sentence of this paragraph—with the armed forces, including the supplying and servicing of the latter, or with public adminis-trative authorities; assignments to occupations connected with supplying and servicing the civilian population shall not be permissible except in order to meet their vital requirements or to guarantee their safety.

4. If, while a state of defense exists, civilian service requirements in the civilian public health and medical system or in the stationary military hospital organization cannot be met on a voluntary basis, women between eighteen and fifty-five years of age may be assigned to such services by or pursuant to a law. They may on no account render service involving the use of arms.

5. During the time prior to the existence of any such state of defense, assignments under paragraph 3 of this article may be effected only if the requirements of paragraph 1 of article 80a are satisfied. It shall be admissi-ble to require persons by or pursuant to a law to attend training courses in order to prepare them for the performance of such services in accordance with paragraph 3 of this article as presuppose special knowledge or skills. To this extent, the first sentence of this paragraph shall not apply.

6. If, while a state of defense exists, the labor requirements for the pur-poses referred to in the second sentence of paragraph 3 of this article. cannot be met on a voluntary basis, the right of a German to give up the practice of his trade or occupation or profession or his place of work may be restricted by or pursuant to a law in order to meet these requirements. The first sentence of paragraph 5 of this article shall apply *mutatis mutandis* prior to the existence of a state of defense.

.    .    .

ART. 14    1. The right to own and inherit property is guaranteed. The content and limits shall be determined by the laws.

2. Property imposes duties. Its use should also serve the public weal.

3. Expropriation shall be permitted only for the public weal. It may take place only by or pursuant to a law that provides for the nature and extent of the compensation. The compensation shall be determined upon just con-sideration of the public interest and of the interests of the persons affected. In cases of disputes regarding the amount of compensation, recourse may be had to the ordinary courts.

ART. 15    Land, natural resources, and the means of production may, for the purpose of socialization, be transferred to public ownership or other forms of publicly controlled economy by a law that provides for the kind and extent of compensation. With respect to such compensation article 14, paragraph 3, sentences 3 and 4, apply *mutatis mutandis.*

## 18. WEIMAR

ART. 119   Marriage, as the foundation of family life and of the maintenance and the increase of the nation, stands under the special protection of the constitution. It rests upon the equal rights of the sexes. . . .

ART. 121   By means of legislation, illegitimate children are to be given the same conditions for their physical, mental, and social development as legitimate children.

. . .

ART. 143   Provision for the education of the young is to be made through public institutions. The federation, the *Länder,* and the communities cooperate in their establishment. The education of teachers is to be regulated uniformly for the federation according to the fundamental principles of general higher education. Teachers in public schools have the rights and duties of state officials. [See 5:17:128–31.]

. . .

ART. 145   There exists universal compulsory education. This obligation is met fundamentally by the public elementary schools with at least eight school years and by connected trade schools [*Berufsschule*] until the completion of the eighteenth year of life. Instruction and school supplies in the public elementary schools and in the trade schools are free.

ART. 146   The public school system must be developed organically. The intermediate and higher school systems are to be based on an elementary school education common for all. The guiding principle is the multiplicity of vocations; a child must be accepted in a given school on the basis of his abilities and talents, not on the basis of the economic and social status or the religious beliefs of his parents.

In the communities, however, public elementary schools of a given denomination or world philosophy must be established if the community so requests and if this does not interfere with an organized school system in the sense of paragraph 1. . . .

In order that those of smaller means may have access to intermediate and higher schools, public funds must be provided by the federation, the *Länder,* and the communities. . . .

ART. 147   Private schools, as a substitute for public schools, require the approval of the *Land* and are subject to *Land* laws. . . .

ART. 149   Religious instruction is a regular teaching subject, except in nondenominational (secular) schools. Religious instruction is regulated by school laws. Religious instruction is given in accordance with the fundamental principles of the religious organization concerned, without prejudice to the supervisory right of the *Land.*

Religious instruction and exercises remain optional for teachers; the decision whether a child is to receive religious instruction and to participate in religious ceremonies must be made by the child's parents or guardian. The theological faculties in institutions of higher learning will continue to exist.

.　　.　　.

ART. 151　The economic order must correspond to the fundamental principles of justice and should guarantee to everyone an existence worthy of mankind. Within these limits, the economic freedom of the individual must be safeguarded.

Freedom of commerce and of industry must be guaranteed in accordance with federal law.

ART. 152　Freedom of economic contract must prevail in accordance with the law.

Usury is forbidden. Legal transactions that violate morals are void.

ART. 153　The right to property is guaranteed by the constitution. Its nature and limitations are defined by law. Expropriation can take place only for reasons of general welfare and on statutory grounds. It must be accompanied by adequate compensation, unless a national law provides otherwise. Legal access to regular courts must remain open in matters relating to the amount of compensation, insofar as national laws do not provide otherwise. Expropriation by the federation, in contrast to expropriation by the *Länder*, communities, and public institutions, can take place only if compensation is paid. Property involves obligations. Its use shall at the same time be of service to the general welfare.

.　　.　　.

ART. 155　1. The distribution and use of land are supervised by the *Land* so as to prevent misuse, to guarantee to every German a healthy dwelling, and to all German families, especially to those with many children, a home that corresponds to their needs. Special consideration must be given to war veterans.

2. Landed property whose acquisition is necessary to meet the need for dwellings, to develop settlements, and to allow land reclamation or to encourage agriculture can be expropriated. Entails must be dissolved. . . .

ART. 156　1. By law, the federation can take over as public property, without compensation and application of the provisions regulating expropriation, private economic enterprises suitable for socialization. It can engage itself, the *Länder*, or the communities in the administration of economic enterprises and associations, or it may use other methods of control.

ART. 157　The labor forces stand under the special protection of the federation. The federation must adopt a uniform labor law.

ART. 158　Intellectual labor and the rights of authors, inventors, and artists enjoy the protection and care of the federation.

.　　.　　.

ART. 161 The federation establishes a comprehensive insurance system with the prominent cooperation of the insured in order to maintain health and working capacity, to protect motherhood, and to provide against the economic consequences of old age, infirmity, and the vicissitudes of life.

. . .

ART. 163 Without injury to his personal freedom, every German has the moral obligation to use his mental and physical powers as the welfare of society demands. Every German shall have the opportunity to earn his living. If no suitable opportunity to earn a living exists, the state must provide minimum maintenance. Federal legislation will regulate details.

. . .

ART. 165 Workers, employees, and entrepreneurs shall cooperate on equal terms in regulating wages and labor as well as in developing the productive forces. The organizations of workers and entrepreneurs and their agreements are recognized.

In order to safeguard their social and economic interests, workers and employees are legally represented in the labor councils of the local industry as well as in district councils organized according to economic areas and in a national labor council.

The district and national labor councils meet with the representatives of the entrepreneurs and of other interested groups in district and national economic councils to deal with matters of common interest and to cooperate in the execution of laws concerning socialization. District and national economic councils must include representatives of all occupational groups according to their economic and social importance.

The federal government must present bills containing fundamental provisions on economic and social policy to the national economic council for discussion before they can be introduced in the Reichstag. The national economic council has the right to propose such bills itself. If the federal government does not approve them, it must nevertheless introduce the bills in the Reichstag and state its own viewpoint. A member of the national economic council can support the bill in the Reichstag. Control and administrative functions in a given economic field may be transferred to the labor and economic councils. To regulate the organization and the functions of the labor and economic councils as well as their relationship to other social self-administering bodies is the exclusive responsibility of the federation.

## 19. FEDERAL REPUBLIC, LAW ON CODETERMINATION OF EMPLOYEES, 1951

ART. 1 1. Pursuant to this act, employees shall have a right of codetermination on boards of directors and in the bodies designated for legal representation in: (1) enterprises whose primary business is the mining

FROM *FLG*, I (1951), pp. 347–50; (1956), p. 707.

of bituminous coal, lignite, or iron ore or the . . . processing of these raw materials and whose business is supervised by the mining administrations; (2) enterprises engaged in the production of iron and steel. . . .

2. This act shall apply only to those enterprises designated in article 1, paragraph 1, that . . . are incorporated and, as a rule, employ more than 1,000 workers. . . .

ART. 4   1. Each board of directors shall consist of eleven members. It shall be composed as follows: (1) four representatives of the shareholders and one additional member; (2) four representatives of the employees and one additional member; (3) one additional member.

2. The additional members referred to in paragraph 1 may not: (1) be the representatives of a trade union or an employers' association . . .; (2) have held a position described in paragraph 1(1) during the year preceding their election; (3) be active in the enterprise as either employee or employer; (4) have any substantial economic interest in the enterprise.

3. All members of the board of directors shall have equal rights and duties. They shall not be bound by orders and instructions.

ART. 5   The members of the board of directors mentioned in article 4, paragraph 1(2), must include one worker and one employee [*Angestellter*] of a plant of the enterprise. These members shall be nominated to the electing body by the works councils [*Werksrat*] of the enterprise's plants after consultation with the trade unions represented in the plants and with their roof organizations [*Spitzenverbände*, federations of associations]. . . .

2. Roof organizations may lodge objections with the works councils within two weeks [after nominations] if there is justifiable suspicion that a nominee does not offer the assurance of responsible cooperation on the board of directors for the welfare of the enterprise and of the economy as a whole. If the works councils reject the objection by a majority vote, the works councils of the objecting roof organizations may appeal to the federal minister of labor, who shall have the power of final decision.

3. Two of the members mentioned in article 4, paragraph 1(2), shall be nominated by the roof organizations after consultation with trade unions represented in the plants and with the works councils. . . . This shall also apply to the additional member mentioned in article 4, paragraph 1(2).

4. The electing bodies shall be restricted to the nomination of the works councils and their roof organizations.

·   ·   ·

ART. 8   The additional member of the board of directors mentioned in article 4, paragraph 1(3), shall be elected by the electing body upon nomination by the other members of the board of directors. The nomination shall be made by a majority vote of all members voting. However, it shall require the approval of at least three members, each elected pursuant to articles 5 and 6 respectively.

# 7. Berlin and East Germany

## INTRODUCTION 1: BERLIN

In 1945, the Allies established Greater Berlin, a municipal unit that had existed since the 1920's, as an area outside the Allied occupation zones in Germany. The city was divided into four sectors and was jointly governed by the occupying powers in the Allied Control Council (Allied Kommand-atura) (documents 1 and 2). A temporary constitution of Greater Berlin (document 3) was approved by the Allied powers in August, 1946, and the Berliners could then participate in the city's government through an elected city assembly (*Stadtverordnetenversammlung*) and a city council (*Magistrat*) established by the assembly. In the first election, in October, 1946, the SPD (outlawed in the Soviet occupation zone) received almost half of the votes; the SED lost decisively, thus barring the Soviets from exercising full control over Berlin through accepted political channels. In the course of time, enormous difficulties arose within the Kommandatura and the German city administration, and, by 1948, Berlin was *de facto* split into two sectors: the Soviet sector (East Berlin) and the Western sectors (West Berlin), consisting of the American, British, and French occupied areas (documents 4, 5, 6, and 7). For all practical purposes, East Berlin was integrated with the Soviet occupation zone and, in 1949, became the capital of the German Democratic Republic. The three Western sectors soon merged; although the Basic Law (article 23) and West Berlin's constitution of 1950 consider the city a *Land* of the Federal Republic of Germany, Berlin cannot be fully integrated into the Federal Republic until the ultimate political status of Germany has been settled. As a city, Berlin was given broad powers of self-government in political and economic matters, although officially it was still under the three-power Allied Kommandatura, which has reserved its right to resume certain powers in cases where it deems it necessary (document 11). In October, 1950, the Kommandatura allowed West Berliners to adopt a new constitution (document 8). Its essential legislative and administrative provisions corresponded to those of the temporary constitution of 1946. Cooperation between city government (*Senat*) and population takes place through a popularly elected city assembly; the city's top official is the governing mayor (*Regierender Bürgermeister*). The constitution sub-divided the city into twelve boroughs, each with its own administrative structure.

While West Germans consider West Berlin an integral part of the Federal Republic (some federal agencies have their headquarters in Berlin, and Bundestag committees meet irregularly in the city), Berlin is granted only limited participation in the political affairs of the Federal Republic. Berlin sends twenty-two representatives to the Bundestag; they are not popularly elected but are selected by the city assembly (document 13). While the Berlin representatives can participate in all parliamentary discussions, they are not permitted to vote in the plenary sessions of either the Bundestag or the Bundesrat. In turn, federal laws enacted in the Federal Republic extend to Berlin only after they have specifically been adopted by the city assembly as applying to Berlin (documents 9 and 11).

Repeated Soviet attempts to persuade the Western Allies to agree to a new status for West Berlin—that of a free city independent of East and West Germany—have so far been unsuccessful (documents 14–18). The Western powers have insisted on the continuation of the city's four-power status and have held the Soviet government (rather than the nonrecognized East German authorities) responsible for obstructing free access to Berlin. In Berlin itself, the erection of the wall in 1961 practically eliminated the access of East Berliners to West Berlin; West Berliners could visit East Berlin occasionally with special passes. Negotiating such and similar agreements, however, has become increasingly difficult in view of the East–West disagreement over the status of Berlin and of the GDR.

# DOCUMENTS

## 1. GOVERNMENTS OF THE UNITED STATES, THE SOVIET UNION, AND THE UNITED KINGDOM, PROTOCOL ON THE ZONES OF OCCUPATION IN GERMANY AND THE ADMINISTRATION OF GREATER BERLIN, SEPTEMBER 12, 1944

The governments of the United States, Soviet Union, and United Kingdom have reached the following agreement with regard to the execution of article 11 of the instrument of unconditional surrender of Germany.

1. Germany, within her frontiers as they were on December 31, 1937, will, for the purposes of occupation, be divided into three zones, one of which will be allotted to each of the three powers, and a special Berlin area, which will be under joint occupation by the three powers. . . .

2. The Berlin area—that is, the territory of Greater Berlin as defined by the law of April 27, 1920—will be jointly occupied by armed forces of the United States, Soviet Union, and United Kingdom assigned by the respective commanders-in-chief. . . . [See 1:3:2.]

FROM *U.S. Treaties and Other International Agreements* (Washington, D.C., 1954), pp. 2079–82. Approved by the United States on February 2, 1945; by the United Kingdom on December 5, 1944; and by the Soviet Union on February 6, 1945.

## 2. REPRESENTATIVES OF THE ALLIED COMMAND, RESOLUTION ON THE QUADRIPARTITE ADMINISTRATION OF BERLIN, JULY 7, 1945

In accordance with article 7 of the agreement on the Allied control machinery in Germany, the conference . . . passed the following resolution.

FROM Elmer Plischke, *Berlin: Development of Its Government and Administration* (Bonn: Office of the U.S. High Commissioner for Germany, 1952), pp. 209–10.

1. For the purpose of exercising the joint administration of Berlin, an inter-Allied military Kommandatura is to be established under a chief military commandant, whose duties are to be performed in turn by each of the military commandants of the inter-Allied military Kommandatura of Berlin during a period of fifteen days. [See 1:3:2.] The chief military commandant will exercise the administration of all Berlin zones, utilizing for this purpose conferences of the Allied military commandants to solve questions of principle and problems common to all zones. The resolutions of such conferences are to be passed unanimously. Orders and instructions of the chief military commandant of Berlin, issued in the Russian, English, French, and German languages, will be transmitted to the governing mayor [*Regierender Bürgermeister*] of Berlin and must be obeyed in all zones of the city. . . .

### 3. TEMPORARY CONSTITUTION OF GREATER BERLIN, AUGUST 13, 1946

#### 1. GENERAL PROVISIONS

ART. 2   1. All German citizens of Greater Berlin manifest their will through their representative bodies.

2. All citizens of Greater Berlin are equal under the law, regardless of race, sex, religion, and extent of property owned.

3. The representative bodies are the city assembly [*Stadtverordneten-versammlung*] and the city council [*Magistrat*].

ART. 3   1. The city assembly is constituted on the basis of universal, equal, direct, and secret elections by the citizens of Berlin who are entitled to vote and according to the principles of proportional representation.

2. The members of the city council are elected by the city assembly for the assembly's legislative term. All officially recognized political parties in the city assembly must be represented in the city council if such parties so demand. The members of the city council must be competent to perform their duties. . . .

#### 4. GOVERNMENT

ART. 40   1. Government functions are exercised by the senate [*Senat*].

2. The senate is composed of the governing mayor, the mayor acting as his deputy, and a maximum of sixteen senators.

ART. 41   1. The governing mayor is elected by the city assembly on the basis of a majority vote of the representatives present.

FROM Elmer Plischke, *Berlin: Development of Its Government and Administration* (Bonn: Office of the U.S. High Commissioner for Germany, 1952), pp. 213–29.

2. The mayor and the senators are elected by the city assembly according to the proposals of the governing mayor.

3. If no senate is established on the basis of the proposals of the governing mayor within a period of twenty-one days, the mandate for forming a senate expires, and new elections must be held.

4. Senators may resign from their office at any time.

. . .

ART. 42   1. The senate must enjoy the confidence of the city assembly.

2. The city assembly may pass a vote of nonconfidence on the senate and on any of its members. The roll call vote may take place not earlier than forty-eight hours after the motion of nonconfidence has been introduced in the city assembly.

3. The vote on a motion of nonconfidence requires the consent of a majority of the elected members of the city assembly. If a vote of nonconfidence is adopted, the senators must resign immediately. If requested to do so, a senator must continue in office until his successor takes over. The vote of nonconfidence becomes invalid if no new election has taken place within twenty-one days.

## 4. GOVERNMENT OF THE SOVIET UNION, STATEMENT ON THE WITHDRAWAL OF THE SOVIET REPRESENTATIVE FROM THE BERLIN KOMMANDATURA, JULY 1, 1948

The Allied Kommandatura in Berlin has for all practical purposes ceased its activity since the American commandant, Colonel Howley, on June 16, at a meeting of the Kommandatura, refused to discuss Soviet proposals for the improvement of the material and legal position of workers and office employees in Berlin industry and transport and, after a number of remarks insulting to the Allied Kommandatura, walked out of the meeting. This defiant behavior of the American commandant wrecked the work of the Allied Kommandatura in Berlin. . . . Later, the American, British, and French commandants in Berlin, ignoring the fact that Berlin is in the Soviet occupation zone and economically forms part of the Soviet zone, issued a tripartite, unlawful order in the Western sectors. It concerned the introduction of the new currency[1] of the Western zones into Berlin with a special stamp B. These acts were aimed at disorganizing currency circulation and at undermining the economy of the Soviet occupation zone and of Greater Berlin; such acts are incompatible with the principles of the Four Power administration of Berlin.

FROM M. O. von der Gablentz, *Documents on the Status of Berlin, 1944–1959* (Munich: Oldenbourg Verlag, 1959), pp. 64–65.

[1] The currency reform of 1948 in the Western zones of occupation changed the currency from *Reichsmark* (RM) to *Deutschmark* (DM).

## 5. GOVERNMENTS OF THE UNITED STATES AND THE UNITED KINGDOM TO THE GOVERNMENT OF THE SOVIET UNION, NOTE ON THE BERLIN BLOCKADE, JULY 6, 1948

The U.S. government wishes to call to the attention of the Soviet government the extremely serious international situation that has been brought about by the actions of the Soviet government in imposing restrictive measures on transport, which amount now to a blockade against the sectors in Berlin occupied by the United States, the United Kingdom, and France. The U.S. government regards these measures of blockade as a clear violation of existing agreements concerning the administration of Berlin by the four occupying powers.

The rights of the United States as a joint occupying power in Berlin derive from the total defeat and unconditional surrender of Germany. The international agreements undertaken in connection therewith by the governments of the United States, United Kingdom, France, and Soviet Union defined the zones in Germany and the sectors in Berlin that are occupied by these powers. . . .

These agreements implied the right of free access to Berlin. This right has long been confirmed by usage. It was directly specified in a message sent by President Truman to Premier Stalin on June 14, 1945, which agreed to the withdrawal of U.S. forces to the zonal boundaries, provided satisfactory arrangements could be entered into between the military commanders, which would give access by rail, road, and air to U.S. forces in Berlin. . . .

It clearly results from these undertakings that Berlin is not a part of the Soviet zone but is an international zone of occupation. Commitments entered into in good faith by the zone commanders and subsequently confirmed by the Allied Control Authority, as well as practices sanctioned by usage, guarantee the United States together with the other powers free access to Berlin for the purpose of fulfilling their responsibilities as occupying powers. . . .

FROM U.S. Dept. of State, *Germany 1947–1949, the Story of Documents* (Washington, D.C.), pp. 205–206.

## 6. SOVIET MILITARY COMMANDANT TO THE CHAIRMAN OF THE EXTRAORDINARY ASSEMBLY OF BERLIN CITY AND DISTRICT DEPUTIES, DECEMBER 2, 1948

The re-establishment of a single administrative body for the city of Berlin is of vital importance for the Berlin population. The Soviet Kommandatura therefore supports the measures directed toward maintaining the unity of the city and toward securing the normal operation of the organs of democratic self-government; it recognizes the provisional democratic city council of Greater Berlin, elected by the extraordinary assembly, as the only legitimate administrative body for the city. . . .

FROM M. O. von der Gablentz, *Documents on the Status of Berlin, 1944–1959* (Munich: Oldenbourg Verlag, 1959), p. 74.

7. WESTERN COMMANDANTS, DECLARATION ON THE CONTINUED OPERATION
OF THE ALLIED KOMMANDATURA, BERLIN, DECEMBER 21, 1948

On July 1, the Soviet authorities withdrew from the Allied Kommandatura and thus disrupted the quadripartite administration of Berlin. The Allied Kommandatura was established by agreements concluded between the four governments; they can be altered or abrogated only with the consent of all governments party to the agreements. . . .

The Allied Kommandatura will therefore resume its work. If the Soviet authorities, either now or at a future date, decide to abide by the agreements to which the Four Powers are committed, the quadripartite administration of Berlin could be resumed. During their abstentions, the three Western Allies will exercise the powers of the Allied Kommandatura, although it is realized that, owing to Soviet obstruction, it will only be possible for them to carry out their decisions in the Western sectors for the present.

FROM M. O. von der Gablentz, *Documents on the Status of Berlin, 1944–1959* (Munich: Oldenbourg Verlag, 1959), p. 74.

## 8. CONSTITUTION OF WEST BERLIN, OCTOBER 1, 1950

### PREAMBLE

In the resolve to protect the freedoms and rights of all individuals, to regulate the community and the economy on a democratic basis, to serve the spirit of social progress and peace, and in the desire to remain the capital of a new united Germany, Berlin has adopted this constitution.

### 1. FUNDAMENTAL PROVISIONS

.     .     .

ART. 2    1. All public power derives from all German citizens residing in Berlin.

2. Under this constitution, the citizens manifest their will directly by election of the popular representative body and by referendum and indirectly through the popular representative body.

ART. 3    1. Legislative power is exclusively vested in the popular representative body and, by means of referendum, in the people. Executive power lies in the hands of the government and of the administration subordinate to it; judicial power lies in the hands of independent courts. . . .

ART. 4    2. Berlin is divided into twenty boroughs [*Bezirke*]. Borough boundaries may be changed, and the number of boroughs may be reduced or increased only by law. . . .

FROM U.S. Commissioner for Germany (Bonn), *Policy Reports* (Washington, D.C., 1951).

### 3. POPULAR REPRESENTATIVE BODY

ART. 25   1. The city assembly [*Abgeordnetenhaus*] is the popular representative body elected by the Berlin citizens entitled to vote.

2. The city assembly is composed of 200 representatives.

ART. 26   1. The representatives are elected for a term of four years in universal, equal, secret, and direct elections.

2. Only political parties can present nomination lists. No seats will be allocated to nomination lists that poll less than 5 per cent of the total vote in the territory of Berlin.

.    .    .

### 5. LEGISLATION

ART. 46   1. Bills are passed by a simple majority of votes in the city assembly unless the constitution provides otherwise. . . .

### 9. TRANSITIONAL AND CONCLUDING PROVISIONS

ART. 87   . . . 2. In the transition period, the city assembly can by law establish that any law of the F.R.G. is applicable in Berlin without alteration.

### 9. ALLIED KOMMANDATURA, BERLIN CONSTITUTION, OCTOBER 8, 1951

1a. The Berlin city assembly may adopt a federal law by means of a *Mantelgesetz* (cover law), stating that the provisions of the federal law are also valid in Berlin.

1b. The provisions for implementing ordinances or regulations under federal law may become valid in Berlin if issued . . . as Berlin ordinances or regulations.

FROM M. O. von der Gablentz, *Documents on the Status of Berlin, 1944–1959* (Munich: Oldenbourg Verlag, 1959), pp. 121–27.

### 10. FEDERAL REPUBLIC, CONVENTION ON THE SETTLEMENT OF MATTERS ARISING FROM THE WAR AND FROM THE OCCUPATION, MAY 26, 1952

ART. 5   In the exercise of their responsibilities with respect to Berlin, the Three Powers will continue to regulate all air traffic to and from the Berlin air corridors established by the Allied Control Authority. The F.R.G. undertakes to facilitate and assist such traffic in every way and on a basis not less favorable than that enjoyed on the entry into force of the present convention.

FROM *FLG*, II (1952), pp. 405–68, as amended, October 23, 1954.

## 11. ALLIED KOMMANDATURA BERLIN, DECLARATION ON BERLIN, MAY 5, 1955

Taking into consideration the new relations established between France, the United Kingdom, United States, and Federal Republic of Germany, wishing to grant the Berlin authorities the maximum liberty compatible with the special situation of Berlin, the Allied Kommandatura makes this declaration:

1. Berlin shall exercise all rights, powers, and responsibilities set forth in its constitution as adopted in 1950, subject only to the reservations made by the Allied Kommandatura on August 29, 1950, and to the provisions hereinafter.

2. The Allied authorities retain the right to take . . . such measures as may be required to fulfill their international obligations, to ensure public order, and to maintain the status and security of Berlin and of its economy, trade, and communications.

3. The Allied authorities will normally exercise powers only in the following fields: (1) security, interests, and immunities of the Allied forces; . . . (2) disarmament and demilitarization, including related fields of scientific research, civil aviation, and prohibitions and restrictions on industry in relation to the foregoing; (3) relations of Berlin with authorities abroad (However, the Allied Kommandatura will permit the Berlin authorities to assure the representation abroad of the interests of Berlin and of its inhabitants by suitable arrangements); . . . (5) authority over the Berlin police to the extent necessary to ensure the security of Berlin.

4. The Allied Kommandatura will not, subject to articles 1 and 2 of this declaration, raise any objection to the adoption by Berlin, under an appropriate procedure authorized by the Allied Kommandatura, of the same legislation as that of the F.R.G., in particular with regard to currency, credit and foreign exchange, nationality, passports, emigration and immigration, extradition, the unification of the customs and trade area, trade and navigation agreements, freedom of movement of goods, and foreign trade and payments arrangements.

FROM M. O. von der Gablentz, *Documents on the Status of Berlin, 1944–1959* (Munich: Oldenbourg Verlag, 1959), pp. 141–44.

## 12. FEDERAL REPUBLIC, CHANCELLOR ADENAUER, DECLARATION CONCERNING AID TO BERLIN, 1955

In view of the special role that Berlin has played and is destined to play for the self-preservation of the free world, aware of the ties connecting the F.R.G. with Berlin as the future capital of a free, reunited Germany, the F.R.G. undertakes to: (1) take all necessary measures to ensure, through appropriate assistance, the maintenance of a balanced budget in Berlin; (2) take adequate measures for the equitable treatment of Berlin in the control

FROM *FLG*, II (1955), pp. 500–502.

and allocation of materials in short supply; (3) take adequate measures to ensure that Berlin also benefits from the resources received by the F.R.G. from outside sources for the necessary further economic reconstruction of Berlin; (4) take all appropriate measures to promote the public and private participation in the Berlin economy; (5) promote the development of Berlin's external trade; to accord Berlin such favored treatment in all matters of trade policy as circumstances warrant; and to provide Berlin, within the limits of possibility and with consideration of Berlin's participation in foreign currency control by the F.R.G., with necessary foreign currency.

## 13. FEDERAL REPUBLIC, FEDERAL ELECTORAL LAW, MAY 7, 1956

ART. 54   As long as the full application of this law to the *Land* Berlin is restricted . . . the following provisions will be in force:

.   .   .

2. Twenty-two representatives of the *Land* Berlin will be added [to the Bundestag] according to the following provisions: (1) The city assembly of Berlin elects the representatives as well as a sufficient number of substitutes in conformity with the composition of the city assembly at the time the German Bundestag is elected. (2) The elected representatives become members of the Bundestag when they state their acceptance to the president of the city assembly. The president immediately transmits the result of the election to the president of the Bundestag, enclosing the statements of acceptance. [See 1:7:145(1).]

FROM *FLG*, I (1956), pp. 383–84. For other provisions of the electoral law, see 4:1.

## 14. GOVERNMENT OF THE SOVIET UNION, NOTE TO THE U.S. GOVERNMENT ON THE SITUATION OF BERLIN, NOVEMBER 27, 1958

The government of the Soviet Union addresses the government of the United States as one of the signatory powers of the Potsdam Agreement on the urgent question of the status of Berlin. The problem of Berlin, which is situated in the center of the German Democratic Republic but whose western part is cut off from the G.D.R. as a result of foreign occupation, deeply affects not only the national interests of the German people but also the interests of all nations desiring to establish lasting peace in Europe. Here, in the historic capital of Germany, two worlds are in direct contact, and at every turn there tower the barricades of the cold war. A situation of constant friction and tension has prevailed in this city for many years.

The policy of the United States, United Kingdom, and France with respect to West Germany has led to the violation of those provisions of the Potsdam Agreement designed to ensure the unity of Germany as a peace-loving and democratic state. When a separate state, the F.R.G., was set up

FROM *DSB*, Vol. XL (January, 1959), pp. 82–89.

in West Germany—at the time occupied by the troops of these three powers —East Germany, under a leadership determined not to allow the German people to be plunged once again into disaster, had no alternative but to create in its turn an independent state. Thus, two states came into being in Germany. . . .

The G.D.R. advocates another program for uniting Germany. It is a program for uniting Germany as a peace-loving and democratic state, and it cannot fail to be welcomed by the people. There is but one way to put this program into effect. That is through agreement and contacts between the two German states and through the establishment of a German confederation. The implementation of this proposal would, without affecting the social structures of the G.D.R. and of the F.R.G., direct into the single channel of a peaceful policy the efforts of these governments and parliaments and would ensure a gradual rapprochement and merger of the two German states. The Soviet Union, as well as other states interested in strengthening peace in Europe, support the proposals of the G.D.R. for the peaceful unification of Germany. . . . If the United States, United Kingdom, and France are indeed staying in Berlin by virtue of the right stemming from the aforementioned international agreements and, primarily, from the Potsdam Agreement, they must abide by these agreements. Those who have grossly violated these agreements have lost the right to maintain their occupation regime in Berlin or any other part of Germany. . . .

The most correct and natural way to solve the problem would be for the western part of Berlin, now detached from the G.D.R., to be reunited with its eastern part and for the unified city to become part of the state in whose territory it is situated. However, the Soviet government, taking into account the present unrealistic policy of the United States as well as of the United Kingdom and France toward the G.D.R., cannot but foresee the difficulties the Western powers will have in contributing to such a solution of the Berlin problem. At the same time, the Soviet government is guided by the concern that the process of liquidating the occupation regime will not involve any painful break with the established way of life of the West Berlin population. . . .

In view of all these considerations, the Soviet government would consider it possible to settle the question of West Berlin by the transformation of West Berlin into an independent political unit—a free city—without any state, including both existing German states, interfering in its life. Specifically, it might be possible to agree that the territory of the free city of Berlin be demilitarized and that no armed forces be stationed in the city. The free city of West Berlin could have its own government and run its own economic, administrative, and other affairs. The Four Powers that shared in the administration of Berlin after the war, as well as both German states, could undertake to respect the free status of West Berlin as they have done, for instance, with regard to the neutrality of the Austrian Republic. For its part, the Soviet government would have no objection if the United Nations shared, in one way or another, in observing the free status of the city of West Berlin.

### 15. U.S. Government, Note to the Soviet Government on the Berlin Situation, December 31, 1958

The three Western powers are there as occupying powers, and they are not prepared to relinquish the rights they acquired through victory. . . . The government of the United States will not and does not in any way accept a unilateral denunciation of the accords of 1944 and 1945, and it is not prepared to relieve the Soviet Union from the obligations it assumed in June, 1949. Such action on the part of the Soviet government would have no legal basis, since the agreements can only be terminated by mutual consent. The government of the United States will continue to hold the Soviet government directly responsible for the discharge of its obligations undertaken with respect to Berlin under existing agreements. As the Soviet government knows, the French, British and U.S. governments have the right to maintain garrisons in their sectors of Berlin and to have free access thereto. Certain administrative procedures have been agreed on with the Soviet authorities accordingly and are in operation at the present time. The government of the United States will not accept a unilateral repudiation on the part of the Soviet government of its obligations in respect of that freedom of access. Nor will it accept the substitution of the regime the Soviet government refers to as the G.D.R. for the Soviet government in this respect.

From *DSB*, Vol. XL (January, 1959), pp. 79–81.

### 16. Soviet Aide-Memoire to President Kennedy, June 4, 1961

2. The Soviet government is earnestly striving to remove the sources of tension between the United States and the Soviet Union and to proceed to constructive, friendly cooperation. The conclusion of a German peace treaty would allow the two countries to come much closer to the attainment of this goal. The Soviet Union and the United States fought together against Hitler Germany. Their common duty is to conclude a German peace treaty and never again to permit the rise of forces that could plunge the world into a new and even more devastating war. . . .

5. The conclusion of a German peace treaty would also solve the problem of normalizing the situation in West Berlin. Deprived of a stable international status, West Berlin is at present a place where the Bonn *revanchist* circles continue to maintain extreme tension and to organize all kinds of provocations dangerous to the cause of peace. We are duty-bound to prevent a development where the intensification of West German militarism could lead to irreparable consequences due to the unsettled situation in West Berlin. At present, the Soviet government does not see a better way to solve

From *DSB*, Vol. XLV (October, 1961), pp. 23–33. Handed to President Kennedy by Premier Khrushchev during their meeting at Vienna, June 3–4, 1961.

the West Berlin problem than by transforming West Berlin into a demilitarized free city. The implementation of the proposal to turn West Berlin into a free city, with the interests of all parties duly taken into consideration, would normalize the situation in West Berlin. The present occupation regime has already outlived itself and has lost all connection with the purposes for which it was established, as well as with the Allied agreements on Germany that provided the basis for its existence. The occupation rights will naturally be terminated upon the conclusion of a German peace treaty, whether it is signed with both German states or only with the G.D.R., in whose territory West Berlin is located.

The position of the Soviet government is that the free city of West Berlin should have unobstructed contacts with the outside world and that its internal regulations should be determined by the freely expressed will of its population. The United States as well as other countries would naturally have every possibility to maintain and develop their relations with the free city of West Berlin. In short, West Berlin, as the Soviet government sees it, should be strictly neutral. Of course, the use of Berlin as a base for provocative activities hostile to the Soviet Union or to any other state cannot be permitted in the future, nor can Berlin be allowed to remain a dangerous hotbed of tension and international conflicts.

. . .

7. The Soviet government is prepared to consider any constructive proposals of the United States government for a German peace treaty and for normalizing the situation in West Berlin. The Soviet government will show a maximum of good will in order that the question of a German peace treaty may be settled by mutual agreement between the Soviet Union, the United States and other states concerned. The signing of a German peace treaty by all the members of the anti-Hitler coalition and the settlement of the question of a neutral status for West Berlin on this basis would create better conditions for trust among states and for the solution of such important international problems as disarmament. But, if the United States does not show that it realizes the necessity of concluding a peace treaty, we shall deplore it because we shall then be obliged to sign a peace treaty, which it would be impossible and dangerous to delay, not with all the states but only with those that wish to sign it.

The peace treaty would specifically define the status of West Berlin as a free city, and the Soviet Union, just as the other parties to the treaty, would of course observe it strictly; measures would also be taken to ensure respect for this status by other countries as well. At the same time, this would mean putting an end to the occupation regime in West Berlin, with all its implications. In particular, questions related to communication by land, water, or air within the territory of the G.D.R. would have to be settled solely by appropriate agreements with the G.D.R. That is but natural, since control over such means of communication is an inalienable right of every sovereign state.

## 17. U.S. NOTE, JULY 17, 1961

The U.S. government has given careful consideration to the Soviet government's aide-memoire received on June 4, 1961, in Vienna. It has consulted with its British and French allies and has found itself in full agreement with them. It has also consulted the government of the F.R.G. and the other member governments of NATO. . . .

With regard to Berlin, the United States is not insisting upon the maintenance of its legal rights because of any desire merely to perpetuate its presence there. It is insisting on, and will defend, its legal rights against attempts at unilateral abrogation, because the freedom of the people of West Berlin depends upon the maintenance of those rights. The support and approval of the people of West Berlin for the system under which they live has been made amply clear over the years. Their overwhelming support for their government in free elections is a dramatic example of this. That the United States is not wedded to one particular arrangement for Berlin is demonstrated by the all-Berlin solution proposed at Geneva in 1959. It has accepted the possibility of practical arrangements intended to improve the present situation in Berlin until such time as an over-all solution of the German problem can be achieved. It is sorry to note that all the proposals it has made to that end have been rejected by the government of the Soviet Union. However, the United States also supports the clearly expressed wish of the West Berliners that no change be made in the status of their city which would expose them, at once or gradually over a longer time, to the domination of the regime that presently controls the surrounding areas. . . .

The counterpart of the Soviet position is that, unless the Western powers accept its German solution, the Soviet government will try to obtain what it wants by unilateral action. . . .

At the end of World War II, the victorious powers entered into a number of agreements to settle the German problem, based on the principle that questions concerning Germany as a whole were a matter for joint action by the victorious powers. A peace settlement with Germany is foremost among those questions. The Potsdam Agreement of 1945, for instance, refers to "the preparation of a peace settlement for Germany to be accepted by the government of Germany when a government adequate for the purpose is established."

Under international law, the Soviet government cannot ignore these agreements in order to conclude unilateral arrangements with part of Germany; nor would such action invalidate the rights of the U.S. government and the other governments responsible for the settlement of the German question, since these rights derive absolutely from the unconditional surrender of Nazi Germany and were not granted by or negotiated with the Soviet Union. . . .

FROM *DSB*, Vol. XLV (October, 1961), pp. 224–30. Delivered to the Soviet Ministry of Foreign Affairs at Moscow on July 17, 1961. Similar notes were delivered on the same day by the French and British ambassadors.

According to the thesis repeatedly expounded by the Soviets, the "separate peace treaty" would, upon its conclusion, terminate the rights of the West in, and with regard to, Berlin. These assertions are untenable and fallacious from a legal point of view, because such a separate treaty would be legally ineffective and because neither the Soviet Union nor East Germany can, for the reasons stated above, unilaterally deprive the three Western powers of their original rights in and regarding Berlin. Rights of access to Berlin are inherent in the rights of the Western powers to be in Berlin. The procedures for the exercise of these rights have been defined in numerous agreements between the four governments and were confirmed by the Soviet government in the Paris Agreement of June 20, 1949, on the termination of the Berlin blockade and in practice over many years. They cannot be unilaterally abrogated by any act of the Soviet government. . . .

The Soviet Union further asserts that a "peace treaty," whether signed by all the interested parties or not, would bring about the establishment of West Berlin as a "demilitarized free city." As proposed, this would bring with it the cessation of the rights of the Western allies in Berlin, including the right of access.

The United States considers entirely unfounded the Soviet claims that this unilateral act could deprive the other three participants in the joint occupation of Berlin of their basic rights in the city—rights derived from the Nazi surrender, as indicated and expressed in binding and valid agreements, to which the Soviet Union is a party. The agreements of September 12, 1944, and May 1, 1945, establishing the occupation arrangements for the city were joint undertakings by the occupying powers, all of whom derived rights and obligations from them. The obligation of the Soviet Union to assure the normal functioning of transport and communication between Berlin and the Western zones of Germany was reaffirmed in the Four Power Agreement of June 20, 1949. This legal situation was thus jointly created by the Four Powers and cannot be altered except by the common consent of all of them.

The United States wishes particularly to reiterate, in discussing the legal aspects of Berlin's status, that Soviet references to Berlin as being situated on the territory of the so-called German Democratic Republic are entirely without foundation. . . .

The Soviet Union claims that the "free city" of West Berlin would be able to freely maintain its communications with the outside world and determine its domestic order by the free expression of the will of its people. Since, however, the "free city" would in fact be isolated within the so-called "German Democratic Republic" which, according to the Soviet proposal, would control all access to and from the city, it is of significance to examine the stated intentions of the leaders of that regime with respect to West Berlin. . . .

It is evident that the present status of the city, which the Soviet Union chooses to characterize as an "occupation regime" that "has already outlived itself," is actually an arrangement that, under the existing abnormal division of Germany, does not constitute any threat to peace. Attempts by the Soviet Union to destroy that arrangement, in pursuit of its political goals, are certain to gravely jeopardize the peace, in the name of which the Soviet action is taken. . . .

The immediate cause of this threat to peace arises from the announced intention of the Soviet government to present the three Western powers with a *de facto* situation based on the false assertion that they would no longer be entitled to remain in Berlin or to have free access thereto. Such a move could lead to highly dangerous developments and would be totally devoid of legal effect. . . .

There is no reason for a crisis over Berlin. If one develops, it is because the Soviet Union is attempting to invade the basic rights of others. All the world will plainly see that the misuse of such words as "peace" and "freedom" cannot conceal a threat to raise tension to the point of danger and suppress the freedom of those who now enjoy it.

### 18. U.S. Note to the Soviet Government, Protest at the Closing of the Soviet Sector Border in Berlin, August 17, 1961

The embassy of the United States presents its compliments to the minister of foreign affairs and, upon instructions of its government, has the honor to direct the most serious attention of the government of the Soviet Union to the following:

On August 13, East German authorities put into effect several measures regulating movement at the boundary of the Western sectors and the Soviet sector of the city of Berlin. These measures have the effect of limiting, to a degree approaching complete prohibition, passage from the Soviet sector to the Western sectors of the city. These measures were accompanied by the closing of the sector boundary by a sizeable deployment of police forces and by military detachments brought into Berlin for this purpose.

All this is a flagrant and particularly serious violation of the quadripartite status of Berlin. Freedom of movement with respect to Berlin was reaffirmed by the quadripartite agreement of New York of May 4, 1949, and by the decision taken at Paris on June 20, 1949, by the council of the ministers of foreign affairs of the Four Powers. The U.S. government has never accepted that limitations can be imposed on freedom of movement within Berlin. The boundary between the Soviet sector and the Western sectors of Berlin is not a state frontier. The U.S. government considers that the measures the East German authorities have taken are illegal. It reiterates that it does not accept the pretension that the Soviet sector of Berlin forms a part of the so-called German Democratic Republic and that Berlin is situated on its territory. Such a pretension is in itself a violation of the solemnly pledged word of the Soviet Union in the agreement on the zones of occupation in Germany and the administration of Greater Berlin. [See 1:3:1.] Moreover, the U.S. government cannot admit the right of the East German

From *DSB*, Vol. XLV (October, 1961), pp. 395–96.

authorities to authorize their armed forces to enter the Soviet sector of Berlin.

By the admission of the East German authorities, the measures just taken are motivated by the fact that an ever increasing number of inhabitants of East Germany wish to leave this territory. The reasons for this exodus are known. They are simply the internal difficulties in East Germany.

To judge by the terms of a declaration of the Warsaw Pact powers published on August 13, the measures in question are supposed to have been recommended to the East German authorities by those powers. The U.S. government notes that the powers that associated themselves with the Soviet Union by signing the Warsaw Pact are thus intervening in a domain in which they have no competence.

It is to be noted that this declaration states that the measures taken by the East German authorities are "in the interests of the German peoples themselves." It is difficult to see any basis for this statement or to understand why it should be for the members of the Warsaw Pact to decide what the interests of the German people are. It is evident that no Germans, particularly those whose freedom of movement is being forcibly restrained, think this is so. This would become abundantly clear if all Germans were allowed a free choice and if the principle of self-determination were also applied in the Soviet sector of Berlin and in East Germany.

The U.S. government solemnly protests against the measures referred to above, for which it holds the Soviet government responsible. The U.S. government expects the Soviet government to put an end to these illegal measures. This unilateral infringement of the quadripartite status of Berlin can only increase existing tension and dangers.

## 19. Tripartite Declaration on Germany and Berlin, June 26, 1964

The governments of France, the United Kingdom, and the United States, after consulting with the government of the F.R.G., wish to state the following with regard to the agreement[1] signed by the Soviet Union and the so-called German Democratic Republic on June 12, 1964. This agreement, among other things, deals with questions related to Germany as a whole and to Berlin in particular.

1. As the Soviet government was reminded before the signing of this agreement, it is clear that any agreement the Soviet Union may make with the so-called G.D.R. cannot affect Soviet obligations or responsibilities under agreements and arrangements with the Three Powers on the subject of Germany, including Berlin and access thereto. The three governments consider that the Soviet Union remains bound by these engagements, and they will continue to hold the Soviet government responsible for the fulfillment of its obligations.

From *DSB*, Vol. XLV (October, 1964), pp. 396–97.

[1] The Friendship and Mutual Assistance Treaty, which emphasized the maintenance of the G.D.R. state borders.

2. West Berlin is not an "independent political unit." Within the framework of their responsibilities regarding Germany as a whole, the Four Powers have put the German capital, the city of Greater Berlin, under their joint administration. Unilateral initiatives taken by the Soviet government in order to block the quadripartite administration of the city cannot in any way modify this legal situation nor abrogate the rights and responsibilities of the Four Powers in regard to Berlin. While reserving their rights relating to Berlin, the three Western powers, taking account of the necessities for the development of the city, have authorized, in accordance with the agreements of October 23, 1954, the establishment of close ties between Berlin and the F.R.G., including permission to the F.R.G. to ensure representation of Berlin population outside Berlin. These ties, the existence of which is essential to the viability of Berlin, are in no way inconsistent with the quadripartite status of the city.

3. The three governments consider that the government of the F.R.G. is the only German government freely and legitimately constituted and therefore entitled to speak for the German people in international affairs. The three governments do not recognize the East German regime nor the existence of a state in East Germany. As for the provisions related to the frontiers of this so-called state, the three governments reiterate that, within Germany and Berlin, there are no frontiers but rather a "demarcation line" and the "sector borders" and that, according to the agreements to which the agreement of June 12 refers, the final determination of the frontiers of Germany must await a peace settlement for the whole of Germany.

4. The charges of *revanchism* and militarism contained in the agreement of June 12 are without basis. The government of the F.R.G., in its statement of October 3, 1954, has renounced the use of force to achieve the reunification of Germany or the modification of the present boundaries of the F.R.G. This remains its policy.

5. The three governments agree that the safeguarding of peace and security is today more than ever a vital problem for all nations and that a just and peaceful settlement of outstanding problems in Europe is essential to the establishment of lasting peace and security. Such a settlement requires the application in the whole of Germany of the principle of self-determination. This principle is reaffirmed in the U.N. Charter, which the agreement of June 12 itself invokes. By ignoring this principle, the agreement of June 12 seeks to perpetuate the arbitrary division of Germany, which is a continuing source of international tension and an obstacle to a peaceful settlement of European problems. The exercise of self-determination, which should lead to the reunification of Germany in peace and freedom, remains a fundamental objective of the three governments.

6. The three governments are convinced that such a settlement should be sought as soon as possible. This settlement should include progressive solutions that would bring about German reunification and security in Europe. On such a basis, the three governments are always ready to take advantage of any opportunity that would peacefully re-establish German unity and freedom.

# INTRODUCTION 2: EAST GERMANY

The German Democratic Republic now constitutes a system complete in itself and completely different from that of the Federal Republic. Its establishment and its international status (in particular, its relations with the Soviet Union) have been documented in chapter 1; its relations with and attitude toward Berlin, in the preceding part of this chapter; documents relating to its attitude to reunification are found in chapter 8. Here, its political and government framework is documented.

East Germany has functioned under two constitutions: one promulgated on October 7, 1949, that masked the reality of single Communist Party control, which its leaders hoped, in vain, to extend to all Germany; the second, presently in force, promulgated on April 8, 1968, reflects more than the first the actual power structure and power relations (document 20).

The first constitution had in some ways been patterned on the Weimar Constitution. For example, it had a section on "the limits of state authority," including a long list of liberal-democratic basic rights, although in reality, the citizen was not protected if these rights were considered to be in conflict with state and Party objectives. It envisaged election by proportional representation of deputies for parliament (*Volkskammer*, People's Chamber); in reality, there were (and are) only single-slate elections of candidates belonging to the National Front, in which the ruling SED (*Sozialistische Einheitspartei*, product of the forced merger, in 1946, of Eastern Communist Party and SPD) joins with puppet parties such as the Eastern CDU and LDP as well as with SED-controlled mass organizations such as the Free Trade Unions and the Free German Youth. (See the introduction to chapter 3 for early party developments.) Votes could (and can) be cast only for or against this list. The subsequent law on elections to the People's Chamber (1958) likewise conceals the reality of a one-list vote behind a competitive façade (document 21). Finally, the 1949 constitution envisaged a Western-style parliamentary system, with members of government responsible to parliament, but in reality the SED from the outset was in complete control of government and of parliament, so that a conflict between the two was unthinkable.

In addition, the structure of government and administration as laid down in this constitution was even formally altered shortly after its promulgation. The federal structure of government based on *Länder* was changed in 1952 in favor of a centralized system; both *Länder* and local self-government were abolished.[1] In 1960, the presidency (whose power and influence had been negligible) was abolished in favor of a Council of State (*Staatsrat*), a body which not only assumed the former presidential powers and also the functions of the presidium of parliament but actually took over top

---

[1] See the Law on the Further Democratization of the Structure and Procedure of the Organs in the *Länder*, July 23, 1952, in *GB*, I, p. 867.

executive power by assuming control over the formal executive, the Council of Ministers.[1] It also controlled (and controls) the newly established National Defense Council,[2] as well as the machinery of justice (document 26). No wonder that top SED-leader Walter Ulbricht emerged as (and has since been) the chairman of this all-powerful body.

The new constitution ratifies this structure. The process of its formulation began with an announcement by Ulbricht, in his capacity as first secretary of the SED's central committee, at a party convention in April, 1967, to the effect that the time had come to draft "a more timely constitution." Thereupon, a committee of parliament was put in charge of drafting it.[3] On January 31, 1938, the chamber, to which Ulbricht had presented the finished draft, resolved that it should be presented to the people for discussion.[4] This so-called *Volksaussprache* took place in the following months. That this was not entirely a meaningless façade was proved by the insertion of certain substantive changes—for example, a provision giving churches certain rights—on which the "discussant" people apparently had strongly insisted.[5] The draft was then adopted by the chamber and referred to popular referendum,[6] which took place on April 6, yielding a 94.5 per cent majority for the new constitution.[7]

The 1968 constitution, like constitutions of other Communist countries, has a double function: to spell out and formulate the reality of government structure and practice (this is primarily done in the second half of the document, parts 3 and 4); and to place all this in the ideological setting of the Marxist-Leninist doctrine (parts 1 and 2 of the document), a procedure through which the constitution assumes the character of exhortation, propaganda, and formulation of ultimate aim. The new East German constitution, in addition, has been made the occasion to strongly emphasize the existence of the republic as an independent unit.

A law on separate East German citizenship enacted in February, 1967 (document 24), also emphasizes the separate statehood of East Germany.

By conferring a monopoly of political power on the National Front

[1] See the Law on the Formation of the Council of State of the G.D.R. of September 12, 1960, in *GB*, I, p. 505; and the Law on the Council of Ministers of the G.D.R. of April 17, 1963, in *GB*, I, p. 505.

[2] See the Law on the Formation of the National Defense Council of the G.D.R. of February 27, 1960, in *GB*, I, p. 89.

[3] See *Neues Deutschland* (December 2, 1967), pp. 3–5.

[4] See the Resolution of the People's Chamber of the G.D.R. on the People's Chamber's Approval to the Declaration of the Chairman of the Council of State in *GB*, I, p. 29; and the Resolution of the People's Chamber on the Formation of a Commission of the People's Chamber for the Drafting of a Socialist Constitution of the G.D.R. of December 1, 1967, in *GB*, I, p. 130. Among the forty members and twenty-two experts of the commission, there were, in addition to Ulbricht, the chairman of the commission and four other members of the Politburo.

[5] About the results of the "*Volksaussprache* to the Draft," see the report of the commission in *Neues Deutschland* (March 28, 1968), p. 2, and for changes of the draft, see *Neues Deutschland* (March 15, 1968), p. 11.

[6] See the Resolution of the People's Chamber in *GB*, I, p. 191; and the Law for the Execution of a Referendum on the Constitution of March 3, 1968, in *GB*, I, p. 192.

[7] See *Neues Deutschland* (April 9, 1968), p. 7.

(article 3), in conjunction with constantly emphasizing the "socialist" nature of the new Eastern society, the constitution implies the dominating role of the "state party," the SED. The SED is completely structured on the pattern of the leading bloc party, the Communist Party of the Soviet Union, and implements its guiding principle of "democratic centralism" (document 22). The party program (document 23), besides summing up the general principles of socialism, formulates long-range perspectives for the socialist future in all realms of life and society.

# DOCUMENTS

### 20. CONSTITUTION OF THE GERMAN DEMOCRATIC REPUBLIC, 1968

The people of the German Democratic Republic—imbued with the responsibility of guiding the whole German nation on its path toward future peace and socialism, fully cognizant of the historical fact that imperialism has divided Germany and that West Germany has become the base for imperialism and for the fight against socialism under the leadership of the United States and with the consent of the West German circles of capitalist monopoly, aware that this division is against the vital interests of the nation, firmly founded on the achievements of the anti-fascist and democratic-socialist transformation of the social order, united in the goal of its working classes and people to continue in the spirit of the Constitution of October 7, 1949, and imbued with the will to pursue peace, social justice, democracy, socialism, and friendship with all peoples—have given themselves freely and with determination this socialist constitution.

PART I: FOUNDATIONS OF THE SOCIALIST SOCIETY AND STATE

### Chapter 1: Political Foundations
ART. 1   The German Democratic Republic is a socialist state of German nationhood [*Staat deutscher Nation*]. The G.D.R. is the political organization of the urban and rural working people. Under the leadership of the working class and its Marxist-Leninist party, it is making socialism a reality. Berlin is the capital of the G.D.R. The flag of the G.D.R. is black, red, and gold with the state emblem of the G.D.R. in the center on both sides. The state emblem of the G.D.R. is the hammer and sickle in a wreath of ears of grain entwined at the base with a black, red, and gold ribbon.

ART. 2   1. All political power in the G.D.R. is exercised by the working people. Man is the center of all endeavors of the socialist society and state. The social system of socialism is constantly being improved.

2. The firm alliance of the working class with the farmers of the cooperatives, the intelligentsia, and other groups; the socialist ownership of the

FROM *G.D.R. GB*, I (1968), pp. 199–300.

means of production; and the planning and direction of social development on the basis of increased scientific knowledge are the unassailable foundations of the socialist order of society.

3. Exploitation of man by man is eliminated forever. What the hands of the people create is their own. The socialist principle that each person gives according to his abilities and receives according to his capabilities will be realized.

4. The conformity of the political, material, and cultural interests of the working people and their collectives with social requirements is the most important driving force of the socialist society.

ART. 3  1. The unity of all forces of the people finds its organized expression in the National Front of the democratic Germany.

2. The parties and mass organizations unite all popular forces in the National Front so that they can jointly work for the development of the socialist society. Everyone is responsible for all, and thus the socialist community becomes a reality.

ART. 4  All power must be used to serve the welfare of the people. Power secures the people's peaceful existence, protects the socialist society, guarantees a planned increase of the standard of living and of man's independent development, upholds his dignity, and secures his rights contained in this constitution.

ART. 5  1. The citizens of the G.D.R. exercise their political power through democratically elected representative organs.

2. The representative organs of the people are the foundation of the state. In their activities, these organs rely on the citizens' active participation in the preparation, execution, and control of their decisions.

3. At no time and under no circumstances can organs other than those listed in this constitution exercise political power.

ART. 6  1. Loyal to the interests of the German people and to the international obligations of all Germans, the G.D.R. has exterminated German militarism and Nazism in its territory. It pursues a foreign policy that serves peace and socialism, understanding between peoples, and security.

2. The G.D.R. cultivates and develops cooperation and friendship with the Soviet Union and with other socialist states, thereby adhering to the principles of international socialism.

3. The G.D.R. supports the efforts of all peoples to achieve freedom and independence and encourages friendly cooperation among all states, based on equality and mutual respect.

4. The G.D.R. aims at a system of collective security in Europe and at a stable and peaceful world order. The G.D.R. supports total disarmament.

5. Militarist and revanchist propaganda in any form, war-mongering, and racial, religious, and ethnic prejudices will be punished as a criminal act.

ART. 7  1. The state organs guarantee the inviolability of the territory of the G.D.R., including air space, territorial waters, and the continental shelf.

2. The G.D.R. organizes the defense of the territory as well as the protection of the socialist order and the peaceful existence of its citizens. The national people's army and other defense institutions guard the socialist

people's achievements against outside aggression. In order to safeguard peace and to secure the socialist state, the national people's army seeks close cooperation with its comrades in the Soviet Union and in other socialist states.

ART. 8  1. The generally recognized provisions of international law that encourage peaceful cooperation among peoples are also binding for all state authorities and citizens. The G.D.R. will never start a war of aggression or use its armed forces against the freedom of another people.

2. The establishment of normal relations between the two German states and their cooperation on the basis of equality is the national concern of the G.D.R. Moreover, the G.D.R. and its citizens seek to overcome the division of Germany that was forced upon the German nation by imperialism and, step by step, to bring about the *rapprochement* of the two German states on the basis of democracy and socialism.

### Chapter 2: Economic Foundations, Science, Education, and Culture

ART. 9  1. Socialist ownership of the means of production is the foundation of the economy of the G.D.R. The economy develops according to the economic laws of socialism, which are rooted in socialist production requirements. Socialist production requirements are the result of the struggle against the economic system of capitalist monopoly, whose aggressive and adventurous policy has brought only misfortune to the German nation. Through the destruction of monopoly holders and big landowners and the liquidation of the capitalist profit-making economy, the source of militarism and of man's exploitation by man has been eliminated. Socialist property ownership has proven to be successful.

2. The economy of the G.D.R. aims at strengthening the socialist order, at steadily increasing the satisfaction of its citizens, and at developing their personality and their socialist social relations.

3. The G.D.R. follows the basic principles of economic and social planning and management. The economy of the G.D.R. is a socialist, planned economy. The socialist economic system coordinates state planning of social development and the individual responsibility of socialist producers and local authorities.

4. The determination of currency regulations and of the financial system is the responsibility of the socialist state. Dues and taxes are levied according to law.

5. Foreign economic policy, including foreign trade and currency exchanges, are a state monopoly.

ART. 10  1. The common property of the people [*Volkseigentum*], the collectivized property of the working people [*Gemeineigentum*], and the property of citizen organizations constitute socialist property of the state.

2. It is the duty of the socialist state and its citizens to protect and increase socialist property.

ART. 11  1. The citizen has a guaranteed right to own personal property and to inherit it. Personal property serves to satisfy the material and cultural needs of the working people.

2. The socialist state protects the rights of authors and inventors.

3. Personal property as well as the rights of authors and inventors may not be used against the interests of society.

ART. 12   1. Mineral wealth, mines, power stations, dams, large rivers, natural resources, larger industrial enterprises, banks and insurance companies, railways and shipping, as well as aviation, post, and telephone installations are the property of the people. Such property may not be privately owned.

2. The socialist state guarantees such use of the property of the people as will yield the greatest benefit for the people. . . .

ART. 13   Tools, machines, and installations, agricultural, handicraft, and other socialist cooperatives, as well as the livestock of agricultural cooperatives and the yields of agricultural and industrial production belong to all.

ART. 14   1. Economic enterprises and institutions that yield private profit must be used and managed so as to serve and improve the well-being of the people and to increase social wealth.

2. The state promotes the close cooperation of socialist workshops and private economic enterprises and institutions. Private enterprises can apply for state participation if the needs of the people so require.

3. The establishment of associations for the exercise of private economic power is not permitted.

ART. 15   1. The land is one of the G.D.R.'s most precious natural possessions. It must be protected and rationally used. Forests and cultivated land can only be used for other than regular purposes with the consent of the responsible state authorities.

2. State and society are responsible for the protection of nature in the interests of the well-being of the citizens. The appropriate organs, as well as every citizen, are responsible for the prevention of water and air pollution, for the protection of plants and animals, and for the beautification of the country.

ART. 16   Expropriations are allowed only for legally justified beneficial purposes and in return for fair compensation. They can take place only if such beneficial purposes cannot be achieved otherwise.

ART. 17   1. Science and scientific research and the application of scientific knowledge are essential foundations of the socialist society. The G.D.R. will promote them in every possible way.

2. Through a uniform socialist educational system, the G.D.R. ensures that all citizens receive an education adequate for the ever growing demands of society. . . .

3. The G.D.R. promotes science and education in order to protect and enrich the society and the life of its citizens, to master the scientific and technological revolution, and to safeguard the constant progress of the socialist society.

4. Any abuse of science that endangers peace, the understanding among peoples, life, and the dignity of men is prohibited.

ART. 18   1. The socialist national culture is part of the foundation of the socialist society. The G.D.R. promotes and protects the socialist culture, which promotes peace, humanism, and the development of the socialist community. The G.D.R. combats barbaric imperialism, which encourages psychological warfare and man's degradation. The socialist society promotes the cultural life of the working people and the humanistic values of the cultural heritage of the nation and of the world and thus develops the socialist culture of the nation as a responsibility of the entire people.

2. The promotion of the arts and of the artistic interests and talents of the working people as well as the dissemination of artistic works and accomplishments is the responsibility of the state and of its social forces. Artistic creation is based on a close relationship between the creators of culture and the life of the people.

3. Gymnastics, sports, and tourism are elements of the socialist culture and serve the physical and mental development of all citizens.

PART II: CITIZENS AND COMMUNITY ASSOCIATIONS IN THE
SOCIALIST SOCIETY

## Chapter 1: Fundamental Rights and Duties

ART. 19   1. The G.D.R. guarantees that all citizens can enjoy their rights and participate in the direction of the society's development. The G.D.R. guarantees socialist legality and legal security.

2. All state organs, all social forces, and all citizens must respect the rights of the individual and protect his dignity and freedom.

3. All citizens enjoy equal rights and opportunities for the full development of their capabilities. They can do so free from exploitation, oppression, and economic dependence, and they can use their capabilities both for the welfare of the socialist society and for their own benefit. . . .

4. The conditions for the acquisition and loss of G.D.R. citizenship are determined by law. [See 7:24.]

ART. 20   1. All citizens of the G.D.R. have equal rights and obligations, regardless of their nationality, race, ideology or religion, social background, and position. All citizens are equal before the law.

2. Men and women enjoy equal rights and legal equality in all spheres of social, government, and personal life. It is the function of the society and of the state to strengthen the position of the woman, especially her professional status.

3. The social and professional development of youth shall be especially promoted. Youth has every opportunity to take a responsible part in the development of the socialist social order.

ART. 21   1. Every citizen has the right to take part in the formation of the political, economic, social, and cultural life of the socialist community and state according to the principle: "Participate in the work, the planning, and the government of the state."

2. The right of codetermination and cooperation is guaranteed since the citizens elect the state organs democratically and participate in the planning, formation, and direction of social life. The representative organs

of the people, their delegates, and the leaders of the state and economic institutions are responsible to the people for their activities. By the authority of their social organizations, the people can express their wishes and demands and submit their requests and proposals to the social, state, and economic organizations. The people can express their will in referenda.

3. To exercise the right of codetermination and cooperation is also a highly moral responsibility of the citizen. Society and state recognize and support the activities of the society and of the state.

ART. 22   1. Every citizen of the G.D.R. who is eighteen years old on election day has the right to vote.

2. Every citizen who is eighteen years old on election day can be elected to the local representative bodies. He can be elected to the People's Chamber if he is twenty-one years old on election day.

3. These socialist electoral principles cannot be waived. Elections are directed by democratic election commissions; popular discussions are held on the fundamental political issues; and candidates are nominated and examined by the voters.

ART. 23   1. The citizens of the G.D.R. have the right and sacred duty to protect peace, the socialist fatherland, and its achievements. Each citizen must serve and defend the G.D.R. according to the law.

2. No citizen is allowed to participate in warlike actions or war preparations that are aimed at the oppression of a people.

3. The G.D.R. can offer asylum to aliens or stateless persons, if, in defending peace, democracy, or the interests of the working people or participating in a social and national liberation struggle, they have been persecuted for political, scientific, or cultural activities.

ART. 24   1. Each citizen of the G.D.R. has the right to work. He has the right to choose his place of work according to his personal qualifications and his social needs. He has the right to earn a wage that corresponds to the quality and quantity of his work. Men and women, adults and youth have the right to equal pay for equal work.

2. It is the duty of every employable citizen to pursue socially useful activities. The right to work and the duty to work form a unit.

3. The right to work is guaranteed by the socialist ownership of the means of production, by socialist planning and management of the social processes of reproduction, by the steady and planned growth of the socialist forces of production and of the productivity of labor, by the determined implementation of the scientific-technological revolution, by the continuous education of the citizens, and by uniform labor laws.

ART. 25   1. Every citizen of the G.D.R. has an equal right to education. The educational institutions are open to everyone. The unified socialist educational system guarantees every citizen a continuous socialist upbringing and a general education.

2. The G.D.R. ensures the progress of the people toward a socialist community of generally educated and harmoniously developed human beings. . . .

3. All citizens have the right to participate in the cultural life of the state, which is increasingly important in view of the scientific-technological revo-

lution and of the rising intellectual demands. State and society promote the citizens' participation in cultural affairs, in physical culture, and in sports, thus molding and perfecting the socialist personality and providing increased satisfaction for the cultural interests and needs of the citizens.

4. The G.D.R. requires ten years of compulsory secondary education; each youth must attend a secondary school [*Oberschule*] for ten years. In specific cases, secondary education can be completed in vocational or technical-training schools for working people. All young people have the right and duty to learn a vocation.

5. Special schools and vocational institutions have been established for children and adults with psychiatric and physical handicaps.

6. The state and all social forces cooperate in the implementation of these educational tasks.

ART. 26   1. The state assures the student of the opportunity of educational advancement to universities and professional academies [*Hochschulen*] on the basis of performance, the needs of the society, and the social structure of the population.

2. Education is free. Scholarships and educational material are granted according to the social needs of the individual.

3. Students enrolled in universities, academies, and professional schools do not have to pay tuition. Scholarships and grants are given according to the social needs and abilities of the individual.

ART. 27   1. According to the principles of this constitution, every citizen of the G.D.R. has the right to express his opinion freely and publicly. This freedom cannot be restricted because of the professional affiliation of the individual. No one may be discriminated against for exercising this right.

2. Freedom of the press, of radio, and of television is guaranteed.

ART. 28   1. All citizens have the right to assemble freely within the framework of the principles and aims of this constitution. . . .

ART. 29   The citizens of the G.D.R. have the right to form associations in order to implement their interests according to the basic principles and aims of this constitution and through joint action in political parties, social organizations, associations, and collectives.

ART. 30   1. The personality and the freedom of every G.D.R. citizen are inviolable.

2. Restrictions are allowed only in case of criminal acts or of mental incapacity; they must be based on legal grounds. . . .

3. Every citizen is entitled to the assistance of the state and of social institutions for the protection of his personality and freedom.

ART. 31   1. Secrecy of postal, telephone, and wire services is inviolable.

2. It can only be restricted by law if the security of the state or the prosecution of a crime so requires.

ART. 32   Every citizen is entitled to freedom of movement on G.D.R. territory within the framework of the law.

ART. 33   1. Every G.D.R. citizen living in a foreign country can ask for legal protection by the authorities of the G.D.R.

2. G.D.R. citizens may not be extradited to a foreign country.

ART. 34  1. Every citizen has the right to leisure and recreation.

2. The right to leisure and recreation is safeguarded by legally restricted daily and weekly working hours, by a fully paid annual vacation, and by planned recreation and vacation facilities.

ART. 35  1. All G.D.R. citizens are entitled to the protection of their health and strength [*Arbeitskraft*].

2. This right will be safeguarded through the planned improvement of working and living conditions, through protection of the citizens' health, through a comprehensive social policy, through the promotion of physical education, school and popular sports, and tourism.

3. A social insurance system guarantees material security, free medical care, medicines, and other medical facilities in case of illness and accident.

ART. 36  1. All G.D.R. citizens are entitled to the care of the state in old age and disability.

2. This right will be safeguarded through increased material, social, and cultural provisions as well as through provisions for old and disabled citizens.

ART. 37  1. According to prevailing economic and local conditions, every citizen of the G.D.R. has the right to a home for himself and his family. The state is obligated to provide for the implementation of this right by building new housing, by maintaining existing housing, and by controlling the just distribution of housing.

2. The citizen is legally protected against eviction.

3. The inviolability of the citizen's home is guaranteed.

ART. 38  1. Marriage, family, and motherhood are under the special protection of the state. Every G.D.R. citizen has the right to see his marriage and family respected, protected, and promoted.

2. This right is safeguarded by the equality of men and women in marriage and family relations and by the support of state and society of the stability and development of marriage and family. Special state measures provide for the care and support of families with many children and of unmarried mothers and fathers.

3. Mother and child enjoy the special protection of the socialist state. Leave for expecting mothers, special medical care, material and financial support at birth, and child support are granted.

4. It is the right and absolute responsibility of the parents to educate their children so that they may become healthy and happy, efficient and generally educated, and dedicated citizens. Parents are entitled to collaborate closely with the educational institutions of the state and society.

ART. 39  1. Every G.D.R. citizen has the right to profess and practice his religion.

2. Churches and other religious associations regulate their affairs and exercise their activities in accordance with the constitution and other legal provisions of the G.D.R. Details shall be regulated by special arrangements

ART. 40  G.D.R. citizens of Sorbic origin have the right to cultivate their language and culture. The state will promote the implementation of this right.

### Chapter 2: Enterprises, Cities, and Communities in the Socialist Society

ART. 41   Socialist enterprises, cities, communities, and community associations, in which the citizens participate as a self-governing body and work and form their social relations, exist within the framework of central state planning and management. These organs ensure the basic rights of the citizens, the effective link between personal and social interests, as well as a many faceted social-political and cultural-intellectual life. They are protected by this constitution. Interference with their rights is only allowed by law.

ART. 42   1. The working people cooperate directly and through their elected organs in the management of the enterprise, whose activities are the basis for creating and multiplying the social wealth.

2. State organs, enterprises, and agricultural cooperatives can develop their own associations and other forms of cooperation to enhance social productivity.

ART. 43   1. In cooperation with the enterprises and cooperatives of their area, the cities, communities, and community associations of the G.D.R. establish the necessary conditions for the growing satisfaction of the material, social, cultural, and other needs of the citizens. Every citizen takes part in this process by exercising his political rights.

2. The responsibility for realizing the social function of the cities and communities rests with the popularly elected representatives of the citizens. They make their own decisions on the basis of the law. They are also responsible for using that part of the citizens' property over which they have control in the most rational way.

### Chapter 3: Trade Unions and Their Rights

ART. 44   1. The free trade unions are united in the German Free Trade Union Association [*Freier Deutscher Gewerkschaftsbund*] and represent broadest class organization of the working people. They protect the interests of the workers, of the employees, and of the intelligentsia through their active participation in the affairs of the state and of the economy.

2. Trade unions are independent. No one is allowed to restrict or hinder their activities.

3. Through their organizations and organs, through their representatives in the popularly elected representative bodies of the people, and through their political and economic proposals, the trade unions take a decisive part in shaping the socialist order, in planning and managing the people's economy, in realizing the scientific-technological revolution, in developing working and living conditions, the protection of health, work, and popular culture [*Arbeitskultur*], as well as the cultural and sports life of the working people. The trade unions participate in the preparation of plans in enterprises and organizations and thus are represented in the social councils of the associations of popularly owned enterprises [*Volkseigene Betriebe*], as well as in the production committees and in other enterprises and combines [*Kombinate*]. They organize the permanent advisory councils on production [*Ständige Produktionsberatung*].

ART. 45   1. The trade unions have the right to conclude agreements on working and living conditions with the state organs, with the management of industrial and agricultural enterprises, and with other economic management bodies.

2. The unions take an active part in shaping the socialist legal order. They have the right to initiate legislation, and they have social control over the constitutionally guaranteed rights of the working people.

3. The trade unions administer the social insurance system of workers and employees, paying full respect to the principle of the insured. They participate actively in the determination of material and financial care for the citizens in case of sickness, accident, disability, and old age.

4. All state organs and managers are responsible for the establishment of close and confident relations with the trade unions.

### Chapter 4: Socialist Production Cooperatives and Their Rights

ART. 46   1. The agricultural cooperatives [*Landwirtschaftliche Produktionsgenossenschaften*] are the voluntary farmers' associations created to promote the material and cultural needs of the farmers and all other people. The cooperatives are responsible, on the basis of law, for determining the working and living conditions of the farmers.

2. The agricultural cooperatives participate actively in state planning and in the management of social development through their organizations and representatives in the state organs.

3. The state assists the agricultural cooperatives in developing large-scale socialist production using advanced knowledge in science and technology.

4. The same principles apply to the cooperatives of fishermen, gardeners, and craftsmen.

PART III: STRUCTURE AND SYSTEM OF STATE CONTROL

ART. 47   1. The structure and functions of the state organs are determined by the objectives and responsibilities of the state laid down in this constitution.

2. The sovereignty of the working people, realized on the basis of democratic centralism, is the sustaining principle of the government.

### Chapter 1: The People's Chamber

ART. 48   1. The People's Chamber [*Volkskammer*] is the highest state organ of the G.D.R. The plenary sessions of the People's Chamber decide on the basic questions of state policy.

2. The People's Chamber is the only organ in the G.D.R. that can authorize the state's constitution and laws. Its rights cannot be restricted. The People's Chamber is guided in its activities by the basic principle of unity of decision and execution.

ART. 49   1. The People's Chamber determines the goals of the development of the G.D.R. through binding laws and resolutions.

2. The People's Chamber determines the principal rules for the cooperation of citizens, communities, and state organs and states their functions in the execution of the social development plans of the state.

3. The People's Chamber ensures the realization of its laws and resolutions. It determines the activities of the Council of State, of the Council of Ministers, of the Council of National Defense, of the Supreme Court, and of the prosecutor-general.

ART. 50    The People's Chamber elects the chairman and the members of the Council of State, the chairman and the members of the Council of Ministers, the chairman of the National Defense Council, the president and the judges of the Supreme Court, and the prosecutor-general. They can be recalled by the People's Chamber at any time.

ART. 51    The People's Chamber ratifies the treaties of the G.D.R. and other international agreements if these treaties change the laws of the People's Chamber. The People's Chamber decides on the termination of these treaties.

ART. 52    The People's Chamber decides on the defense mobilization of the G.D.R. In case of emergency, the Council of State is authorized to decide on defense mobilization. The chairman of the Council of State proclaims the defense mobilization.

ART. 53    The People's Chamber can decide to hold referenda.

ART. 54    The People's Chamber consists of five hundred deputies. Deputies are elected by the people in free, universal, equal, and secret elections for a term of four years.

ART. 55    1. The People's Chamber elects a presidium for the duration of its legislative term. The presidium consists of the president of the People's Chamber, a deputy president, and other members.

2. The presidium directs the plenary meetings of the People's Chamber. Other business of the People's Chamber is regulated by standing orders.

ART. 56    1. The deputies of the People's Chamber fulfill their responsibilities in the interest and for the welfare of the entire people.

2. The deputies promote the participation of the citizens in the preparation and realization of the laws in cooperation with the committees of the National Front of the G.D.R., with the social organizations, and with the state organs.

3. The deputies are in close contact with their voters. It is their duty to consider the proposals, suggestions, and the criticism of their voters and to deal with them conscientiously.

ART. 57    1. The deputies of the People's Chamber must hold regular hours for consultation and discussion and must report about their activities to the voters.

2. A deputy who flagrantly misuses his office can be recalled by the voters in accordance with legal procedures.

ART. 58    The deputies of the People's Chamber may attend the local meetings of popularly elected representative bodies as advisers.

ART. 59    Each deputy of the People's Chamber has the right to direct questions to the Council of Ministers and to each of its members.

ART. 60   1. It is the duty of all state and economic organs to support the deputies in the performance of their duties.

2. The deputies of the People's Chamber enjoy immunity. Restriction of a deputy's personal freedom, house search, seizure, or criminal prosecution are only allowed with the consent of the People's Chamber or of the Council of State if the People's Chamber is not in session. A decision of the Council of State requires confirmation by the People's Chamber. A member of the People's Chamber can refuse to testify about a person, if this person has confided facts to him in his capacity as deputy or if the deputy has entrusted facts to this person in his capacity as deputy; the deputy can also refuse to give evidence on the facts themselves.

3. The deputies may not suffer any professional or other personal disadvantage as a result of their deputy status. They are released from their professional activities if their work as deputies so requires. Salaries and wages must be continued.

ART. 61   1. The People's Chamber establishes its own committees. The committees must discuss proposed legislation with the voters and supervise the execution of law.

2. The committees may request the presence, for the purpose of obtaining information, of ministers and leaders of other state organs. It is the duty of all state organs to provide the committees the necessary information.

3. All committees have the right to request the permanent or temporary assistance of experts.

ART. 62   1. The People's Chamber convenes not later than thirty days after its establishment. Its first meeting is called by the Council of State.

2. The sessions of the People's Chamber are open to the public. The public may be excluded if two-thirds of the deputies present so request.

ART. 63   1. A quorum exists if more than half of the deputies are present.

2. Resolutions of the People's Chamber are adopted by a majority vote. Laws changing the constitution are adopted with at least a two-thirds majority vote of the deputies.

ART. 64   1. Before the conclusion of a legislative term, the People's Chamber may be dissolved only by its own resolution.

2. The consent of more than two-thirds of the deputies is needed for such a resolution.

3. A new People's Chamber must be elected not later than sixty days after the conclusion of the legislative term or forty-five days after the dissolution of the People's Chamber.

ART. 65   1. Deputies of the People's Chamber who represent parties and mass organizations, committees of the People's Chamber, the Council of Ministers, and the free trade unions have the right to introduce bills.

2. The Council of State, which prepares the sessions of the People's Chamber, deals with such bills and examines their constitutionality.

3. The committees of the People's Chamber deliberate the bills and present their views to the plenary session of the People's Chamber. The Council of State supports the activities of the People's Chamber.

4. Drafts of basic laws are presented to the people before they are passed.

The results of the discussion by the people are taken into consideration in the final draft.

5. The chairman of the Council of State promulgates the laws of the People's Chamber in the *Law Gazette* within a month.

6. If not otherwise stated, laws enter into force fourteen days after their promulgation.

### Chapter 2: The Council of State

ART. 66   As an organ of the People's Chamber, the Council of State [*Staatsrat*] fulfills all basic duties arising from the laws and resolutions of the People's Chamber. The Council of State is responsible for its activity to the People's Chamber.

2. The chairman of the Council of State represents the People's Chamber in international relations. The Council of State decides on the conclusion of the treaties of the G.D.R. The chairman of the Council of State ratifies them, and the Council of State terminates them.

ART. 67   1. The Council of State consists of the chairman, his deputies, its members, and its secretary.

2. The chairman, the deputy-chairman, the members, and the secretary of the Council of State are elected by the People's Chamber at the first meeting of each four-year legislative term of the People's Chamber.

3. After the expiration of the legislative term of the People's Chamber, the Council of State continues its activities until the People's Chamber has elected a new Council of State.

ART. 68   On assuming office, the chairman, the deputy-chairman, the members, and the secretary of the Council of State take the following oath before the People's Chamber: "I swear that I shall dedicate my strength to the welfare of the people of the German Democratic Republic, defend its constitution and laws, discharge my duties conscientiously, and do justice to all."

ART. 69   The chairman directs the work of the Council of State.

ART. 70   1. The Council of State handles the bills to be submitted to the People's Chamber and initiates their deliberation in the committees of the People's Chamber.

2. The Council of State convenes the sessions of the People's Chamber on the decision of the People's Chamber or on its own initiative.

3. It is the duty of the Council of State to convene the People's Chamber at any time if at least one-third of the deputies so requests.

ART. 71   1. The Council of State regulates the basic functions that arise from the laws and resolutions of the People's Chamber by decrees. They are submitted to the People's Chamber for endorsement.

2. The decrees and resolutions of the Council of State are legally binding.

3. The interpretations of the constitution and of the laws by the Council of State are binding insofar as such interpretation has not been provided by the People's Chamber.

ART. 72   The Council of State announces the elections of the People's Chamber and of other popularly elected representative organs.

ART. 73  1. The Council of State makes the fundamental decisions that are related to the defense and security of the country. It organizes the defense of the country in cooperation with the National Defense Council.

2. The Council of State appoints the members of the National Defense Council. The National Defense Council is responsible to the People's Chamber and to the Council of State.

ART. 74  The Council of State ensures the permanent supervision of the constitutionality and legality of the work of the Supreme Court and of the prosecutor-general on behalf of the People's Chamber.

ART. 75  1. The chairman of the Council of State appoints the diplomatic representatives of the G.D.R. to other states and recalls them. He receives the credentials and letters of recall of accredited foreign representatives.

2. The Council of State determines military service ranks, diplomatic ranks, and other special titles.

ART. 76  The Council of State creates state orders, awards, and titles of honor, which are conferred by its chairman.

ART. 77  The Council of State exercises the right of amnesty and pardon.

### Chapter 3: The Council of Ministers
ART. 78  1. On behalf of the People's Chamber, the Council of Ministers [*Ministerrat*] organizes the implementation of the political, economic, cultural, social, and those defense tasks of the socialist state with which it has been charged. It is a collectively working state organ.

2. The Council of Ministers formulates scientific forecasts, organizes the construction of the socialist economic system, and directs the planned development of the economy.

ART. 79  1. The Council of Ministers functions on the basis of the laws and resolutions of the People's Chamber and also of the decrees and decisions of the Council of State.

2. The Council of Ministers directs, coordinates, and supervises the activities of the ministries, of the other central state organs, and of the district council in accordance with the findings of organizational expertise [*Organisationswissenschaft*].

3. The Council of Ministers decides on treaties concluded in its name and on their abrogation.

ART. 80  1. The chairman of the Council of State proposes the chairman of the Council of Ministers to the People's Chamber; the People's Chamber authorizes him to form the Council of Ministers.

2. The People's Chamber elects the chairman and the members of the Council of Ministers for the duration of four years.

3. The chairman and the members of the Council of Ministers take the oath on the constitution before the chairman of the Council of State.

4. The Council of Ministers consists of the chairman, the deputy-chairman, and the ministers. The chairman directs the business of the Council of Ministers.

5. The Council of Ministers constitutes its presidium from among its

members; the chairman of the Council of Ministers presides over the presidium.

6. Every minister is directly responsible for his ministry. All ministers are collectively responsible for the business of the Council of Ministers.

7. The Council of Ministers is responsible and accountable to the People's Chamber.

8. After termination of the legislative term, the Council of Ministers continues its business until the new Council of Ministers has been elected by the People's Chamber.

### Chapter 4: The Local Representations of the People and Their Organs

ART. 81   1. The local representations of the people consist of state organs that have been elected by eligible voters in the districts, counties, cities, city districts, communities, and community associations.

2. The local representations of the people decide independently on all matters concerned with their area and its citizens on the basis of the law. They organize the citizens' participation in the formation of the political, economic, cultural, and social life and cooperate with the social organizations of the working people.

3. The activities of the local representations of the people are directed toward enlarging and protecting socialist property, toward improving working and living conditions of the citizens, toward promoting the social and cultural life of the citizens and of their associations, toward elevating the awareness of socialist state authority and justice, toward securing the public order, and toward guaranteeing the rights of the citizens.

ART. 82   1. The local representations of the people pass resolutions that are binding for their organs and institutions as well as for the people, for the representations of the people, and for their associations. The resolutions must be published.

2. The local representations of the people have their own revenues and are authorized to use them at their own discretion.

ART. 83   1. Every local representation of the people elects its council and commissions to carry out its duties. The members of the council should preferably be deputies. But also members who are not deputies can be appointed to the commissions.

2. The council ensures that the activities of the representation of the people develop and that the management of social development in the area under its jurisdiction is organized. The council is responsible to the representation of the people for all activities, and it is accountable to the respective superior council. The council is a collectively working organ.

3. The commissions organize the competent cooperation of the citizens in the preparation and execution of the resolutions of the people's representation. The commissions supervise the execution of laws, decrees, ordinances, and resolutions of the people's representation through the council and its specialist groups.

ART. 84   The local representations of the people can form associations for the implementation of their responsibilities.

ART. 85   The duties and powers of the local representations of the people, of their deputies, and of their commissions as well as of their councils in the districts, counties, cities, city districts, communities, and community associations will be determined by law.

PART IV: SOCIALIST LEGALITY AND THE ADMINISTRATION OF JUSTICE

ART. 86   The socialist society, the political power of the working people, and their state and legal system are the basic guarantees for observing and implementing the constitution in the spirit of justice, equality, brotherhood, and humanity.

ART. 87   State and society guarantee legality by including citizens and their associations into the administration of justice and by employing social and state control for the observation of socialist law.

ART. 88   A system of accountability assures the citizens of the sense of duty of all leading officials of the state and of the economy.

ART. 89   1. Laws and other generally binding legal regulations of the G.D.R. are published in the *Law Gazette* [*Gesetzblatt*] and elsewhere.

2. Legal regulations of the local representations of the people and their organs are published in suitable form.

3. Legal ordinances cannot contradict constitutional provisions. In cases of doubt, the Council of State decides on the constitutionality of the legal ordinances of the Council of Ministers.

ART. 90   1. The administration of justice aims at the realization of socialist legality, at the protection and development of the G.D.R., its state and social order. It protects freedom as well as the peaceful existence and the rights and dignity of man.

2. To combat and prevent crimes and other offenses is the common concern of the socialist society, of the state, and of all citizens.

3. The participation of the citizens in the administration of justice is ensured. Details will be regulated by law.

ART. 91   The generally recognized norms of international law for the punishment of crimes against peace and humanity as well as war crimes are also binding in the G.D.R. The statute of limitation cannot be applied in this case.

ART. 92   Justice is administered in the G.D.R. by the Supreme Court, by district courts, county courts, and social courts, each within its own field of legal competence. Military crimes are adjudicated by the Supreme Court, the higher military courts, and the military courts.

ART. 93   1. The Supreme Court is the highest judicial organ.

2. The Supreme Court directs the judicial business of the courts on the basis of the constitution, of laws, and of other legal provisions of the G.D.R. It ensures the uniform application of justice by all courts.

3. The Supreme Court is responsible to the People's Chamber and, between sessions of the People's Chamber, to the Council of State.

ART. 94   1. Only those persons can become judges who are loyal to the people and its socialist state and possess a high degree of knowledge, wisdom, maturity, and stability of character.

2. The democratic election of all judges, lay judges, and members of the social courts guarantees that justice is exercised by women and men of all classes and of all population sections.

ART. 95　All judges, lay judges, and members of the social courts are elected by popularly elected representative bodies or directly by the citizens. They report to the voters who can dismiss them, if they have violated the constitution or the laws or have grossly misused their office otherwise.

ART. 96　1. Judges, lay judges, and members of the social courts act independently. They are bound only by the constitution, by the laws, and by other legal provisions of the G.D.R.

2. Lay judges and professional judges perform the same functions and have equal votes.

ART. 97　1. The supervisory authority of the prosecutor-general ensures the observance of socialist justice in the socialist society and state as well as the rights of its citizens on the basis of existing laws and other legal regulations.

2. The prosecutor-general directs the fight against crime and ensures that persons who have committed a crime or a misdemeanor stand trial.

ART. 98　1. The prosecutor-general directs the prosecutor's office.

2. The district and county prosecutors as well as the military prosecutors are under the jurisdiction of the prosecutor-general.

3. Prosecutors are appointed and dismissed by the prosecutor-general. They are responsible to him and bound by his instructions.

4. The prosecutor-general is accountable to the People's Chamber and, between sessions of the People's Chamber, to the Council of State.

ART. 99　1. The laws of the G.D.R. determine criminal responsibility.

2. An act can be punished only if it was a legally punishable offense at the time the act was committed, if the offender's act involved guilt, and if his guilt has been proved beyond doubt. Penal law is not retroactive.

3. Criminal prosecution is only possible in accordance with criminal laws.

4. During criminal procedure, the rights of the citizen can be restricted only insofar as this is legally permitted and absolutely necessary.

ART. 100　1. Only the judge can decide whether pre-trial detention is justified. Arrested persons must be brought before the judge at the latest on the day following their arrest.

2. The judge or the prosecutor-general must examine at any time whether continued detention is justified.

3. The prosecutor-general must inform close relatives of the arrested person within twenty-four hours after the first judicial examination.

ART. 101　1. No one may be removed from the jurisdiction of his judge.

2. Extraordinary courts are not allowed.

ART. 102　1. Every citizen has the right to be heard before a court.

2. The right of defense is ensured during the entire prosecution.

ART. 103　1. Every citizen can submit presentations (proposals, suggestions, requests, or complaints) to the representative bodies of the people, to its deputies, or to the state and economic organs. The same right exists with regard to social organizations and associations. No disadvantage shall arise from making use of this right.

2. The organs responsible for the decision are obliged to consider the presentations of citizens or associations within the time limits set by law and to inform the proposer of the result.

ART. 104   1. The Council of Ministers deals with complaints against the decisions of the central organs of the Council of Ministers.

2. The Council of State deals with complaints against the decisions of the Council of Ministers, the Supreme Court, or the prosecutor-general.

ART. 105   1. As regards complaints against the decisions of the local state organs, the chairman of the organ concerned deals with the complaint. If the chairman does not alter the decision, the complainant can appeal to the complaint committee of the appropriate people's organization.

2. The rights and duties of the complaint committees are regulated by decree.

ART. 106   1. The state organ is responsible for the damages an official of this organ inflicted upon a citizen or his personal property through unlawful measures.

2. Prerequisites and procedures for liability by the state are regulated by law.

#### PART V: CONCLUDING PROVISIONS

ART. 107   This constitution has the direct force of law.

ART. 108   This constitution can be amended only by the People's Chamber of the G.D.R. and only by a law that expressly amends or supplements its wording.

#### 21. G.D.R., PEOPLE'S CHAMBER ELECTION LAW, SEPTEMBER 24, 1958

ART. 1   1. Members of the People's Chamber shall be elected for terms of four years in general, equal, direct, and secret elections on the basis of proportional representation.

2. Every man or woman of German citizenship who has reached the age of eighteen on election day and resides in the territory of the G.D.R. shall be eligible to vote. . . .

ART. 6   1. Four hundred members shall be elected to the People's Chamber.

2. The capital of the G.D.R., Berlin, shall be entitled to sixty-six representatives in the People's Chamber. . . .

FROM *GB*, I (1958), pp. 677–830. Another election law was promulgated on July 31, 1963; see *GB*, I (1963), pp. 97–99.

ART. 8　1. Members shall be elected to the People's Chamber from election districts

2. The number of members to be elected from an election district shall depend on the size of its population. As a rule, ten to twenty members of the People's Chamber shall be elected from a single election district. . . .

ART. 29　. . . 2. Democratic parties and mass organizations that aim at the democratic formation [*Gestaltung*] of government and social life of the entire republic and whose organization comprises the entire territory of the state shall be entitled to make nominations for elections to the People's Chamber. They shall have the right to combine their nominations in a joint nomination of the National Front. . . .

ART. 49　1. The voters shall have the right to petition for the recall of a member of the People's Chamber in voter meetings that have been properly convened by the appropriate committees of the National Front of democratic Germany.

2. In such cases the People's Chamber shall rule on continued membership in accordance with article 59 of the constitution.

## 22. G.D.R., SED STATUTE ADOPTED AT THE SIXTH PARTY CONGRESS, EAST BERLIN, JANUARY 15–21, 1963

The SED is the conscious and organized vanguard of the German working class and of the working people. It combines in its ranks the progressive members of the working class, of the cooperative farmers, and of the intelligentsia. . . .

To be a member of the SED is a great honor. Membership in the SED imposes high obligations. Every working person who recognizes the program and the statute of the Party, who actively participates in building socialism, who is active in an organization of the Party, who submits himself to the decisions of the Party, who carries them out, and who pays the fixed dues regularly can be a member of the SED. . . .

It is not sufficient for a Party member to only agree with the decisions of the Party. The Party member is obliged to struggle for the realization of these decisions. He must participate in the life of the Party and must attend Party meetings regularly. . . . The Party member is obliged to perform his work in the organs of the state and of the economy as well as in mass organizations according to the decisions of the Party and in the interest of the working people. He is obliged to preserve the discipline of the Party and of the state, which is equally binding for all Party members. He who violates the discipline of the Party and of the state must be held responsible regardless of his merits and of the position he occupies. . . .

The Party member has the following rights:

1. in Party organizations, in Party meetings, and in the Party press, to participate in the discussion of all problems of Party policy and in the

FROM *Neues Deutschland* (January 26, 1963).

practical work of the Party, and to make suggestions and express his opinion openly, until the organization has taken a resolution

2. in Party meetings, in Party conferences, in Party congresses, as well as in plenary sessions of the leading Party organs, to criticize the activity of the Party members and functionaries regardless of their position. Party members who suppress criticism or consciously tolerate the suppression of criticism must be called to account

3. to participate in the election of Party organs and to stand for election

4. to request to be present if, in Party organizations, his attitude and activity are discussed or if a resolution is passed concerning his person

5. to submit every problem to a higher organ of the Party, if necessary to the central committee, and to request an answer to his petition that thoroughly deals with the nature of the subject. Only individuals are admitted as Party members; each person's admission is decided separately. Politically conscious and active workers, cooperative farmers, members of the intelligentsia, employees, and other workers who are faithfully devoted to the Party and to socialism are admitted as Party members at the end of their candidacy.

The following regulations hold for the admission of a candidate as a Party member. The candidate whose candidacy has expired and who wishes to become a Party member submits to his primary Party organization an application for admission accompanied by recommendations from two Party members. The recommendations must be given by Party members of at least two years' standing, who must have known the candidate for one year as a colleague or as a friend. . . . If a member of the Free German Youth organization [*Freie Deutsche Jugend*] applies for membership in the Party, the recommendation of the district leaders of the Free German Youth Organization is equivalent to the recommendation of a Party member.

Admission to the Party takes place at a meeting of the members of the primary Party organization. If the Party decides favorably, admission becomes effective after confirmation by the district leaders. . . . Party members or candidate-members who do not have the will or the strength to fulfill their duties as Party members can be dropped as members or as candidates by a resolution of a membership meeting of the primary Party organization; the resolution must be confirmed by the district leader. He who offends the unity and purity of the Party, who does not fulfill its resolutions, who does not respect democracy within the Party, who violates Party discipline, or who abuses his membership and the functions entrusted to him, who proves himself in public and private life unworthy of Party membership must justify his actions before the primary Party organization or before a higher Party organ.

According to the type of violation, the following Party punishments can be decided upon: (1) reprimand, (2) severe reprimand, (3) demotion to candidate status for one year, (4) expulsion from the Party. . . . Expulsion from the Party is the most severe punishment. The decision to expel a member from the Party must be made with extreme care, and a thorough investigation of the accusations against the Party member must be allowed. Expulsion from the Party is valid only if at least two-thirds of the Party members present at the meeting vote for it and if this resolution is confirmed by the district and regional leaders. . . . A member against whom legal Party proceedings are *sub judice* must be invited to the meeting by the Party membership. The member concerned has the right to participate in all stages of the primary Party organization's discussion of his case, and he has the right to express his opinion personally on the accusations made against him. Expulsion from the Party or any other punishment by the Party must be communicated orally to the member and must include a statement of reasons; the member must acknowledge receipt of the statement with his signature. . . .

Punishment or expulsion of members or candidate-members of the central committee is decided by the Party congress; during the period between Party congresses, a two-thirds majority of the central committee decides. An expelled member of the central committee must be replaced by a candidate-member. . . . The member or candidate-member can protest to the central committee against the resolution to punish him and against the confirmation of this resolution by the district leaders. . . . The district leaders must deal with this protest within four weeks, and the central committee must consider the protest within six weeks. . . . An expelled member or candidate can apply for readmission to the Party after a specified probationary period. . . .

A period of candidacy is set for admission to the Party so that the candidates can, during this period, become thoroughly acquainted with the program and the statute of the Party. . . . The period of candidacy is limited to one year. . . . The candidate must apply for membership immediately after the termination of his period of candidacy and must request that the primary Party organization give his application prompt consideration. . . .

The Party organization is based on the principle of democratic centralism: (1) all Party organs are elected democratically; (2) the elected Party organs must give regular reports about their activities to the organizations that elected them; (3) the resolutions of the higher Party organs are binding; strict Party discipline must be exercised, and the minority as well as the individual must submit to the resolutions of the Party majority. The highest principle of the Party is collectivity. All Party leaders must collectively discuss and decide the problems, tasks, and plans of the Party. . . .

The highest Party organs are: (1) the meeting of the members for the primary Party organization; (2) the conference of the delegates for the Party organizations in large enterprises and administrations as well as in towns, districts, cities, and regions; (3) the Party congress for the whole Party. The meetings of the Party members and the conferences of the delegates elect the Party leaders. The Party congress elects the Party's central committee. All are executive organs concerned with the daily work of the Party. Elections for the highest Party organs are held by secret ballot. Every proposed candidate is discussed and voted on individually. Every member and candidate-member has the unrestricted right to put questions to the nominated candidates, to raise objections against them, and to make new proposals. The candidate who receives a simple majority vote of the Party meeting, Party conference, or Party congress is elected. . . . Democracy within the Party guarantees to every Party member and candidate the right to express his opinion freely and objectively. . . . The highest Party organ is the Party congress. Ordinary Party congresses are, as a rule, held every four years. The central committee can convene extraordinary Party congresses upon two months' notice, either on its own initiative or on the request of more than one-third of the Party members. . . .

The Party congress accepts and judges statements of accounts of the central committee, the inspection committee, and other central organs; determines the program and the statute of the Party as well as the general outline and strategy of the Party; elects the central committee according to the number of members and candidates determined by the Party Congress. . . .

The central committee implements the resolutions of the Party congress; it supervises the Party's activities and represents the Party in its relations with other parties and organizations. The central committee appoints the Party's representatives to the highest organs of the state and of the economy, and it confirms the Party's candidates for the People's Chamber. The central committee directs the activities of the elected central organs and organizations of the state and of the society through Party groups organized in them. At least every six months, the central committee holds a plenary session. The candidates of the central committee participate in the plenary session in an advisory capacity. . . .

The central committee elects the Poliburo to direct the political work of the central committee in the period between plenary sessions; it elects the secretariat to direct its administrative work and, in particular, to organize the implementation of the Party resolutions; it also selects the administrative staff of the Party. Furthermore, the committee confirms the department heads of the central committee. The central committee appoints the members of the central commission for Party control. . . .

The central committee directs and controls the Party units; it distributes Party materials and administers the Party's treasury. The central committee informs the Party organization regularly of its activities. The central committee appoints the editorial boards of the organs under its control. The central committee has the right to convene Party conferences between Party congresses.

The regional and city Party organizations as well as the rural, urban, and industrial district Party organizations are guided in their work by the Party's program and statute; they are responsible for the implementation of the resolutions and directives of the central committee in their area. The highest organ of a regional, city, or district organization is the conference of Party delegates; in the period between conferences, the regional, city, or district leadership is the highest authority. The ordinary conference of the Party delegates in a region, city, or district is convened at least once every two years by the competent Party organ. . . . The regional, city, and district leaders elect the secretaries of their units and establish secretariats according to the instructions of the central committee. . . . In the period between plenary sessions, the secretariat directs the political work of the Party unit. The regional secretaries must be Party members of at least five years' standing. The district secretaries must be Party members of at least three years' standing. . . .

The primary Party organizations are the foundation of the Party. They exist in factories, agricultural cooperatives, machine-tractor stations, repair and technical survey stations, craftsmen's cooperatives, and state-owned farms, in units of the German people's police and of the people's army, in the administrative bodies of the state and of the economy, in research institutes, and in educational institutions. . . . At least three Party members are needed to form the organizations. The highest organ of the primary Party organization is the meeting of the members, which must be convened at least once every month. . . . Daily work is carried out by leaders of the primary Party organization elected for terms of one year. . . .

The Free German Youth organization is the reserve organization of the Party. It assists the Party in educating the young in the spirit of and for active participation in socialism as well as for the defense of their socialist fatherland. . . .

Party groups are organized at all congresses and meetings as well as in elected organs of the state and of mass organizations with at least three Party members. It is the duty of these Party groups to strengthen the Party's influence, to represent its policy among non-Party people, to support the discipline of the Party and of the state, to fight against bureaucracy, and to control the implementation of the Party and government directives.

Membership dues, revenues from Party enterprises and activities, as well as from other sources, constitute the financial resources of the Party. The monthly membership dues of Party members and candidate-members are determined as a percentage of the member's total income. . . .

## 23. G.D.R., SED Program Adopted by the Sixth Party Congress, East Berlin, January 15–21, 1963

A new era in the history of the German people has begun: the era of socialism. It is the era of peace and social security, of human dignity and brotherhood, of freedom and justice, humanity and enjoyment of life. The old exploitation of man by man, which lasted for centuries, is abolished. The people, creator of all values, now shape their own destiny, that is, the fate of the nation. The principle of the new society is: with the people, by the people, for the people.

Socialism means that the most progressive class of society, the working class, has taken power in its strong hands, guided in this effort by its Marxist-Leninist party alliance with the working farmers and with other working groups of society. Capitalists and landowners have lost their power

From *Neues Deutschland* (January 25, 1963).

forever. The power of the state, which is essentially a democratic power, is exercised by the working class in alliance with the farmers and with other working people in the interest and for the welfare of the whole people. This alliance, which expresses the firm friendship of all working people, is the foundation of the power of the German workers and farmers. All organization of power in the state, such as the administration of justice, the army, the people's police, and so forth, serve the interests of workers and farmers as well as of the working nation as a whole. Socialism means that all wealth, all important means of production, factories, works, and railroads, all mineral wealth, fields, water, and forests belong to the people who make them available, work them and continuously increase and create new wealth. They no longer belong to capitalist exploiters or feudal landowners. The work of millions of industrious members of our gifted nation no longer helps a handful of capitalists and *Junkers*. Instead, it increases the wealth of the whole society and satisfies its needs as well as the needs of all working people. The causes of economic crises and unemployment have been abolished forever. The anarchism of the capitalist economy has been replaced by the planned guidance and development of the socialist economy, observing the highest standards of science and technology.

Socialism means to strive for high productivity. It means to achieve and participate in the determination of the world's production standard. It requires the application of advanced science and technology, the mastery of the most modern production methods as well as the expert guidance and organization of the economy. It is the basis for a continuous and planned improvement of the nation's living conditions.

The conquest of power by the working classes, the development of capitalist exploitation, and the establishment of the power of workers and farmers have cleared the way for this struggle. Now the improvement of living conditions depends on the performance of the workers and, more particularly, on the continuous increase of productivity. Socialism recognizes and respects the individual's performance. From each according to his abilities and to each according to his performance is the principle of socialism.

Socialism means freedom from exploitation and from fear of the future; it means equal development opportunities for all. Education is no longer the monopoly of the capitalist classes. All cultural, scientific, and technological achievements are at the disposal of the working people. Everybody has a chance to develop his abilities, to obtain an education, and to develop his personality. Men and women, as all citizens, are equal, regardless of their philosophy [*Weltanschauung*], religion, race, nationality, and social status.

Socialism means that relations among men are characterized by friendly cooperation and mutual help. Through socialism, the union of all free people, united already by common, free, and creative work, begins to become real. The ideals of socialist morality (socialist patriotism and internationalism, conscious responsibility toward society, love for work and working people, and socialist work discipline) enables society and the individual to work for the welfare of the nation and for the peace of the world.

Socialism means that no class interested in the exploitation and suppression of its own or of other people or in war and conquest will be in power any longer. Socialism, therefore, is a secure foundation for the friendship of peoples and for their peaceful coexistence; socialism is peace. . . .

A new period in German history began with the destruction of Hitler's fascism by the Soviet Union and its allies in the anti-Hitler coalition. The German people had to face the imperative necessity of learning from the consequences of two world wars and a fascist regime. Under the leadership of the working class, the nation had the great opportunity to abolish German imperialism and militarism once and for all. The main objective was to end war and aggression forever, to lead Germany to the road of peace, democracy, and socialism, and to secure a policy of friendship, above all with the Soviet Union.

The foundation of the SED was the greatest achievement of the German working class since the Communist Manifesto, that is, since the beginning of the workers' revolutionary movement in Germany and since the founding of the German Communist Party in 1918. . . .

The objectives of the anti-fascist democratic revolution were fulfilled in the East. Protected by the Soviet army from an imperialistic military intervention, the working people were able to create the example for a peaceful and democratic revolution, to develop their strength, and to break reactionary resistance. The fascist state apparatus was destroyed and replaced by an anti-fascist democratic state power. Essentially, this power was a revolutionary democratic dictatorship of workers and farmers, in which the working class held the decisive positions. In the struggle to realize the anti-fascist democratic revolution, the basis for the development of a true democracy was created. The bourgeois democratic revolution was completed by a democratic land reform, the power of the *Junkers* and landowners was broken, and the land and soil were given back to those who tilled them. Thus, with the help of the working class and its revolutionary party, the injustice committed against farmers for centuries was redressed. The alliance of the working class with the working farmers received a firm foundation. The punishment of war criminals and Nazi activists as well as the expropriation of the property of those who profited from, and were interested in, the war broke the power of the capitalist monopoly. The people took over their industries and enterprises. Thus the state-owned production centers became the firm social and economic foundation of the anti-fascist democratic order. Democratic school reform abolished privileged education for the propertied class, and the foundation for a democratic education of youth was laid. . . .

THE FUNDAMENTAL TASKS OF THE ECONOMY

Decisive for the economic development of the G.D.R. are: (1) the chemical industry, in particular the petrochemical industry, because it is an increasingly important branch of industry; (2) the metallurgic industry, because it yields products that are decisive for technical progress in engineering and in other important branches of industry; (3) electrical engineering, in particular electronics and those branches of engineering that determine the rapid progress of mechanization and automation; (4) the development and construction of scientific instruments; (5) the rapid development of the power industry and transportation; (6) the further industrialization of agricultural production. . . .

The trade of the G.D.R. with the socialist countries will be developed more and more on the basis of coordinated economic planning. . . . Industrial production will double between 1960 and 1970, and there will be an increased use of G.D.R. raw materials and a further division of labor in the socialist camp. This increase will be achieved through scientific and technological progress, increased productivity, and expanded production.

### FURTHER DEVELOPMENT OF SOCIALIST AGRICULTURE

The socialist transformation of agriculture is a general law of the socialist revolution and corresponds to the essence of our time. After the completion of the socialist land reform, the suppression and exploitation of the farmers, which lasted for centuries, was terminated. . . . Through the development and employment of new technological discoveries, through the application of the most modern management methods, and through the organization of cooperatives and state farms, the further intensification and gradual transition to industrialized agricultural production is achieved. . . .

The task of reshaping the economy of the G.D.R. requires the full development of the creative activity of the working people through a uniform economic plan. The materialistic and moral incentives of work must complement each other. These incentives must be directed: (1) toward the encouragement of model performances in production, particularly when new techniques are introduced; (2) toward the application of new methods that have already been tested and proved; and (3) toward the further rationalization of manpower and machinery. These technological and scientific incentives shall be so employed as to make it financially rewarding for working people to perform creatively. . . .

The accomplishment of socialism requires the planned growth and development of science. In the second half of the twentieth century, the natural sciences and technology play a greater role than ever before in the history of mankind. Their field of application is continuously expanding. Freed from the claims of capitalist monopoly control, science can develop freely in a socialist society. Science becomes more and more an immediate force in production and permeates all technological processes. . . . In order to solve complex tasks by modern scientific methods, the coordination of technology, the natural sciences, and economics in particular becomes more and more important. It is necessary to direct research uniformly in order to eliminate uncoordinated investigations in important fields of research. This applies in particular to complex research problems of a scientific, technological, and economic nature. . . .

The prerequisite for recognizing objective truth in all fields of research is a comradely, open, and principled discussion of all disputed issues. This means that all dogmatic approaches to the solution of theoretical problems must be avoided or overcome with determination. Dogmatism favors revisionism, which conveys bourgeois ideology and will remain a permanent danger in Germany as long as the struggle between the two social systems continues. The Party, therefore, struggles against both distortions in order to create a systematic and consistent socialist ideology. . . .

The producers of manufactured consumer goods have the obligation to produce useful, durable, modern, and attractive goods. . . . The waste of great sums of money in the production of unnecessary goods and foods of poor quality is henceforth prohibited. . . . Trade must be modernized so as to assure the population of a sufficient supply of goods. The trading organs will see to it that industry produces high-quality goods. . . . As a consequence of a decreased birth rate during the fascist war, the number of workers will decrease further until 1970. Yet the number of pensioners will increase. This means that a decreasing number of working people will have to provide for an increasing number of people who are either no longer or not yet able to work. Under these conditions, the existing planned working hours are fully needed for production purposes. Whether working hours can be reduced further will depend on whether productivity can be increased beyond the planned goal and whether illness can be reduced. The minimum vacation time for workers is to be extended. Labor unions and government organs will help the workers restore their strength during their vacation and find recreation with their families in the beautiful areas of their home country and of fellow socialist countries. . . .

The Party will try to provide all workers with sufficient housing. The most serious housing problem in coming years will be housing shortage, which is one of the disastrous consequences of Hitler's criminal war and must be overcome. The construction of housing will therefore be continuously furthered according to the economic plans. . . .

It is the duty of the socialist state to supervise the full realization of socialism according to existing plans, to develop the conditions and forces of socialist production, to improve the materialistic and cultural living conditions for the people, to further the creative initiative of the workers, to strengthen socialist consciousness, and to protect the socialist system from hostile intrigues. . . . The SED considers it necessary that the state organs coordinate their strength and efforts to fulfill the economic, technical, and cultural objectives of the economic plan. . . .

The performance improvement of the representative bodies of the people promotes the participation of large groups of the people in the governing functions of the state. Improvements must be made in the electoral system, in the replacement of at least one-third of the representatives in every election, in the conscientious popular discussion of the principal problems of socialist development, national politics, and drafts of important bills and resolutions. . . .

The State Council safeguards the unanimity of the state's leaders on the basis of the laws and resolutions of the People's Chamber. . . .

The SED sets itself the task of improving and expanding the socialist legal norms that regulate man's social life. In particular, the legal norms that regulate the economic and organizational as well as the cultural and educational activities of the organs of the state and of the economy as well as the relations between them must be improved. The legal norms that contribute to the free development of the strength, abilities, and gifts of man must also be improved. New codes of civil, criminal, and family law must be written. . . . The rights and duties of the public prosecutors must be expanded so that strict observance of socialist laws is ensured. . . . Citizens who violate criminal laws will be taught to respect the law by penalties that do not deprive them of their freedom and by the influence of society on them.

Together with the Soviet Union and other socialist states, the national people's army makes an important contribution to the strength of the defense forces of the socialist camp. As long as imperialistic forces are engaged in an armaments race and remain opposed to the prohibition of nuclear weapons, to the dissolution of their aggressive military blocs, and to general disarmament, the military superiority of the socialist camp is indispensable for the maintenance of peace and for the protection of socialist development. Protection of the socialist German fatherland and service in the national people's army are the honorable national duty of every citizen of the G.D.R. . . .

The SED is concerned with the propagation of its doctrines and with the study of the classic works of Marxism-Leninism. It favors a close relationship between theory and practice as well as the creative use of these doctrines in the building of socialism. . . .

Job training will be combined with the creation of real and necessary social values. Practical instruction in school workshops and polytechnical instruction in factories are therefore organized systematically. The polytechnical high schools provide basic training in several related professions; students apply their theoretical knowledge in factories and agricultural cooperatives, using the most modern technological standards. At the end of his school training, the student can perfect his special training by becoming an apprentice in a factory or in a cooperative. . . . Special attention must be given to the steady improvement of mathematical-scientific training and to the perfect mastery of our native language as well as to the cultivation of foreign languages and, in particular, to the active use of Russian. . . .

The SED believes that socialist realism creates a new socialist spirit of life through profound ideas, a more fertile imagination, true innovation, and innumerable creative possibilities in the various forms, styles, and fields of art. The works that demonstrate the new essence of our society require artistic mastery based on the close relation between art and life. Socialist art is the art of the Party and of humanism and requires a determined fight against the militarist and clerical forms of art in imperialist West Germany, a fight against all influences of decadent art, which is an expression of the process of cultural decay of the capitalist society. . . .

The Party exists for the people; it serves the people. The Party members have the duty to explain the policy of the Party to the masses and, in turn, to learn from the masses. In fulfilling the economic, government, and cultural tasks of the Party, its members should be examples for all working people. The creative application of Lenin's norms to the activities of the Party is the fundamental prerequisite for the fulfillment of the new tasks. As a conscious and organized vanguard of the working class, our Party works according to the living principle of democratic centralism. It combines the principles of subordination of the minority to the majority, of elected centralized leadership in the whole Party, and of the implementation of the decisions of the central committee by all primary organizations in the fight against conservatism and dogmatic stagnation. The Party fights against the cult of the individual and against its consequences. . . .

## 24. G.D.R., CITIZENSHIP LAW, FEBRUARY 20, 1967

### 1. CITIZENSHIP OF THE G.D.R.

ART. 1   A citizen of the G.D.R. is anyone who: (1) was a German national at the time of the founding of the G.D.R., had his domicile or regular abode in the G.D.R., and has not lost his G.D.R. citizenship since then; (2) was a German national at the time of the founding of the G.D.R., had his domicile or regular abode outside the G.D.R., did not acquire citizenship of any other country afterwards, and is recorded as a citizen of the G.D.R. according to his own will through registration with a G.D.R. authority competent for such matters; (3) has acquired citizenship of the G.D.R. in accordance with valid regulations and has not lost it since then.

ART. 2   1. G.D.R. citizenship guarantees the citizens of the G.D.R. the protection of their constitutional rights and demands from them the fulfillment of their constitutional duties.

2. The G.D.R. grants its citizens protection and supports them in making use of their rights outside the G.D.R.

ART. 3   1. Citizens of the G.D.R. cannot assert any rights or duties arising from citizenship of another state toward the G.D.R., according to generally recognized international law.

2. A citizen of the G.D.R. who intends to acquire the citizenship of another state must have the approval of the competent state authorities of the G.D.R.

3. Regulations on questions of citizenship that have been concluded in agreements of the G.D.R. with other states are applicable.

FROM *Foreign Affairs Bulletin*, Vol 7 (March 15, 1967), pp. 62–63, published by the Press Department of the Ministry of Foreign Affairs of the G.D.R.

II. ACQUISITION AND LOSS OF CITIZENSHIP OF THE G.D.R.

## Acquisition

ART. 4   Citizenship of the G.D.R. is acquired by: (1) descent, (2) birth on G.D.R. territory, and (3) grant.

ART. 5   A child acquires G.D.R. citizenship with its birth if one or both parents are citizens of the G.D.R.

ART. 6   1. A child born on G.D.R. territory acquires G.D.R. citizenship if, by its birth, it has not acquired the citizenship of another country.

2. A child found on G.D.R. territory (foundling) is a citizen of the G.D.R. if citizenship of another country cannot be proved.

ART. 7   1. Citizenship of the G.D.R. can be granted to a citizen of another state or to a stateless person on his application if he proves worthy of being granted citizenship of the G.D.R. through his personal behavior and attitude toward the state and social system of the G.D.R. and if there are no urgent objections to the granting of citizenship.

2. The applicant for citizenship must, as a rule, have his domicile or regular abode in the G.D.R. . . . .

ART. 8   1. Minors acquire G.D.R. citizenship if their parents are granted citizenship of the G.D.R. and if the application for citizenship is also made in their name. This also applies when only one parent is granted citizenship of the G.D.R.

2. If the minor has completed his fourteenth year, his consent is required.

## Loss

ART. 9   Citizenship of the G.D.R. is lost by: (1) release, (2) revocation of the grant of citizenship, (3) dispossession.

ART. 10   1. With the consent of the competent G.D.R. authorities, a citizen can be released from G.D.R. citizenship on his application if he has or wants to have his domicile outside the G.D.R., if he is a citizen of another country or intends to become one, and if there are no urgent objections to the release from G.D.R. citizenship.

2. A certificate is issued stating that the person is released from G.D.R. citizenship.

ART. 11   1. If parents are released from G.D.R. citizenship, the release also applies to their minor children, provided the application was also made for them. If the application is made by one parent only, the other parent must be heard.

2. If the minor has completed his fourteenth year, his consent is required.

ART. 12   1. Citizenship of the G.D.R. can be revoked if: (1) the citizen has made false statements on the application or has concealed facts that would have excluded him from G.D.R. citizenship, (2) the citizen proves unworthy of G.D.R. citizenship through flagrant disregard of the obligations assumed when acquiring G.D.R. citizenship.

2. The revocation of citizenship can occur within a period of five years after citizenship of the G.D.R. has been granted.

ART. 13   Citizens having their domicile or abode outside the G.D.R. can be dispossessed of their G.D.R. citizenship if they have flagrantly violated the duties of citizenship.

ART. 14   Revocation or dispossession of citizenship applies only to persons against whom the revocation or dispossession was expressed.

III. COMPETENCE AND PROCEDURE

ART. 15   1. The Council of Ministers of the G.D.R. decides on the granting of and release from citizenship. . . .

IV. FINAL REGULATIONS

ART. 18   The Council of Ministers of the G.D.R. issues the necessary regulations for the implementation of this law.

ART. 19   1. This law comes into effect upon proclamation. . . .

25. DECLARATION OF THE GOVERNMENTS OF POLAND AND OF THE
G.D.R., DEMARCATION OF THE ODER-NEISSE BOUNDARY, WARSAW,
JUNE 6, 1950

The delegation of the provisional government of the G.D.R. and the government of the Republic of Poland have agreed to demarcate the peace and friendship border of the Oder and Lausitzer Neisse, which was laid down and exists inviolably between the two states. This agreement is based on the interest of the German and Polish people to develop further and to deepen good and neighborly relations as well as peace and friendship between them. The German and Polish people were motivated by their desire to strengthen peace and to invigorate the peace camp, led by the Soviet Union in its struggle against the plots of the imperialistic forces; furthermore, they were motivated by their desire to support the efforts of the G.D.R. to strengthen the new democratic order and the development of all forces gathering around the National Front of democratic Germany.

FROM *Documents of the G.D.R.*, No. 8 (1950). For agreements between the G.D.R. and Poland, Hungary, and Czechoslovakia, see *Europa Archiv*, V (July 20, 1950), p. 3215; for parliamentary discussion in the Bundestag, see 68th Plenary Session (June 13, 1950).

26. G.D.R., JUDICIARY ORDINANCE, 1963

1. The Supreme Court shall be the highest organ of the administration of justice in the G.D.R. The Supreme Court shall supervise the jurisdiction of

FROM *GB*, I (1963), pp. 21–56.

all courts in the G.D.R. on the basis of the statutes and resolutions of the People's Chamber, of the ordinances and resolutions of the Council of State, and of other legal regulations. It shall guarantee the uniform and correct application of the law by all courts. The Supreme Court shall assure that adjudication serves the requirements of the objective laws of socialism as well as the strengthening and protection of the socialist order of society, particularly the development of the citizen's political and legal consciousness. The Supreme Court shall be responsible to the People's Chamber and, between sessions, to the Council of State. The president of the Supreme Court shall participate in the sessions of the People's Chamber.

2. The president, vice-president, and justices of the Supreme Court . . . shall be elected by the People's Chamber, on the nomination of the Council of State, for terms of four years. . . .

3. The Supreme Court is responsible for the constant guidance of the jurisdiction of all courts so as to assure that adjudication accords with the law and serves to solve the basic problems of general socialist construction —particularly, problems of the development of the national economy and of the struggle against all violations of the law. . . .

ORGANS OF THE SUPREME COURT

1. The plenum of the Supreme Court shall be the highest organ of the Supreme Court. . . .

2. The presidium of the Supreme Court shall be responsible for the organization of the Supreme Court's activities. . . . An inspection group shall be formed in the presidium to assist the Supreme Court in its supervision of the jurisdiction of the courts. . . . The inspection group . . . shall assist, control, and utilize the work of the district and county courts. . . . The presidium can suggest that the Minister of Justice recommend to the district or county assemblies the election or recall of a director or judge of a district or county court. . . . The district court shall be the highest judicial organ of each district. . . . The director, judge, and lay judges [*Schöffen*] of the district courts shall be elected by the district assemblies for terms of four years. . . .

County courts shall decide all criminal, civil, family, and labor-law matters assigned to it by law. . . . In order to include more effectively all forces of society in the fight against violations of the law, particularly against crimes and misdemeanors and their causes, and in order to protect the socialist order of society, particularly the development of the citizens' political and legal consciousness, the county courts shall cooperate closely with the county assembly and with other local government organs as well as with the social organizations united in the National Front. The director and the judges of the county court shall be elected by the county assembly for terms of four years; the lay judges of the county court shall be elected in direct elections in workers' meetings for terms of four years. They may be recalled before their terms expire. . . .

LAY JUDGES

The participation of lay judges elected by the people as equal judges in judicial proceedings assures the direct participation of the workers in the adjudication process of the G.D.R. . . . In particular, lay judges help to tie adjudication more closely to social developments; they assist professional judges in drawing correct conclusions from political, economic, and social developments . . . thus helping the judge to work more competently; they increase the social effectiveness of adjudication; they intensify the struggle against violations of the law, particularly against crimes and misdemeanors, and mobilize the workers for removing the causes of these violations; they develop the socialist political and legal consciousness of the citizens and widen their knowledge of the laws of the workers' and peasants' state. . . .

PUBLICITY OF JUDICIAL PROCEEDINGS

1. The participation of the public in judicial proceedings contributes to developing the workers' political and legal consciousness, to strengthening their respect for the institutions of their socialist state, to increasing the educational effect of judicial proceedings, and to channeling the power of the public in overcoming violations of the law.

2. The court, therefore, shall, in all appropriate cases and, especially, in criminal cases, give timely notice of the proceedings to the appropriate trade union offices, to the offices of the Free German Youth organization, to factory offices, to committees of the National Front, to other appropriate organs, and to institutions and collectives that are affected by the case. Specifically, the court shall indicate how important their participation in the proceedings will be to their work and shall schedule appropriate proceedings in socialist factories, collectives, and institutions at such times that the workers can participate in them. . . .

THE SOCIAL PROSECUTOR AND THE SOCIAL DEFENDER

Representatives of the people, of committees of the National Front, of the trade unions, of honorary organs of the workers' and peasants' inspection, of other social organizations, as well as of socialist workers' collectives designated by their organization or collective, may participate in criminal proceedings as social prosecutors or as social defenders during the trial [*Hauptverhandlung*]. . . .

INCREASE IN EDUCATIONAL EFFECT OF PENALTIES WITHOUT IMPRISONMENT

1. Socialist workers' collectives may propose that the court impose a penalty that does not involve imprisonment, and they may obligate them-

selves to act as sureties for the accused. By standing surety for the accused, the collective shall be responsible for the education of the accused. . . .

## JUDICIAL CRITICISM

1. In order to utilize the findings of judicial proceedings more effectively for the mobilization of social forces in the struggle against violations of the law and for the removal of shortcomings, particularly in the guidance of the economy and in the work of government organs, judicial criticism shall be employed more intensively. . . .

## CONFLICT COMMISSIONS

.  .  .

2. Conflict commissions shall deliberate and decide minor offenses and lesser disputes in civil law. In doing so, they shall influence the offender educationally through comradely and critical discussion and, in cooperation with his labor collective, shall attempt to overcome the causes and to abet the conditions of the offense. Conflict commissions shall be established in nationalized and similar enterprises, in enterprises with government participation, and in the administrative organs of the socialist state. . . .

## STATUS AND FUNCTIONS OF THE PUBLIC PROSECUTION

.  .  .

3. The attorney-general [*Generalstaatsanwalt*] shall be responsible to the People's Chamber and, between sessions, to the Council of State. He shall participate in the sessions of the People's Chamber and in the meetings of the Council of State. He may participate in meetings of the Council of Ministers.

4. The attorney-general shall be elected by the People's Chamber after nomination by the Council of State; he serves a term of four years. An election shall be held after each election of the People's Chamber. The attorney-general may be recalled by the People's Chamber on the recommendation of the Council of State. . . .

6. The attorney-general shall ensure that all public prosecutors: (1) exercise their responsibilities always and solely for the benefit and welfare of the working people and of their workers' and peasants' state; (2) devote their authority to securing socialist legality and justice for everyone; (3) associate closely with the workers, maintaining an open ear for their suggestions and problems, and participating actively in social life; (4) appreciate deeply the laws of social development and have a command of the fundamental policies of the G.D.R.; (5) constantly improve their knowledge and study thoroughly the problems of socialist construction and, particularly,

the development of the socialist economy; and (6) draw the necessary conclusions in order to constantly improve their work. . . .


STATUS AND FUNCTIONS OF THE MINISTRY OF JUSTICE

.        .        .

2. The Ministry of Justice shall be responsible for: (1) the execution of
government personnel policy [*Kaderpolitik*] of district and county courts
and notaries public; (2) the supervision [*Revision*] of the activities of district
and county courts; (3) the direction of the lawyers [*Rechtsanwaltschaft*]
of the G.D.R. and the supervision of its activities.

# 8. German Foreign Policy

# INTRODUCTION

German foreign policy since the end of World War II has been marked by the fundamental fact that, in view of the demise of the Reich and the emergence of two units on its territory, there could not be one German foreign policy. There are two, that of West Germany and that of East Germany. The leaders of both units had to accept partition from the outset, but the direction of their respective foreign policies and their foreign policy objectives have been basically different for over twenty years.

This section documents "the German question"—the conflict over policy aims and approaches between East and West. The articles of the Weimar Constitution and the Basic Law that deal with conduct of foreign affairs, as well as excerpts from Hitler's *Mein Kampf*, illustrating Nazi racist philosophy and the expansionist foreign policy aims based on it, are presented as background material. (See documents 1–4.) Other documents in this chapter are statements by leaders of East Germany and West Germany showing the progress of disunity about the German question. See also in this connection documents 14–18 in chapter 7, which illustrate the backing the two Germanys received in their attitudes from the Western powers and the Soviet Union, respectively, as well as the portions of party programs in East and West that refer to foreign policy (chapter 3, documents 10, 11, 14, 15, and chapter 7, document 23). While initially, in the West, there was considerable difference between government foreign policy and the policy advocated by the opposition SPD (the latter opposing Chancellor Adenauer's policy of allying West Germany with the West and favoring a more neutralist policy), there has been, since the early 1960's, agreement about fundamentals among all parties, except the new NPD (see chapter 3, document 15); they now differ chiefly over matters of implementation and detail.

Adenauer, who presided over West German policy throughout the 1950's, based his policy entirely on integrating the Federal Republic into the political, economic, and military community of the U.S.-led Western bloc, through joining NATO, the EEC, and so forth. In this he was strongly backed by the United States in particular and, especially, by State Secretary John Foster Dulles. The hope was that, negotiating "from strength," the West might compel the Soviet Union to yield to Western demands for reunification through all-German free elections (documents 5, 6, 7, 9). One conclusion from this attitude was what has become known as the *Alleinvertretungsanspruch* of the Federal Republic—that is, its claim to be the sole German unit legitimately representing the nation. The so-called Hallstein doctrine (document 8)

221

implemented this claim by refusing having or continuing diplomatic relations with any country, except the Soviet Union, that recognized East Germany.

This policy, instead of leading to rapprochement and unification, rendered the East, which in the early 1950's had seemed willing to at least talk about reunification, intransigent. The Soviet Union insisted on the "two-Germanys" approach, which, subsequently, with the crisis over Berlin, became a "three Germanys" approach, adding West Berlin to the two other "independent" units. The Soviet Union encouraged the East German government to insist on recognition as equal partner in any approaches to and negotiations with West Germany. Adenauer and every subsequent Bonn chancellor, backed by the Western powers and the United States in particular, have steadfastly refused this recognition. In the 1960's and especially since the entrance of the SPD into the government (with SPD leader Willy Brandt as foreign minister), emphasis was placed on a policy of gradual détente, a policy of "little steps" that aims at resumption or strengthening of economic ties (for example, inter-German trade), of cultural exchanges (permitting East German papers to circulate in West Germany), and of enabling travel and visits of individual persons, in order to alleviate the personal hardships engendered by partition (document 10). Ulbricht, however, backed by the Soviet government, has continued to insist on the establishment of official relations between the two governments as a precondition of everything else—that is, on Bonn's giving up its "sole representation" approach and other "recognitions," such as the recognition of the Oder-Neisse boundary between Germany and Poland, as definite (implying renunciation of claims to former German territory east of that line). With the assumption of power, in 1969, of the Willy Brandt-led SPD-FDP coalition, however, West Germany has come closer to recognition of this boundary line as well as close to a renunciation of the *Alleinvertretungsanspruch* and the Hallstein doctrine. Steps toward re-establishment of official relations with Eastern European countries such as Poland were likewise undertaken. However, Ulbricht's basic demand for full diplomatic recognition was not granted. The split, as it existed in 1967, is illustrated by the exchange of letters between then federal chancellor Kiesinger and East German minister-president Stoph (documents 11–14). And thus divided they still stand.

# DOCUMENTS

### 1. FEDERAL REPUBLIC

ART. 24   1. The federation may, by legislation, transfer sovereign powers to international institutions. [See 5:20:115e(1).]

2. For the maintenance of peace, the federation may join a system of mutual collective security; in doing so, it will consent to such limitations

upon its sovereign powers as will bring about and secure a peaceful and lasting order in Europe and among the nations of the world.

3. For the settlement of disputes between nations, the federation will accede to agreements concerning a general, comprehensive, and obligatory system of international arbitration.

ART. 25 The general rules of public international law form part of the federal law. They take precedence over the laws and directly create rights and duties for the inhabitants of the federal territory.

ART. 26 1. Activities tending and undertaken with the intent to disturb peaceful relations between nations, especially to prepare for aggressive war, are unconstitutional. They shall be made a punishable offense.

2. Weapons designed for warfare may be manufactured, transported, or marketed only with the permission of the federal government. Details will be regulated by a federal law.

. . .

ART. 32 1. The conduct of relations with foreign states is the concern of the federation. [See 5:1:59(1).]

2. Before the conclusion of a treaty affecting the special interests of a *Land*, this *Land* must be consulted in sufficient time.

3. Insofar as the *Länder* have power to legislate, they may, with the consent of the federal government, conclude treaties with foreign states. [See 2:4:30; 5:20:59a(3).]

## 2. THIRD REICH, PHILOSOPHY UNDERLYING RACISM

In opposition to this [Marxist doctrine], the "folkish" view recognizes the importance of the racial subdivisions of mankind. In principle, it sees in the state only a means to an end, and it considers the preservation of the racial existence of men as its end. Thus, it by no means believes in the equality of all races, but with their differences it also recognizes their superior and inferior nature, and by this recognition it feels the obligation, in accordance with the Eternal Will that dominates this universe, to promote the victory of the better and stronger and to demand the submission of the worse and the weaker. Thus, it is in agreement with the fundamentally aristocratic character of nature and believes in the validity of this law down to the last individual. It recognizes not only the difference in the value of the races but also the difference of individual men. In its opinion, out of the masses emerges the importance of the person, but this has a constructive impact, as contrasted with the disorganizing effect of Marxism. It believes in the necessity of idealizing mankind, as, in turn, it sees in this the only presumption for the existence of mankind. But it cannot grant the right of existence to an ethical idea if this idea represents a danger to the racial life of the bearers of higher ethics, for, in a hybridized and negrified

FROM Adolf Hitler, *Mein Kampf*, Harcourt, Brace, & World.

world, all conceptions of the humanly beautiful and sublime, as well as all conceptions of an idealized future of mankind, would be lost forever.

In this world, human culture and civilization are inseparably bound up with the existence of the Aryan. His dying-off or his decline would again lower upon this earth the dark veils of an era without culture.

### 3. THIRD REICH, FOLKISH THEORY OF RACE

. . . The right to soil and territory can become a duty, if decline seems to threaten a great nation unless it extends its territory. All the more so if what is involved is not some unimportant Negro people or other but the German mother of all life, who has given the contemporary world its cultural imprint. Germany either will be a world power or will not exist at all. To be a world power, a nation must be large in size; this gives it its power, which gives life to its citizens.

Because of this awareness, we National Socialists consciously erase the foreign policy trend of our prewar period and take up where the German nation stopped 600 years ago. We terminate the endless German drive to the south and west of Europe and direct ourselves toward the lands of the east. We terminate the colonial and trade policy of the prewar period and proceed to the territorial policy of the future.

But, if we talk about new soil and territory in Europe today, we think primarily of Russia and its border states. Fate itself seems to direct us toward the east. When Russia surrendered to Bolshevism, the Russian people were robbed of that intelligentsia that had theretofore produced and guaranteed the stability of the state. For the organization of a Russian state structure was not the result of the political talents of Russia's Slavs but rather the wonderful example of the state-building activities of the German element in a country of inferior race. Thus have innumerable mighty empires of the earth been created. Inferior nations, with German organizers and lords as their leaders, have more than once expanded into powerful states and have endured as long as the Germanic racial nucleus maintained itself. For centuries, Russia profited from this superior Germanic leadership nucleus. Today it is uprooted and obliterated. The Jew has replaced it. Impossible as it is for the Russians alone to shake off the yoke of the Jews through their own strength, it is equally impossible in the long run for the Jews to maintain their mighty empire. Jewry itself is not an organizing element but a ferment of decomposition. The Persian empire, once so powerful, is now ripe for collapse, and the end of Jewish domination in Russia will also be the end of the Russian state itself. We have been chosen by fate to witness a catastrophe that will be the most powerful verification of the folkish theory of race.

Our task, the mission of the National Socialist movement, is to give our nation political insight and to make it see its future goal fulfilled, not by the

FROM Adolf Hitler, *Mein Kampf*, Harcourt, Brace, & World.

intoxicating vigor of a new Alexandrian campaign but by the industrious labor of the German plow, which only needs to be given land conquered by the sword.

## 4. WEIMAR

ART. 4   The generally accepted rules of international law are binding for the German federation.

. . .

ART. 78   The conduct of relations with foreign states is the exclusive concern of the federation. [See 5:3:45.]

The *Länder* may conclude treaties with foreign countries on matters that fall within the legislative competence of a *Land*; such treaties require the consent of the federation.

Agreements with foreign powers in respect to changes in national boundaries are made by the federation with the consent of the *Land* affected. Changes in boundaries can be made only on the basis of a federal law, unless the change involves only a correction of the boundaries of uninhabited regions.

In order to assure that the interests of individual *Länder* arising from special economic relationships with, or geographical proximity to, foreign countries are represented, the federation decides on such arrangements and measures after the consent of the *Länder* has been obtained.

## 5. FEDERAL REPUBLIC, CHANCELLOR ADENAUER, STATEMENT TO THE BUNDESTAG ON A FREE, ALL-GERMAN GOVERNMENT, JULY 1, 1953

After the catastrophe of 1945, it had to be the foremost task of any German government to regain for Germany a respected place within the community of nations. This could be achieved only by making every effort to free Germany from occupation and occupation law, to transform it from being the object of the will of others into being the master of its own political decisions. This road was hard and thorny. Today, owing to the fact that the great treaties have not yet come into force, we have not reached the end of this road. In looking back upon the path pursued by us since the federal government took office in September, 1949, we may, however, note with satisfaction that there has been so much improvement in innumerable fields. The F.R.G. is already the master of its decisions in most fields of domestic and foreign policy. This could be accomplished only by tenacious endeavors. Step by step, by patience and consistency, the federal government recovered lost confidence and political credit; this was achieved by its performance—and by nothing else.

The federal government has been aided and supported in this course by

FROM *Handbook of German Affairs* (Washington, D.C., 1954), pp. 61–64.

its firm determination to favor and pursue a policy of European integration, which is imperative for many reasons. The important factor is to overcome, by freely cooperating with other European nations, by establishing a closer union, and by working for practical objectives, the false and exaggerated nationalism that caused so many wars in the past. For the F.R.G., the landmarks on this road have been membership in the Council of Europe, the conclusion of the treaty constituting the ECSC, the treaty establishing the EDC, and also our activity in the development of a European political community that is to stand above the two other great communities. This road, too, is difficult and hard. . . .

The association of the free peoples of Western Europe, to which the F.R.G. has made such an important contribution, has turned disorganized postwar Europe into a vigorous community. This association—I am firmly convinced—is a decisive cause of the tactics the Soviets have developed since Stalin's death. If anything brought home to the Russians the fact that they could not undermine and take possession of the European world by cold war methods, it was the association of the European peoples in the communities to which I have just referred. . . .

6. Federal Republic, Chancellor Adenauer, Statement on the EDC, Bonn, September 4, 1953

The Soviet Union is now violently opposed to the establishment of the European Community and to its association with NATO because it believes that this constitutes a threat to the Soviet Union, which therefore tries to prevent the integration of Europe by all means presently at its command. It has initiated a so-called peace campaign to create the impression among European peoples that the Soviet government no longer represents a threat and that unification is therefore unnecessary.

In this context, it must be said that the integration of Europe as was also stated at the Washington Foreign Minister's Conference (September 14, 1951) is a wise and sensible move in itself and that it will be effected whether Europe is threatened by the Soviet Union or not. Nor does the European Community contain elements that might threaten the Soviet Union, instead, it contains elements that give security to the Soviet Union. In the EDC, for example, the strength of the national contingents and the armament of the member states are limited and internationally controlled. This limitation alone is an important security factor for the Eastern bloc nations. As its name suggests, the internal and external structure of the EDC has been designed for defense purposes and renders any aggression against third powers impossible. . . .

From *Handbook of German Affairs* (Washington, D.C., 1954), pp. 166–68.

## 7. FEDERAL REPUBLIC, CHANCELLOR ADENAUER, STATEMENT TO THE BUNDESTAG ON FOREIGN POLICY, OCTOBER 20, 1953

### REUNIFICATION

The supreme aim of the F.R.G. remains the reunification of Germany in peace and freedom. It has, therefore, done everything in its power to help bring about a Four Power conference and to bring us closer to this aim. In this connection, the federal government is fully aware that the German problem forms only one aspect of the great complex of tension existing between the Eastern bloc and the states of the free world. The Soviet note of September 28, 1953, must fill us with profound disappointment, for it gives no indication that the Soviet government is interested in an early solution of the German question....

### ODER-NEISSE LINE

Following the numerous statements of the Bundestag and of the federal government, the German people will never recognize the so-called Oder-Neisse frontier. But let me emphasize once again that the problems connected with the Oder-Neisse line shall never be settled by force but only by peaceful means....

I have repeatedly stated that the endeavors for European integration, as exemplified in the EDC and ECSC, do not clash with Germany's reunification policy. It would be misjudging the real possibilities and existing facts if one tried to construe a conflict between the policy of peaceful and free reunification and European integration. Peace and freedom are impossible without security. No one who says that an insoluble contradiction exists between peaceful and free reunification and European integration has yet revealed his secret of how and by what other means reunification in peace and freedom can be achieved and secured than by European integration. There is no way to reunification other than European integration, unless one is ready to renounce freedom and to surrender all Germany to the Soviet Union....

FROM *Handbook of German Affairs* (Washington, D.C., 1954), pp. 169–72.

## 8. FEDERAL REPUBLIC, MINISTER OF FOREIGN AFFAIRS VON BRENTANO, STATEMENT ON THE HALLSTEIN DOCTRINE, OCTOBER 19, 1957

The government of the Federative People's Republic of Yugoslavia, having expressed . . . its decision to establish diplomatic relations with the

FROM *News from the German Embassy* (Washington, D.C., 1957), p. 17. With the resumption of diplomatic relations by the F.R.G. with Yugoslavia and Rumania, the Hallstein Doctrine has been tacitly dropped as far as the Communist bloc countries are concerned.

so-called German Democratic Republic, the government of the Federal Republic of Germany has the honor to communicate to the Yugoslav government the following:

The federal government has never left any doubt that it would have to regard as an unfriendly act, directed against the vital interests of the German people, the establishment of diplomatic relations with the government in central Germany—which lacks all democratic legitimacy—by governments with which the F.R.G. maintains diplomatic relations. Nor has the federal government left any doubt that such a step would render inevitable reconsideration of mutual relations on the part of the federal government.

With the exception of a few states, which form one of the power blocs, nearly all the other states of the world maintain diplomatic relations with the F.R.G. alone and not with the so-called G.D.R. This applies, in particular, to those states that have purposely abstained from joining in the world's system of alliances. By the decision now taken, the Yugoslav government ranges itself unequivocally on the side of the states first mentioned and identifies itself with a policy toward the German people that is pursued only by these states.

In the situation created by the unilateral decision of the Yugoslav government, the federal government finds itself constrained to terminate diplomatic relations between the Federal Republic of Germany and the Federative People's Republic of Yugoslavia.

### 9. ALLIED POWERS, TRIPARTITE DECLARATION ON GERMANY, AUGUST, 1957

Twelve years have elapsed since the end of the war in Europe. The hopes of the peoples of the world for the establishment of a basis for a just and lasting peace have nevertheless not been fulfilled. One of the basic reasons for the failure to reach a settlement is the continued division of Germany, which is a grave injustice to the German people and the major source of international tension in Europe.

The governments of France, the United Kingdom, and the United States, which share with the Soviet Union responsibility for the reunification of Germany and the conclusion of a peace treaty, and the government of the F.R.G., as the only government qualified to speak for the German people as a whole, wish to declare their views on these questions, including the question of European security, and the principles that motivate their policies in this regard.

1. A European settlement must be based on freedom and justice. Every nation has the right to determine its own way of life in freedom, to determine for itself its political, economic, and social system, and to provide for its security with due regard to the legitimate interests of other nations. Justice requires that the German people be allowed to re-establish their national unity on the basis of this fundamental right.

FROM *DSB*, Vol. XXXVII (August, 1957), pp. 304–306.

2. The reunification of Germany remains the joint responsibility of the Four Powers, who, in 1945, assumed supreme authority in Germany, a responsibility reaffirmed in the directive issued by the four heads of government in Geneva in July, 1955. At the same time, the achievement of German reunification requires the active cooperation of the German people as a whole under conditions ensuring the free expression of their will.

3. The unnatural division of Germany and of its capital, Berlin, is a continuing source of international tension. So long as Germany remains divided, there can be no German peace treaty and no assurance of stability in Europe. The reunification of Germany in freedom is not only an elementary requirement of justice for the German people but is the only sound basis of a lasting settlement in Europe.

4. Only a freely elected all-German government can undertake, on behalf of a reunified Germany, obligations that will inspire confidence on the part of other countries and that will be considered just and binding in the future by the people of Germany themselves.

5. Such a government can only be established through free elections throughout Germany for an all-German national assembly.

6. There should be no discrimination against a reunified Germany. Its freedom and security should not be prejudiced by an imposed status of neutralization or demilitarization. Its government should be free to determine its foreign policy and to decide on its international associations. It should not be deprived of the right recognized in the Charter of the United Nations for all nations to participate in collective measures of self-defense.

7. Re-establishment of the national unity of Germany in accordance with the freely expressed wishes of the German people would not in itself constitute a threat to Germany's neighbors, nor would it prejudice their security. Nevertheless, so as to meet any preoccupation that other governments may have in this respect, appropriate arrangements, linked with German reunification, should be made that would take into account the legitimate security interests of all the countries concerned. It was for this reason that, at the Geneva Foreign Ministers' Conference, the Western powers made proposals for a treaty of assurance on the reunification of Germany.

8. The Western powers have never required as a condition of German reunification that a reunified Germany should join NATO. It will be for the people of a reunified Germany themselves to determine through their freely elected government whether they wish to share in the benefits and obligations of the treaty.

### 10. FEDERAL REPUBLIC, CHANCELLOR KIESINGER, STATEMENT ON EAST-WEST TENSIONS IN GERMANY, APRIL 12, 1967

We want . . . with all our strength to foster human, economic, and intellectual relations with our countrymen in the other part of Germany. . . .

FROM *Bulletin* (Bonn: German Press and Information Service, April 1, 1967). See also *Efforts of the Government of the F.R.G. Toward Intra-German Détente* (German Federal Foreign Office, 1968), p. 3.

1. Measures to ease the daily life of people in both parts of Germany: (1) improve travel conditions, above all for relatives, with the aim of developing normal traffic; (2) establish border-pass regulations within Berlin and between . . . both parts of Germany; (3) facilitate financial transactions through intra-German accounting and through the mutual provision of funds for travel expenses; (4) facilitate the exchange of medicines and gift parcels; (5) permit family meetings, especially the return of children.

2. Measures to strengthen political and economic cooperation: (1) expand and facilitate intra-German trade, including public guarantees and the establishment of credit lines; (2) set up exchanges between the two energy-source markets and establish adequate power networks; (3) cooperate in developing or installing new transport facilities, especially bridges, motor highways, water transport, and railways; (4) improve postal and telephone connections, particularly by re-establishing telephone service for all Berlin; (5) discuss economic and technical *ad hoc* cooperation.

3. Agreements on economic, technical, and cultural cooperation: (1) to encourage more informal contacts among universities, research institutions, and scientific associations; (2) to promote scientific and technical cooperation; (3) gradually to remove obstacles against the receipt of books, magazines, and newspapers; and (4) to promote visits of youth groups and school classes, free intra-German athletic contacts, and free exchange and contacts among cultural associations and institutions.

The federal government is ready to examine additional suggestions. It wishes to do everything it can by means of conciliation to end the division of Europe and of Germany.

### 11. G.D.R., PREMIER STOPH, REPLY TO CHANCELLOR KIESINGER'S STATEMENT, MAY 10, 1967

The Council of State and the Council of Ministers of the G.D.R. have on several occasions taken the initiative with a view to normalizing relations between the two German states. . . .

In his New Year message for 1967, the chairman of the Council of State of the G.D.R., Walter Ulbricht, made proposals for the next steps that should be taken in the interest of peace and relaxation of tension, which he has recently reaffirmed. With those proposals in mind, I suggest that we open direct negotiations with a view to establishing regular agreements on: (1) the establishment of normal relations between the two German states; (2) the renunciation by both German states of the use of force in mutual relations; (3) the recognition of present frontiers in Europe, especially the frontier between the two German states; (4) a 50 per cent reduction of defense expenditure by both German states; (5) the renunciation by the two German states of the possession, control, or share in control of nuclear

FROM *SBZ Archiv*, XVIII (Bonn), p. 159; and *Efforts of the Government of the F.R.G. Toward Intra-German Détente* (German Federal Foreign Office, 1968), pp. 6–8.

weapons in any form, as well as on their readiness to participate in a nuclear free zone in central Europe; (6) the support by the government of the G.D.R. and the government of the F.R.G. of normal relations between the two German states and the other European states as well as the establishment of diplomatic relations between all European states and the two German states. The government of the G.D.R. is also prepared to consider proposals by the government of the F.R.G. for settling these and other fundamental questions.

It is clear that an arrangement on the normalization of relations between the two German states is the first and most important step. It would remove an essential source of tension in Europe and at the same time make possible a regular settlement of many questions between the G.D.R. and the F.R.G. In this connection, we repeat our proposals for the development of normal international relations, *inter alia*, in the fields of industry and commerce, transport, post, and telecommunications and reiterate that we are prepared to conclude appropriate regular agreements.

It will be necessary for the federal government to accept the realities and to abandon its claim to be the sole representative of the German people, which is both illegal and unpeaceful. If the federal government were really in favor of a renunciation of force between the two German states, as it has repeatedly maintained, it cannot bypass the G.D.R. and seek to achieve this via third states. To give such a renunciation of force the necessary peace-securing and internationally binding effect it can only be agreed upon between those directly concerned, namely, the government of the G.D.R. and the government of the F.R.G.

If your government is really interested in easing relations between the two German states, then it would be a compelling necessity for the federal government to meet its financial and other obligations toward the G.D.R. These, as you know, are extensive obligations of the F.R.G. and the heavy debts of some federal ministries.

Occasional statements made by the federal government to the effect that it is interested in the development of trade with the G.D.R. or in other economic arrangements conflict with the barriers set up by the federal government, which discriminate against the G.D.R. and on whose removal the government of the G.D.R. has always insisted and still insists.

At a time when the solution of urgent problems is essential in the interest of preserving peace and security, the government of the F.R.G. should now at last be guided by realities. The obstinate refusal to recognize the realities in Europe that have emerged as a result of World War II is contrary to the interests of European security and can only redound to the disadvantage of the West German people themselves. It is time to normalize relations between the two German states.

With a view to opening appropriate negotiations, which could be prepared by the foreign ministers of the two German states, I invite you to come to the official seat of the government of the G.D.R. on a date to be fixed later. I would also be prepared to meet you at your official seat in Bonn.

I am looking forward to your reply.

## 12. Federal Republic, Chancellor Kiesinger, Reply to Premier Stoph's Letter, June 13, 1967

I have received your letter of May 10, 1967. Unfortunately, it does not respond to my policy statement of April 12, 1967; I enclose a copy herewith. The meaning and purpose of that statement is that as long as basic differences of opinion prevent a just solution of the German problem, it will be necessary in the interest of the peace of our nation and of détente in Europe to seek intra-German arrangements that will promote as far as possible the human, economic, and cultural relations between Germans in East and West.

But you say: All or nothing! You raise demands for the political and international recognition of a division of Germany, which is contrary to the will of the people in both parts of our fatherland. You make talks conditional on the prior fulfillment of these demands. If I were to take the same line as yourself, I would have to insist on an immediate, secret, and internationally controlled plebiscite. But in the present situation such a confrontation will get us nowhere. I rather feel it imperative that we should talk about how we can prevent the Germans from drifting apart in their human relations during the period of enforced separation. That must not happen, even less in an age when European nations that have long been hostile to each other are coming closer and closer together. Life in the divided Germany must become more tolerable, and it is the duty of all those who bear responsibility to contribute to this end to the best of their ability.

It is essential to the welfare of our nation that tensions in Germany should be reduced, not increased. Our legal standpoint, which we unreservedly uphold, in no way intends to place the people in the other part of Germany under tutelage. Only as long as these people are denied the right to express beyond any doubt their will regarding the destiny of our nation will it remain incumbent on the freely elected federal government to speak for them as well.

You, too, affirm the responsibility of preserving peace for our people. One of the numerous steps the federal government has undertaken to secure peace is its solemn renunciation of force in seeking to achieve political aims. That renunciation applies generally and permits of no exception. The federal government must therefore adamantly insist that the use of force will be renounced in the other part of Germany as well.

You call on me to proceed from the "realities." The reality you and I must recognize is the will of the Germans to be one people. I therefore propose that emissaries, to be nominated by you and me, should begin talks without political preconditions on such practical problems of co-existence of the Germans as are contained in my statement of April 12.

From *Bulletin* (Bonn: German Press and Information Service, June 15, 1967). See also *Efforts of the Government of the F.R.G. Toward Intra-German Détente* (German Federal Foreign Office, 1968), pp. 9–10.

### 13. G.D.R., PROPOSED TREATY FOR THE ESTABLISHMENT AND MAINTENANCE OF NORMAL RELATIONS BETWEEN THE G.D.R. AND THE F.R.G. JUNE 19, 1967

Desirous of making an effective contribution toward guaranteeing peace and security in Europe and to create a peaceful relationship between the two German states as the precondition for their rapprochement in the interest of the nation's future, the government of the G.D.R. and the government of the F.R.G. have agreed as follows:

1. The G.D.R. and the F.R.G. shall establish normal relations with each other.

2. In relations between the G.D.R. and the F.R.G., which constitute relations between sovereign states of the German nation that aspire to peaceful coexistence and a step-by-step rapprochement, the generally accepted principles of international law shall be applied. The governments of the two German states shall conclude an arrangement on the renunciation of force.

The government of the G.D.R. and the government of the F.D.R. undertake to base their mutual relations on the following principles: respect for sovereignty, equality, and noninterference in domestic affairs; respect for the territorial integrity of the European states; recognition of existing frontiers in Europe, including the Oder-Neisse frontier and the frontier between the G.D.R. and the F.R.G.; recognition of West Berlin as an independent political entity; acceptance of the invalidity of the Munich Agreement from the outset as well as the undertaking by the two German states not to acquire, in any form, access to nuclear weapons, nor to stockpile nuclear weapons in their territories.

3. For the purpose of establishing and maintaining normal relations between the G.D.R. and the F.R.G., such direct contacts shall be established as are customary between states.

4. On the basis of the mutual benefits to be gained and with the aim of establishing an orderly peaceful coexistence, the necessary agreements shall be concluded in the fields of economics, trade, transport, posts, and telecommunications, as well as in other fields.

5. The government of the G.D.R. and the government of the F.R.G. undertake to conclude agreements with regard to further contributions of the two German states toward safeguarding European security, as well as toward disarmament and, in particular, with regard to the renunciation of access to nuclear weapons in any form and of their stockpiling.

6. The governments of the two German states declare their willingness, upon the normalization of their relations, the completion of an agreed process of disarmament and the conclusion of an agreement on European security, as well as on condition that militarism, neo-Nazism, and the

FROM *Efforts of the Government of the F.R.G. Toward Intra-German Détente* (German Federal Foreign Office, 1968). For Stoph's accompanying letter, see *Efforts*, pp. 11–14.

power of monopolies is broken, to enter into negotiations with each other with the aim of achieving a peaceful solution to national problems.

The present treaty shall be registered with the secretariat of the United Nations in accordance with article 102 of the U.N. Charter.


### 14. FEDERAL REPUBLIC, CHANCELLOR KIESINGER, REPLY TO G.D.R. TREATY PROPOSAL, SEPTEMBER 28, 1967

I have received and published your letter of September 18, 1967.

The things we are discussing concern all Germans. It would therefore help matters if you would not deny the people in the other part of Germany the chance to read this letter and the letter I sent on June 13, 1967. We are convinced that the German nation, which you too agree exists, is politically of age and should therefore be allowed to make its own judgment of our standpoints. Polemics will not bring us any further.

The only sovereign, the German people, wants, we are convinced, to live united in one state. This will of the nation governs our action. The right of self-determination is undisputed among the peoples of the world. The day will come when this right can no longer be denied to the German people either. It is the duty of all Germans to prepare the way for this solution of the German problem in peace and justice.

On the way to reunification we might jointly elaborate and implement a program of the kind I have already outlined in my proposals of April 12 and in my letter of June 13, 1967, in order at least to mitigate the distress caused by the division of the country and to ease relations between Germans in their divided fatherland.

The federal government is prepared, to serve the interest of all Germans but also the cause of détente and peace, to enter into negotiations on such a program. The state secretary of the federal chancellery will be available for such negotiations at any time either in Bonn or in Berlin.

FROM *Efforts of the Government of the F.R.G. Toward Intra-German Détente* (German Federal Foreign Office, 1968), pp. 18–19.

# Glossary of Abbreviations

CDU      Christlich Demokratische Union (Christian Democratic Union)
CSU      Christlich Soziale Union (Christian Social Union)
DGB      Deutscher Gewerkschaftsbund (German Trade Union Federation)
*DSB*      *Department of State Bulletin*
ECSC      European Coal and Steel Community
EDC      European Defense Community
FDGB      Freier Deutscher Gewerkschaftsbund (German Free Trade Union Association)
FDP      Freie Demokratische Partei (Free Democratic Party)
*FLG*      *Federal Law Gazette (Bundesgesetzblatt)*
F.R.G.      Federal Republic of Germany
*GB*      *Gesetzblatt*
G.D.R.      German Democratic Republic
KPD      Kommunistische Partei Deutschlands (Communist Party)
NATO      North Atlantic Treaty Organization
NPD      Nationaldemokratische Partei Deutschlands (National Democratic Party)
NSDAP      Nationalsozialistische Deutsche Arbeiterpartei (National Socialist Party)
SED      Sozialistische Einheitspartei (Socialist Unity Party)
SPD      Sozialdemokratische Partei (Social Democratic Party)
SRP      Sozialistische Reichspartei (Socialist Reich Party)

# Index of Documents in Each Chapter

*1. International Status and Establishment of the Two Germanies*
   1. Yalta Conference, February 4–11, 1945: Sections III–IV.
   2. Allied Powers, Declaration on the Defeat of Germany and the Assumption of Supreme Authority, Berlin, June 5, 1945: Arts. 1, 13.
   3. Governments of the United States, the Soviet Union, the United Kingdom, and the Provisional Government of the French Republic, Statement on Zones of Occupation in Germany, June 5, 1945.
   4. Potsdam Conference, July 17–August 2, 1945: Section II.
   5. Government of the Soviet Union, Note to the Governments of the United States, the United Kingdom, and France on the London Conference, February 13, 1948.
   6. London Documents, Directives About the Future Political Organization of Germany, Frankfurt, July 1, 1948.
   7. The Basic Law of the Federal Republic of Germany, May 23, 1949: Arts. 144–146.
   8. Law on the Constitution of the G.D.R., October 7, 1949: Arts. 1–2.
   9. Dean Acheson, U.S. Secretary of State, Statement on the Illegality of the East German Government, October 12, 1949.
   10. Convention on Relations Between the Three Powers and the F.R.G., May 26, 1952: Arts. 1–7.
   11. Government of the Soviet Union, Statement on Relations with the G.D.R., March 25, 1954.
   12. Allied High Commission, Joint Declaration on the Status of East Germany, April 8, 1954.
   13. Treaty between the Soviet Union and the G.D.R., September 20, 1955.

*2. Basic Constitutional-Governmental Framework*
### Constitutional Forms
   1. Federal Republic: Preamble, Art. 20.
   2. Weimar: Preamble, Art. 1.
   3. Empire: Preamble.

### Federal Structure
   4. Federal Republic: Arts. 23, 28–31, 37, 70, 83.
   5. Third Reich, Law for the Reorganization of the Reich, January 30, 1934; Arts. 1–6.
   6. Weimar: Arts. 2, 5, 12–14, 17–18, 48, 127.
   7. Empire: Arts. 1–2, 19.

11. Federal Republic, SPD, Basic Program, Adopted at the Extraordinary Party Congress, Bad Godesberg, November 13–14, 1959.

12. Federal Republic, SPD, Organization Statute, Adopted May 23, 1950, and Amended by Party Congress, Dortmund, 1966: Arts. 1–3, 5, 7, 10, 12, 13–14, 17, 22–25, 27–29, 33.

13. Federal Republic, SPD, Parliamentary Party Standing Orders, 1962: Arts. 1–5, 10–11, 14–17, 20–26, 33–34, 36.

14. Federal Republic, FDP, Program Adopted at the Eighteenth Party Congress, Hannover, April 3–5, 1967.

15. Federal Republic, NPD Manifesto, 1965.

16. Adolf Hitler, NSDAP Party Program, Munich, February 24, 1920.

## 4. Elections and the Legislative Process
### VOTING AND ELECTIONS

1. Federal Republic, Federal Electoral Law, May 7, 1956, as Amended February 14, 1964: Arts. 1, 3–6, 17–19, 22, 28, 31, 33–35, 45–46, 48–49.

2. Federal Republic: Art. 41.

3. Weimar: Art. 31.

4. Empire: Art. 27.

### LEGISLATIVE TERM

5. Federal Republic: Art. 39.

6. Weimar: Arts. 23–24.

7. Empire: Arts. 12–13, 24, 26.

### FEDERAL DIET: RULES OF PROCEDURE

8. Federal Republic: Arts. 40, 42–48.

9. Weimar: Arts. 26–30, 32–40.

10. Empire: Arts. 1, 21–22, 28–32.

11. Federal Republic, Bundestag, Standing Orders, January 1, 1952: Arts. 1–2, 5–7, 10, 12–14, 24, 30, 32–33, 37, 42–44, 46, 54, 56–57, 60, 62–63, 68–70, 72–75, 77, 79–81, 84–85, 117.

12. Federal Republic, Bundestag, Rules on the Question Period, June 29, 1959.

13. Federal Republic, Rules on Discussion of Questions of General Interest, 1965.

### FEDERAL COUNCIL: RULES OF PROCEDURE

14. Federal Republic: Arts. 50–53.

15. Weimar: Arts. 60–61, 63–67.

16. Empire: Arts. 6–10, 12–15.

17. Federal Republic, Bundesrat, Standing Orders, July 1, 1966: Arts. 1–2, 5–6, 11, 15, 19, 25–26, 29–30, 37–39, 42–43.

### LEGISLATIVE PROCESS

18. Federal Republic: Arts. 76–78.

19. Third Reich, Enabling Act to Combat the National Crisis, March 24, 1933: Arts. 1–2, 4–5.

# GERMAN CONSTITUTIONAL DOCUMENTS SINCE 1871

## Selected Texts and Commentary

### Edited by LOUISE W. HOLBORN
### GWENDOLEN M. CARTER
### and JOHN H. HERZ

In the midst of its centennial anniversary as a modern nation-state, Germany—split into two distinct political units that dramatically mirror the bipolarity of the postwar era—is perhaps less unified than at any time since Bismarck forged the Empire. Ironically, this very division has made the role of Germany in European affairs and its potential influence on world peace more significant than ever before. Poised between the two superpowers, central to the European landmass, of vital economic importance—Germany today is a critical subject for study and analysis. GERMAN CONSTITUTIONAL DOCUMENTS SINCE 1871 offers a solid basis for just such study. Invaluable both as a source book and as an analytical tool, it offers scholar and student alike a unique perspective on the German nation.

The most innovative feature of this work is its organization, which combines a synoptical approach with a structural and sequential framework. With the exception of those segments devoted to the establishment of the two Germanies, to the peculiar status of Berlin, and to the East German regime, each chapter deals with a particular constitutional element: parties, elections, the legislature, basic rights, the executive, and so forth. Within each chapter, the pertinent documents are arranged sequentially—ranging back from the Federal Republic to Weimar and the Empire. This technique makes it possible to trace the extraordinary persistence of German institutions, a persistence broken only by the Third Reich—as the relevant documents from the Nazi period amply illustrate.

Extensively cross-referenced to enable the student to compare not only the different regimes but also the allocation of powers within each regime, the volume provides a unique picture of a century of German government in which constitutional differences have been